The Human Centered Brand

# A Practical Guide to
# Being Yourself in Business

NELA DUNATO

**Nela Dunato**
ART & DESIGN

*The Human Centered Brand* by Nela Dunato

First Edition: July 2018

PUBLISHED BY
Nela Dunato Art & Design
Markovići 15, 51000 Rijeka, Croatia
neladunato.com

EDITED BY
Siobhan Colgan
siobhancolgan.com

DESIGNED & ILLUSTRATED BY
Nela Dunato
neladunato.com

PRINTED BY
Lightning Source
lightningsource.com

ORDERING INFORMATION
humancenteredbrand.com

A CIP catalogue record for this book is available from the Rijeka University
Library under 140417005.

ISBN 978-953-48171-1-7 (Paperback)
ISBN 978-953-48171-0-0 (Ebook)

*The mention of people, companies, tools, and websites throughout this book is not an endorsement. The author of the book is not receiving any financial benefit from mentioning or recommending these resources. The author and the publisher of the book are not responsible for the content of those websites, or any damage they may cause. Please report any errors or issues to hi@neladunato.com*

# Contents

# Introduction

I knew since I was a kid that I would write a book someday, but it never occurred to me that it would be on the topic of branding. I was just a passionate artist who was trying everything she could think of, in an effort to survive in a world that wasn't very nurturing towards artists. All I wanted to do was draw, paint, design, code, write, take photos, and experiment with digital media to express what I was feeling and imagining. After each successful experiment, I'd share my knowledge with others in the form of tutorials and workshops. I'd be perfectly happy if that was all I did.

Sadly, being skilled and passionate about your craft is not enough to make a living. Many skilled and passionate people end up broke, and many low-skilled people find their way to fame and fortune. The business world (and the world in general) isn't fair. To expect that we'll be rewarded simply because we work hard is naïve—we know from experience that's not how the world works. But as much as I enjoy complaining about it, complaining does not help nor does it change this. So, what do we *do* about it?

In my quest to answer that question, in the past decade I've learned as much as I could about business and marketing—mainly digital marketing, which was just starting to rise in importance at the time. In addition to that, I've dedicated myself to the practice of personal growth and emotional integration, so that I could break free from the family and cultural programming that kept me from being fully present and authentic in front of other people.

By riding both of these tracks—one towards business success, the other towards self-actualization and 'enlightenment' if you will—I could see where they apparently contradicted each other, and where they worked in tandem. There were times when it appeared that pursuing one would pull me away from the other. At other times following my dream career felt like

I was following my Purpose with a capital P. Within this tension, and in the intersection of business and self-discovery is where I've found the seed of what I now call the **Human Centered Brand**.

What started off as a necessity and a curiosity, grew into a passion of its own. I started enjoying the process of examining *why* people started businesses, what they wanted from them, what their process of working with clients was like, and what their clients received from this work. I wanted to know how this related to graphic design, and what I needed to know about business owners and their clients to become a better designer, one that is focused on substance and meaning, and not only on superficial aesthetics and numeric data.

By working closely with clients over the span of several years, and by getting an intimate view into their business, I could examine how they worked, and make hypotheses about what made their brands more or less effective. As I learned from my clients, I would test my theories in my own business. If it worked, I would then use this knowledge to improve my clients' brands.

At first, it was sheer luck that most of my clients were small service based businesses. When I realized that my experience in this segment gave me an edge, I became more intentional about only working with that type of client. I realized that regardless of industry or niche, all of these businesses had something in common—something that made them very different from large corporations. These tiny businesses were still based on the vision of the individuals who founded them, and there was at least one real human with a name and a face that people knew, doing the client-facing work. This defining characteristic of small service based businesses became the basis of the approach I describe in this book.

Developing this approach wasn't as straightforward as I'd like. Both the business and the personal growth paths taught me many valuable lessons, but they were also ridden with harmful, manipulative practices that I didn't recognize at first. I got burned more times than I can count, wasting time, money and confidence. Only in recent years have prominent business people started speaking out against such predatory business and personal development practices. Before I had any good role models on how to do business and marketing with integrity, I felt like I was doing everything 'wrong' because the 'right' way, the one taught by big names in the marketing industry, felt gross.

In a typical 'rags to riches' story that authors share in their book introductions, now would be the moment when I tell you *"But luckily, you won't have to make the same mistakes I did—in this book, I will teach you my super-secret system for stellar success!"* And... No, I'm not going to do that. Why not? Because a) that's exactly the sort of manipulative tactic I'm talking about, and b) I can't promise you that.

While I fully believe in my work, I don't think there are one-size-fits-all solutions that will work for *everyone*. In fact, the main premise behind my approach to branding is: **we're all uniquely different, and our businesses should reflect that**. I'm sharing this with the intention to help, but *you* need to decide whether something is helpful to you or not.

I won't ask you to *"suspend your judgment and just do the work and see what happens"*. Please, use your judgment and your intuition, and weigh every single piece of advice I put before you. Use this book however you see fit, and take from it only what serves you—I don't know what serves you better than you do. I'm truly passionate about the ideas I'm sharing, but it's okay if you disagree. It's okay if you question me. It's okay to skip chapters that bore you out of your mind (though I sincerely hope that won't happen). It's okay to finish half the book and come back to it in a year, when you've finally found a moment to breathe.

Ideally, I wish for this book to become your companion during the shifts and transformations that your business is bound to have, probably more than once in its lifetime. I wish for it to become a useful reference whenever you're testing a new marketing channel, or revisiting your old ones. I've poured everything I think a small service based business owner needs to know about branding into it, and I've had immense help from amazing people who gave me pointers on how to make it better. It's a labor of love, late nights, early mornings, and working weekends and I'm beyond happy, honored, and grateful that it has found its way into your hands.

## Do We Need Yet Another Book on Branding?

There are many, many books on branding out there. Perhaps you've already read a few. Why did I bother to write yet another book on this topic?

As a branding professional, I want to stay on top of the industry's pulse, and keep improving my knowledge all the time. In the reading I've done for my own research, I've found that the majority of literature was created for corporations. The basic premise was that the reader is an employee in a large enterprise—an enterprise that sells *products*. This wasn't very helpful for me personally, since nearly all of my clients were either small service based businesses, independent creatives, or non-profits. (*Book Yourself Solid* by Michael Port, which echoed many of the same thoughts I came to independently, is a notable exception.)

I hang out with a vibrant community of creatives of all stripes: painters, illustrators, writers, graphic designers, developers, musicians, jewelry designers, architects, inventors... Many of my friends are in the 'helping' industries, such as therapists, coaches, and healers. Looking at all these people trying to make a living doing what they love gives me plenty of opportunity to examine how they approach their business, and to identify what works and what doesn't.

Many of these creative, sensitive folks have an aversion to the kind of marketing and branding that is common nowadays. They're put off by the glitz and glamour which is only used to make overpriced products more desirable. I've been told by friends that they distrust anything that looks like too much money was spent on design, and assume not enough was spent on the product itself. I can't blame them—the entire advertising industry has made, and still makes, unethical and harmful decisions in the name of profit. Small, passionate business owners don't want to be associated with that.

Consumers are becoming more educated and careful as well. Decades ago, you would go downtown in search for a service provider who could mend your shoes, do your hair, or write up a contract, and had no idea how to even compare different options, except by price. Nowadays, we have many tools that help us make better decisions: online reviews, client testimonials, galleries of previous work... We follow hundreds of people on social media and get to know them as people, years before we even need their services. We can ask all of our online friends for recommendations, instead of just a couple of friends or family members. We've gotten savvier and more discerning.

With so many options at their fingertips, clients can go *anywhere*. It's more important than ever to be helpful, honest, friendly, and accessible—in short, to be human. Instead of pouring money into hit-or-miss advertising campaigns, you have an opportunity to use the natural magnetism you already possess and bring it online, so more people can get to know you. Instead of waiting for random people to stumble into your office, you can be proactive and make meaningful connections in your everyday life, so that people recommend you to everyone they know.

The approach I share in this book is an alternative to the glossy and complicated approaches that big corporations use. It doesn't require any manipulation or giving false promises. It doesn't require glamorous photo shoots, thinking up clever jokes to suck up to Millennials, complicated marketing funnels, buzzwords, or complex and expensive marketing systems. You don't have to 'sell out' or pretend to be someone you're not in order to make money doing what you love. You can be your unapologetic, wild, quirky self and still grow a loyal audience and meet amazing clients who understand you. You only need to discover who you already are, what makes your work unique, and how to express that in your business relationships.

Instead of telling you what to do, this book offers lots and lots of questions that only you know the answers to. It encourages you to write down your own insights and *take action*. It's not just a feel-good book that tells you *"Be yourself, you're awesome"* and leaves you hanging. I wanted to take this age-old advice further, and go past the inspirational greeting card material, into deep exploratory work that gives real-world results. I wanted to write a useful resource for all my creative friends who are struggling to attract the attention their work deserves.

**The Human Centered Brand is a guide on how to be yourself in your business, so you can enjoy your work every single day, and connect with a community of people who appreciate you just as you are.** Let the big guys and unicorn startups have their way. I know we can do things *our* way, and thrive. Before we do that, let's get some basics out of the way.

## Defining the Terms 'Brand' & 'Branding'

If this is the first book you're reading on the subject of branding, it will help if we defined what these words even mean. If you ask a hundred different designers and marketers to explain what branding is, you'll get a hundred different answers. A lot of these terms are used to describe multiple concepts, which complicates things further. The following definitions explain the meaning of the words as I use them throughout this book.

A **brand** is a collection of impressions the audience has about an organization, a product or a person. A brand is intangible: it exists in the minds of other people. Every business has a brand, whether they're consciously doing something about it or not. The first chapter goes into great detail on what a brand is, how it works, and why it works. The following chapters explain how to consciously create a brand of your own using the Human Centered Brand framework.

A **brand strategy** in a greater sense is a conscious approach to creating and maintaining your brand. In a narrower sense, it signifies a document outlining the key aspects of your brand so that you, and any anyone who works in your business, can refer to it and make business decisions that are *aligned* with your brand. If you answer the questions and follow the exercises from this book and the free bonus resources, by the end of the book you'll have figured out your own brand strategy!

A **brand identity**, also called a brand identity system, or a visual identity, consists of all the graphic brand assets that are used in a specific way. This includes the logo and its variations, colors, fonts, patterns, icons, illustrations, photo treatment, etc. We'll cover these elements in detail in the seventh chapter. All of these elements and assets are documented in the **brand style guide**, which is described in chapter eight.

**Branding** as a verb is the process of creating and managing a brand, for example: *"We're branding our new service"*. Branding as a noun is typically used as a synonym for brand strategy and/or brand identity, like in the sentence: *"We've hired an agency to do our logo design and branding"*.

A **brand strategist** is a person who helps business owners discover what makes their business unique, who their target audience is, how to communicate with them, and which aspects of their business they should highlight through the process of branding. The role of this book is to help you become your own brand strategist.

A **brand designer** is a person who designs brand identities, and provides all the graphic assets so that other people can use them. I've given some background on the work that brand designers do, and provided do-it-yourself brand design tips in the seventh, eighth, and ninth chapter.

Now that we're hopefully on the same page regarding the meaning of brands and branding, let's dive into what makes 'small-biz' brands different from corporate brands, and the impact branding has on the success of your business.

## Whose Rules Do You Play By?

The 'rules' of branding are very different for small service providers and for large product-oriented corporations. Books that are written for startups may offer some insight that's applicable across industries, but there are specifics of service-oriented businesses that these frameworks do not cover. To understand why advice for product-based businesses and startups isn't tailored for service providers, let's examine how each of them creates value.

**Product businesses** create ready-made artifacts (physical or digital) that do not require input from individual customers in order to be designed and produced. The customer is able to choose from the available options, exchange money for the goods they want, and that's pretty much it. Product businesses with no maintenance and low customer service needs may *never* come in touch with the majority of the people who buy from them. This is how big retail brands like Unilever, Coca-Cola, and Levi's operate: you go into a store, buy the thing you want, consume it shortly afterward, and never look back again. Customers contact these companies only if they feel they've delivered a sub-par product to ask for a refund.

For **service businesses** and product businesses with high-touch customer service, it's a completely different story. They remain in contact with the client for the entire duration of the project, and often for months afterwards. The client-professional relationship in this type of engagement is *intense*. You spend a tremendous amount of time talking, brainstorming, debating, presenting and supporting. Every interaction has potential for things to go wrong because of miscommunication, misunderstandings, difference in expectations, unclear responsibilities or simply different standards of politeness and professionalism.

Product based businesses are focused on presenting their product in the best light. Their entire brand hinges on how this particular product compares with others in its category. With services, it's quite different. As Marty Neumeier, author of several popular books on branding, puts it (emphasis mine):

> *"[...] the degree to which a customer trusts a product (or company making that product) determines whether he or she buys that product or a competitor's product. The same principle is true if a company sells services—**but in a service company, it's the people—not the product—who must earn the customer's trust.**"* *

A brand that's focused on your services alone is not nearly as helpful as a brand that helps to present *you* as a professional.

As a service provider, you also need much thicker filters than a product based business. A product based business can afford to take on anyone with a pulse as a customer, since their interaction is minimal. For service based businesses, it's just as important to advertise what type of client your service is *not* intended for, as it is to attract those who would benefit from it.

## Poor-Fit Clients Cost You More than You Think

Poor fit clients are like dead weight for your business. They demand a disproportionately large amount of energy for the value that they're giving back to you. They drag your process out of proportion, and you end up working

---

\*  *"Branding By Business Type"* by Marty Neumeier (October 3, 2016).

more hours than you budgeted for, eating up the cost. At the same time, you're unavailable for the great clients who glide through your process, and enable you to profit from your work.

Poor fit clients won't enjoy the experience of working with you, so they won't recommend you to other people. (If they do, the folks they recommend you to will probably be a poor fit as well—we hang out with people who are similar to us.) Great clients will enjoy their experience so much, that they'll refer people at every chance they get, and come back over and over again. Poor fit clients pick apart and strip down your services based on their badly planned budget. Great clients want to have the best, and trust your professional recommendation. **Constantly taking on people who are a poor fit will *destroy* your business.** Designer and entrepreneur Sean McCabe paints a sobering picture about noticing red flags, and proceeding to work with a client anyway:

> *"One red flag immediately disqualifies a potential client—don't justify red flags. Don't try and fix them so you can work with this person. Red flags are like roaches. For every one you see, there are 50 you don't."* *

After a few years of working with clients, you learn what types of people you play with well, and you're able to recognize them more easily. From the first email interaction, it's clear as day whether this person is your ideal client, a client from Hell, or anything in between. However, you don't even have to wait to interact with people to filter out those you don't want to work with—you can do that even before you ever hear from them, using a strong, polarizing brand. This is exactly what this book is about.

## Branding: The Bridge to Overcome the Trust Gap

Try to imagine yourself in the shoes of your potential client. The client needs just the kind of service you offer, and since they don't personally know

---

\*   *"The One Rule You Must Remember to Get High-Value Clients Who Pay You More to Work Less"* by Sean McCabe and Ben Toalson, Seanwes podcast (April 6, 2016).

anyone who can help them with that, they're researching online. They've identified five people who advertise such a service on their website in the first ten minutes alone, and one of those websites is yours. How will they decide which one is the right business for them? How will they be sure that they've made the right decision? When examining websites, clients are typically looking for **trust indicators**. They have many questions on their mind, such as:

- Is this a legitimate business?
- Who works there?
- Can they really do what they claim?
- Is this a realistic price for this service?
- Can I get a better deal elsewhere?
- Who can vouch for them?
- Who are their previous clients?
- But can they help *me*? I'm a special case.
- How can I reach them if I want to ask a question before buying anything?

There are explicit trust indicators in the form of information you offer on your website: company registration information, licenses and certifications, employee and office photos, references list, portfolio, testimonials, case studies... There are also subtle trust indicators that create a certain experience or mood in your client: a user-friendly website, quality photos, professional design, and engaging copy with no spelling errors... Before you've had the chance to exchange a single sentence with a prospect, your brand is communicating both on the conscious and the subconscious level.

Your marketing materials can elicit trust and excitement, or skepticism and frustration. When you're the only one providing a certain service in your local area and everyone knows who you are, it's easy. When there's several people in a given community who do the same thing, and none of them stand out in a meaningful way, everyone loses—you, your competitors, and your clients.

Today, having a strong brand is a must, because the market is supersaturated. Those of us whose businesses are location independent compete with peers from all over the world. This means that in order to charge the prices we need to charge in order to survive, we must demonstrate to our clients why our prices are *worth it*. We can't be hiding our uniqueness and blending in. Weak brands don't cut it anymore.

Having a weak brand has real-world impact on your business. It's not just about not having a polished website, or fancy brochures. **The biggest problem with having weak brand is that your business attracts all kinds of weirdos**: clients that don't pay on time, try to drive down your rates, disappear for months and come back with an urgency, call you on the weekend and expect you to cater to their every whim, treat you badly, or who think they know how to do your job better than you.

Working with clients like these leads to dissatisfaction, to you doubting your career choices, prompting you to consider leaving everything behind in order to start a sheep farm, or to drown your disappointment in a glass. If you want to work with the best clients in the world—and there are some pretty wonderful people out there, believe me—you need to develop trust with them. Thankfully, this is easier than you think.

## The Small Fish Advantage

The main reason you don't have to play by the same rules as the big brands, is that you have a huge advantage over them. Let me tell you a story about a freelance web designer turned author called Paul Jarvis.* Paul was a marketing agency employee for the first few years of his career. After becoming fed up with how the agency and the projects were run, he decided to leave. When the clients found out, they started calling him and saying *"Let us know when you find a new job, because we want to keep working with you."* After several clients did the same thing, Paul realized he didn't need another job—he could serve these clients directly as a freelancer. That was the start of his

---

* This story was shared by Paul in an interview on the $100k Freelancing Podcast episode *"Make Freelancing Serve Your Own Dreams with Paul Jarvis"*

long, successful freelancing career.

Who would you say had a stronger brand—Paul, or the agency he used to work for? Paul, of course. This story illustrates perfectly the advantage you have: **Clients don't connect with companies—they form relationships with *people*.** The relationships Paul formed with clients were stronger than their sense of loyalty toward the company he used to work for. They were ready to follow him wherever he went. They were personally invested in the relationship, and were unwilling to risk working with someone else who yet had to prove themselves to them. Trust is not easily formed, and once we find someone we can trust, we want to stick to them for as long as we possibly can.

Corporations face a huge challenge: they often don't have personal contact with their customers, and even when they do, it's usually a negative experience, i.e. a customer is complaining about something that went wrong. When a customer calls support, a different person will answer each time, and they'll have to repeat their story all over again as the rep goes through a checklist that has nothing to do with their issue. They're painfully aware that there's no real relationship between themselves and the person answering the phone. They may hear that infamous sentence *"I'm sorry sir/ma'am, I'm just doing my job."*

Contrast this with an experience you have with your hairdresser, or your favorite stall at the local market. Every time you come in, you exchange pleasantries and pick up where you left off last time. They may even know that you have school-aged kids and ask you how they're doing, or they offer a treat to your dog. If they had to close their shop, you would be seriously bummed. Such events disrupt our routine and we have to go looking for someone else who is deserving of our trust, and create a new relationship all over again. This new person never saw your kids, and doesn't have any doggie treats on hand. It's just not the same.

Being small is an advantage, because you can do 'unscalable' things. You could send each and every one of your clients a snail mail greeting card for the holidays or their birthday. You can email them just because, and check in on how their business or their family is doing. You can invite them to your office, or meet at a local café. These are the things that CEOs of large corporations might do for their 'big fish' clients, but not for the regular Joe or Jane like you and me.

Some of the larger service based companies, such as creative agencies and law firms, have already gotten the memo. They've become aware that their clients highly value passion, personality, and social responsibility, and that professional excellence goes without saying.* These companies have started including larger employee photos on their corporate websites, using first names in their communication, and incorporating founder's signatures in their logos. They don't want to be perceived as big and untouchable anymore—they want to create this authentic personal connection, because it works.

You're not in the same league with huge product-based companies—and that's *good*. You don't have the pressure of having to make millions of people like you. Branding for services is more simple and straightforward, and you don't need all the super complicated branding and marketing tools that corporations use.

In this book, we'll go over the branding framework that involves only the elements that service based businesses need, and not a single thing you don't need. In each of the chapters, I'll examine one of those branding elements in more detail, and provide guidance on how to define them for your business, and create your own unique brand strategy. In the last three chapters, you'll learn different ways to apply the branding strategy you've developed in your everyday communication, on your website, at live events, and as well as how your brand interacts with your business offers, pricing, company culture, social impact, and fashion style. Branding affects everything about your business, and with this book you'll learn how to make the best of it.

## How to Put This Information into Practice

The book itself covers theory behind the Human Centered Brands with examples of how other small businesses have implemented it. It also provides

---

* *"Shearman & Sterling Spent Three Years Rebranding Itself"* by Stephanie Russell-Kraft, Bloomberg Law (February 1, 2018).

questions you can answer for yourself to start discovering the unique characteristics of your own brand. To make this even easier for you, I've created a companion **workbook** that follows the lessons in the chapters and takes the inquiry practice even deeper.

The Human Centered Brand Workbook is completely free, and you can download it here: **humancenteredbrand.com/bonus**

I recommend that you download it immediately and either print it, or keep it on your phone so that you can take notes right after you finish reading each chapter. In addition to the workbook, I've included a few other checklists, workbooks, and templates to help with implementation.

Whether you choose to read the book in one go and then complete the workbook, or follow along by answering the questions in each chapter, it's all good—but to get the most out of it, I advise that you complete the chapters *in order*, because the advanced lessons lean on the previous ones.

I tried to cover as much ground as I possibly could in this book that a small business owner would need on their journey, but unfortunately I couldn't cover *everything*. Wherever I wasn't able to go into more detailed explanations, I offer recommendations for additional resources like books, websites, and courses created by other people. Some of these resources I've used myself and loved, and others came highly recommended by my friends and colleagues. I'm not getting any financial compensation for including any of these resources. If one thing is true in business, it's that the learning never stops.

In the next chapter, I'll explain the basics of my Human Centered Brand framework, and why the order of the lessons is significant.

*chapter I*

# The Human Centered Brands

Human Centered Branding is about identifying your unique strengths and quirks, and relying on them to create the feeling of **distinction** (*"I'm not like those other people"*) and **belonging** (*"If you like what I'm saying and doing, we'll get along great"*).

Human Centered Brands are rooted in the core values and the essence of their founders. As these businesses grow to employ more people, they attract employees who also share these core values, and whose personalities are aligned with the way the brand communicates. This way, instead of being diluted as the company grows, the brand is strengthened by additional perspectives that new team members bring to the whole. The Human Centered Brand framework can be applied to a freelancer, an agency, a small business, an artist, or a non-profit organization.

Human Centered Branding is distinct from corporate branding and personal branding, and fills the void that these two leave behind. Human Centered Branding is **relationship-focused**. Its main imperative is to help you have successful and harmonious interactions with your clients.

I believe that business is not only about commerce—it also has a deep human component to it. **Services change people**, both the provider and the recipient. Each project we do for a client helps us learn more about ourselves, and enables us to grow as professionals, as well as people. After working with us, our clients are able to achieve the things they weren't able to achieve before, and gain confidence as they see themselves in new light.

This is not the way most of us think about business. We're focused on tools, methodologies, artifacts we create, and numeric results. We use these tools, methodologies, artifacts, and results to lure new clients and justify our rates. We like to "keep things professional" because letting bits of our personality show would be bad for business, or so we've been trained to believe.

I'm just as guilty of this as the next person: what I'm about to share with you did not come naturally to me. It took me years of trial and error to realize why I was unhappy with the agency jobs I've had, even though I was supposedly doing what I love, and why my own business took its sweet time to elevate from the ground to the level where I can breathe freely and find some time and headspace to write a book. Every mistake I mention in this book is something I've committed as well, so I say this without a hint of judgment. The struggles with clients that I've mentioned in the introduction are real world examples from my personal experience, or stories people told me. Trying to operate from a purely corporate level, while you're deep in the trenches of working with clients every day doesn't work. Here's what does.

The Human Centered Brand approach relies on the natural human magnetism that each of us possesses. By magnetism, I don't necessarily mean attraction: depending on their poles, magnets can attract each other, or repel each other. This is what powerful brands do as well: they act as a strong attractor for the 'right' people, and a strong repellant for the 'wrong' people.

This natural magnetism is already working in your favor in your personal relationships, but the Human Centered Brand framework can help you bring that into your professional relationships. Instead of hiding and shying away from the things that make us unique and potentially 'weird' to the general public, we embrace this uniqueness and weirdness and use it as a leverage. This enables us to attract the attention of the people who love what we do.

**Your unique combination of skills, interests and personality traits becomes a point of resonance with people who appreciate those aspects.** While I believe all brands could benefit from showing more humanity, small service based businesses have some advantages, because your business processes are working in your favor:

1.  High-touch services provide plenty of opportunity to create meaningful connections that go beyond mere transactions.

2. Face-to-face or video meetings enable you to project your personality more vividly than through email and chat alone.

3. You have room to experiment on a small scale and see how your clients respond, before making any changes public.

4. You don't need as many clients as big businesses, so you can be brave and know that you'll be okay even if some people don't like what you do.

Human Centered Brands know that if a client hires a competitor, it was because they were not our right person to begin with. There is no feeling of scarcity or envy, because we don't *want* clients who are better suited for someone else. We want to work with people who are perfect for *us*. This is a healthier approach that encourages collaboration and mutual support between peers, as opposed to cut-throat competition.

When you know that people can't steal your secret sauce because your secret sauce comes from the combination of personality traits and life experiences that are unique to you, you feel more willing to teach your methods and be more generous with your knowledge. Instead of making this framework exclusive for my clients and creating a mystique about it, I'm offering it for a cheap price of a book for *anyone* to use in their business, including fellow brand strategists and designers. I'm not intimidated by competition, because I know that the clients who need *me* will find me.

**Your goal is not to fight for market share with your competitors—it's to connect with a small, but engaged community that brings an equal amount of value to you as you bring to them, and not only in the financial sense.**

Before we go into the details of the Human Centered Brand framework, I want to speak to the resistance that a lot of small business owners have to the concept of branding. It's a loaded word with a rich history, and your current perception of it may be miles away from what I've described above. I want to honor that, and help you process this new perspective and get accustomed to it before we roll up our sleeves to do the work.

## Deconstructing Branding

Perhaps you fall into the camp of people who have picked up this book *despite* its title, not because of it. Maybe you're annoyed with the word 'brand', and think branding is for cattle, not for people. I don't blame you at all— many of my friends are entrepreneurs in healing, therapy, yoga, and similar fields. I identify as a sensitive tree-hugger as well. 'Sensitive types' can often feel apprehensive towards marketing and branding. It sounds expensive, complicated, and useless—like something that the 1% invented to keep us competitive and distracted.

I agree in a way. Many of the rules we're taught about business are not necessary. Many tactics that are popular today are manipulative and short-sighted. It's too easy to throw out the baby with the bathwater, when a lot of conventional business wisdom seems like a steaming pile of crap. I'm on your side. The 'systems' and 'frameworks' I describe in this book are not about it *having* to be a certain way. I won't think you're a loser if you do it differently. I'm not a fan of having to follow a certain process, either. I often get distracted by random bursts of inspiration (like artists tend to do), and recognize it as a strength. I like to let things evolve organically, serendipitously, and unexpectedly. My best work comes from experimentation and doing something other than what I *should* be doing. And yet, I have a tendency to craft neat visualizations, systematize things, and optimize processes—create clarity and structure where there was once confusion and chaos. Visually organizing information makes it easier for me to understand, memorize, and apply.

I'm aware that real life is messy, and can't be boiled down to a simple process. It's just *easier* for me to digest information in this way. I get that not everyone will respond well to this approach. So, before we get into my nerdy, neatly ordered system, I want to preface it with a complementary view on branding that is more fluid and chaotic.

### THE HISTORY OF CONVENTIONAL BRANDING

Branding is the process of marking cattle with a heated metal stamp called 'brand'. No wonder we don't like this expression—it's loaded with a history of animal cruelty, and we don't want that kind of energy anywhere near our shiny, purpose-driven business. This old school brand represented **owner-ship**: *"These cows are mine."* Again, the idea of living creatures being owned by other living creatures is not very humane, and certainly not a model to mimic. However, this is not the origin of the word itself. The Proto-Germanic word *brandaz*, from which all the other language variants originated, means 'a burning'.* The Old English word *brand* included the meanings: fire, flame, piece of burning wood, torch, and destruction by fire. It was only centuries later that the process of cattle branding, and the subsequent word association, developed.

Later, around the seventeenth and eighteenth centuries, producers of goods wanted to mark their creations (such as furniture, ale and wine) to prove their origin.† This was seen as a mark of quality, one which guaranteed to the buyers they were getting the real deal. In the 1820s in the United States it became possible to register a **trademark**—the name and the graphic that represent a company or a product—so that counterfeit items would become illegal. Companies also started using **slogans** that spoke to the value of the product in the most concise manner possible.

Branding became more complex as the marketplace and the media developed. Companies spreading into distant parts of the world needed to develop robust systems that could be reproduced by different people, no matter where they are. This has led to choosing specific language, imagery, colors, and type treatment that would remain consistent and recognizable. Large restaurant and store chains designed custom uniforms, and even manuals on how their employees must behave and talk to the customers. The goal of this very expensive and time consuming effort was to make sure that every single point of purchase radiates the same qualities that increases their buyers' trust.

Multinational companies have entire teams dedicated to managing their corporate brands, because this isn't something any single person can do on their own. This complex process with thousands of tiny cogs in the

---

\*    Source: *etymonline.com*
†    *"A Brief History of Branding"* by Matt Shadel, Convoy (January 08, 2014).

machinery is what most people associate with the word "branding" today.

Unfortunately, we do not yet have a different word that encompasses only the positive aspects of branding that are applicable to small businesses, without any of the historical, negative connotations. Some people have attempted to create their own word combinations to describe the concept of a 'brand', but it hasn't caught on outside some very narrow communities.

The way I'm using the words brand and branding in this book is tailored for small businesses, and it can get as simple or as complex as you want it to be. I'll offer a different perspective that may help you see beyond these mainstream and historical ideas, and understand how this type of branding applies to you and your business.

## Why Does Branding Matter?

Back in the day when people lived in small villages, we only had a need for one bakery, one cobbler, one metal smith shop, one tailor, one barber, one midwife, one tavern, and one priest for the entire population of the village. Sometimes we didn't even have all the facilities in our village, so people travelled to nearby towns to buy and sell goods. When you needed your shoes mended and you couldn't do it yourself, there wasn't much choice: you went to the only cobbler that was *there*.

Industrialization changed everything. Suddenly we had the ability to produce more physical goods than was realistically needed. There were tens and hundreds of thousands of people living in a single city who moved there for the work opportunities in factories. We could travel farther with our gas-guzzling vehicles, so we weren't limited to what our small town could provide. Now there wasn't only one shoe shop in town, there were *dozens*. Since proximity was no longer the governing principle to base our buying decisions on, other factors became more and more important, such as:

- Quality of craftsmanship
- Price
- Reliability
- Aesthetics
- Exclusivity
- Convenience

Instead of one regular, undifferentiated shoe shop, you had the poor people's shoe shop (cheap!), the rich people's shoe shop (exclusive! fashionable!), the military and work boots shoe shop (durable! reliable!), etc.

**You had to distinguish yourself as a business in some way from other people who offered the same products or services in order to attract enough buyers.** If everyone does the same thing the same way, then people will buy the cheapest option, right? But we know from experience that people don't always *want* the cheapest option. Sometimes we're prepared to pay more, because the business addresses a specific need we have that others don't.

Nowadays, the competition is tougher than ever before. Through the technological magic that is the Internet, we're able to order stuff from literally across the globe without leaving our house. Every single one of us, no matter what our profession, has thousands or potentially millions of competitors.

## THE ONLY COBBLER IN TOWN EFFECT

When you're the only service provider in a local community, all the people who need this service come to you, because there's no alternative. We experience this effect with every new industry. In 2005 when I first started freelancing as a web designer, finding clients was easy. I never once had to apply for a job or pitch to anyone. Somehow word got out that I was making websites (my own website and blog had something to do with it), and I started making money. I wasn't a super awesome designer at the time. I was okay—but that was enough, because the marketplace looked very different from today: a) web design was a new profession, and there wasn't a lot of competition, and b) there were no freelance marketplaces like oDesk, Toptal or Fiverr, so most of us found clients locally. People starting out now have a more difficult time than I did breaking into the industry. Back then, I didn't need a brand. I had no idea what a brand was: I thought it had something to do with logos, color palettes, and typography. I wasn't strategic. I was just fooling around in my free time after classes, and somehow it made me money. I'm still pretty amazed when I think about it.

If you happen to be one of the first people in a completely new, never seen before industry, you won't need to bend over backwards to prove how you're different and better. The fact that you're doing something original and unique is enough.

This happened with social media marketers. And life coaching. And group business coaching programs. And the first people who sold online courses. And the guy who crowdfunded a potato salad.* People who are the first at something don't need to work hard to differentiate—their **newness** is their difference. Sometimes people throw money at you just for the kicks (like the potato salad guy). It's refreshing and ridiculous, and we want to take part in a historical moment. Never before in the history of mankind have thousands of people from across the world put their resources together in an effort to make a potato salad.

**Originality sells.** Finding a unique angle that no one else has pursued before, sells. For some industries, it's a challenge to find a new angle. Some of us have hundreds or thousands of competitors just in our city. That's where the need for a concept such as branding comes in.

## Differentiation: The Main Purpose of Branding

When looking at our own industry from the inside, we clearly see the differences between this professional and that one, between our work and the work of other people. Since we're spending so much time immersed in our creative work, the subtle details jump out at us immediately. In a minute, we can see a colleague's website and analyze what they're doing great, and what's not so great. Our clients can't do that. They haven't spent decades learning about our profession. They often miss the subtleties and take the presented information at face value, in order to save time. We can't expect our clients to be able to see our industry the way we see it. We simply need to accept that they have an *outsider's perspective*. If we want them to pay attention to what we believe is important, and notice the slight differences between us and other professionals, we need to spell it out for them in big, bold letters.

**We communicate how we're different from our peers, and why this**

---

\*   In 2014, Zach Brown launched a *Kickstarter campaign for a potato salad* that reached a goal of $55,492 USD, and garnered a lot of media attention.

**should matter to our clients, through our branding.** It's not enough to just say you're different—you should be able to demonstrate or prove it (for example through photos, videos, and client testimonials). If it's not completely obvious why the client should care, then you need to explain the *benefits* of your unique approach.

## The Second Purpose of Branding: Connecting with the People You Most Care to Help

**Human Centered Branding helps clients find the best professional to hire: one that understands their needs, communicates in a way that they like, and offers the level of quality they expect.** It's not about manipulating people into buying from you if that's not in their best interest. It's not about being competitive, and tarnishing the reputation of your peers. Branding will help your clients make the best decision *for them*, which is also the best decision *for you*—because, as we've established in the introduction, clients who aren't the right fit do your business more harm than good.

The effort to create a brand may seem contrived and dishonest to you at the moment. It may feel like you're building an image designed to portray you in the light that the largest possible number of people will appreciate. Corporate and startup branding can sometimes be that way, because they're putting the product at the center, but that's not how we do branding here.

Maintaining a constructed, synthetic brand gets exhausting if communicating with people is a big part of your business model. What I mean by communicating can be literally talking to people—writing emails, consulting over phone, attending meetings, writing reports—but also creating other forms of communication such as stories, visual art, videography, commissioned crafts, theatre plays, performances etc. For a micro-business owner, artificially manufactured brands are not sustainable. If you're forced to put on a mask every day, after a while you might start hating your business, resenting the people you work with and feeling like you want to quit. The purpose of the approach to branding I subscribe to is to avoid that, and to *enjoy your career as much as possible*. Because if it's not fun, why bother? There are easier ways to make money than running your own business.

## Great Branding Creates Resonance

Resonance is a phenomenon in physics where object A can cause object B to oscillate with a greater amplitude (or intensity), if it hits object B's *natural frequency*. I think this is a great metaphor for what happens emotionally in people when they encounter other people and businesses whose essence mirrors their core values and worldview. Resonance comes from a match of the *broadcasted* frequency in person A and *natural* frequency in person B. The graphic below illustrates this concept.

**YOU**   **NOT YOUR IDEAL CLIENT**

(nothing happens)

**YOU**   **YOUR IDEAL CLIENT**

**RESONANCE**

Here's the interesting part: in Human Centered Branding, the 'frequency' you're broadcasting at is also *your* natural frequency. Essentially, finding the clients you want to work with is a search for people whose natural frequency matches yours. (In this book, frequency is used a metaphor for the person's mental and emotional state. If you subscribe to the "everything is energy" worldview, you can also understand it literally, as a person's energy field vibrating in a certain pattern.)

## HUMAN CENTERED BRANDING CREATES CONDITIONS FOR RESONANCE

Imagine for a moment that every single person in the world has a string of tiny bells inside of them. Each bell has a different tone, and each person has a different combination of bells. (Hint: these bells represent the **personal core values**, which we'll discuss in the third chapter.) There are literally millions of different combinations available, so no two people have the exact same set of bells. Some people share a few of the tones with you. You go through the world, dangling these bells like you're Santa's reindeer. When you come close to someone whose bell matches one of the bells you have, theirs starts vibrating in response. Now you're making music together, which gets louder, and attracts even more people who share that tone to join you.

Creating your work and publishing it, appearing on the stage, and talking to the people you meet at events are all you ringing your bells. Listening to other people's stories, watching other people talk, and following other people's creative work is being quiet in anticipation for their bells to ring. Somewhere in that process, *resonance happens.*

You can't force resonance. It's not like you know precisely what the specific person's frequency is, and then go crafting your message to strike at that frequency. That's not how it works. Each time you're in a conversation with someone, you'd have to pretend in order to adapt to their expectations. This is not about adapting, pretending, or hiding behind a mask—**it's about being clear, unapologetic, and natural.**

## Human Centered Branding is about Self-Knowledge

Really, branding is simply a dance between self-knowledge and knowledge of the other. The knowledge of the other serves to better know yourself through the contrast. You learn where the boundary of your identity is. *"This is me. That is not me."* Once you're aware of your identity, it's time to claim your place in the world—for proclaiming:

> *"This is who I am,*
> *this is what I care about,*
> *this is what I do,*
> *and this is who I help."*

Branding and marketing principles for service based businesses are actually the same principles we use in making friendships and romantic relationships. You make sure to look presentable, which at a minimum means showering regularly and wearing a clean shirt. You go out to places where like-minded people hang out. You introduce yourself. You conduct entertaining and meaningful conversations. You gather impressions on whether the person shares your values and seems like someone you'd like to spend time with. When you feel the time is right and the other party is receptive, you make the ask: would you like to have dinner some time?

In a business context, we make up all sorts of rules to follow. This is how you do marketing. This is how you do networking. This is what a sales conversation is supposed to look like. When really, *"Just be a decent human being"* is the thing that matters the most. The corporate types can have their SWOT analysis, their business model canvases, their KPIs, their 9-block models or whatever. You can use it if it helps you to find new ideas and feel safer, grounded, and more prepared—but you don't *have to*. Showing up in a business context the same way you show up in a friendship or romance context is plenty. The reason people aren't generally doing that (apart from not knowing it's even an option) is that they aren't conscious enough in their personal relationships to apply the same to professional relationships. It's hard to reproduce something if you don't know how it works.

The Human Centered Brand framework guides you through a series of questions that encourage you to think and learn more about who you are, what you care about, and who you most want to help. You don't *need* this framework. You could go on a weekend hiking trip and think while surrounded by fresh mountain air and a gorgeous view, and still come up with the same realizations on your own. But when was the last time you chose to dedicate time to thinking about such subjects? If anything, this book is a reminder that these are the questions worth asking, whether you choose to do it at home, at a retreat, or with a group of friends. If you already know how to *resonate*, and are successfully reaching the people you want to help, you're doing just fine. That's all there is to branding. My tools are just a path that can get you there faster.

## Do We Need to Be Strategic about It?

Strategy is a term used in wars and competitive games. Again, it's not something we necessarily like to associate with our business, so upon launching our own creative business, we tend to throw it out and do things on the fly. Instead of making elaborate yearly and quarterly action plans, we do what we feel like doing at the moment, or what other people expect us to do.

Maybe you've made an honest effort in the past to create detailed plans, but the fact that things didn't turn out the way you planned demotivated you, so now you may think there is no point in planning. That's what happened to me many times, and I no longer even use the word 'plan' to describe what I'd wish to do in the future—instead, I use the word 'intention'. This subtle change in wording transformed my approach to planning, i.e. setting intentions, and removed all the feelings of guilt that came up when things don't go according to plan, because we're just humans who suck at predicting our future.

If a plan is a railroad track, an intention is a beacon. It's always glowing in sight, but the path toward it can be fluid and flexible. We're often forced to respond quickly to opportunities and challenges, and our weekly plans get scrambled by Monday, noon. Instead, setting an intention is like saying: *"This is what I'd wish to have happened by the end of the year, but I'm aware that I don't have all the information yet, and I'm open to better possibilities."*

The point of all this is to say that even if you're not the planning sort of person, it's helpful to know in which direction you're headed if you want to get anywhere specific. I assume that you do wish to get *somewhere*. You probably have a vivid vision of some big project you'd like to accomplish in the future. Maybe this project seems impossible at this time, because you still don't have all the resources you'd need to make it happen. What you can do now is lay the groundwork and slowly work toward it, and gather the resources you need.

Branding strategy can work in a similar fashion. If you've anything like me, you could be changing your mood a dozen times a day, or an hour. Maybe you carry a whole lot of emotional baggage from years past, and it has no place in your business. There are moments when you're vulnerable and cranky and say things you don't mean, and later regret. We aren't always able to uphold our most grounded, centered, loving presence. While displaying some flaws is perfect and natural (yay for being human!), making decisions based on a temporary crisis can set you back.

One of the tenets I try to live by is: **if I feel bad, I don't make any decisions.** If I'm able to get some time for myself, I apply self-help techniques until I feel better (I'll mention a few later in this chapter). If outside obligations make this impossible, I keep on truckin' down the path that past me (who was in good spirits) has charted.

The point of strategy is to have a path laid out for you so you don't need to overthink it when you're having a less-than-stellar day. If the word strategy bothers you because of its war-generals or old-school-businessmen-in-suits or Silicon-Valley connotations, just use a different word.

Large companies spend months or years working on their brand strategy documents. These are very helpful for large organizations, because it makes it easy to share among employees and stakeholders, to make sure everyone is on board and understands the goals they're working towards. As a very small business owner, you probably don't need that. In this book, we'll focus only on the parts that you do need, and they can fit on a single page.

Here's another metaphor on strategy that might help bring this point more to the ground.

**THE COMPASS ALWAYS POINTS TO THE NORTH**

The compass doesn't care what people think. It doesn't care which direction you want to go. It doesn't depend on data or popular opinion. It just states the fact: *"Earth's magnetic North is that way."* Your inner compass, rooted in your core values (which we will explore in detail in the next chapter), always points in the direction toward fulfillment.

People call this compass intuition, inspiration, Spirit, inner wisdom, or purpose. Whatever you want to call it, it's there for you at all times. It will show you the way if you would just stop shaking the damn thing and become still and quiet. Your inner compass is always, always available to you.

The problem is, when things in our lives or in the world are going badly, it's difficult to achieve stillness and feel the compass. That's why we make maps, and write down intentions and action plans. When we're in a good mood and good health, our vision extends farther—like being at the top of a mountain, and seeing clearly where all the meandering roads lead, and where to the obstacles like boulders and canyons are. We can chart a route we think will take us to our goal the fastest. Once we get down to the valley, or get lost in a thick forest or a swamp, it's hard to see past the nearest turn. The mapped route and our travel plan is the only thing we can rely on.

Theoretically, if you could get calm, quiet, present, and centered at any moment, you would never need any plans. You'd just check in with your inner compass and know: *"This is the next step."* Strategies, maps, and action plans are just tools for when we feel lost and want to keep going instead of getting stuck. Sometimes these tools save you from wasting your time and second-guessing yourself. You don't *need* a strategy. It's just good to have something written down for when you feel like nothing makes sense, and you need a reminder that *you know what you're doing*. Sometimes, just the reassurance that it will all be okay is enough to kick us into gear.

You don't have to use the words I use, unless you happen to like them. There are other terms that kind of mean the same thing, and other authors may be using something different. Throughout the remainder of this book, whenever I use the word you don't particularly like because it holds the 'icky' energy for you, replace it with a word of your choice. If you own a printed copy, feel free to scribble your corrections all over it! If it makes you more receptive to these ideas and opens up new creative possibilities, I'll be more than happy.

## Why Human Centered Branding Works

There are many benefits of designing a brand that's based on personal values and unique characteristics of the business owner and their employees. I'm going to list some key ones, though the list is not exhaustive, and I keep finding new benefits as I get deeper into this work.

### 1. BEING 'ON BRAND' IS EASY

If you've ever had to work in a place like McDonald's, Starbucks, H&M or a similar large chain, you know that they expect you to wear a certain type of clothing or a uniform and behave in a certain way, all the way to using pre-written scripts. Working in a place like that is exhausting, not only because it's physically demanding, but because you're forced to wear a mask of the brand you're working for, which may not be aligned with your personality. Acting is a respectable job that people get paid for. Yet here, low wage employees need to act *while* tending to their regular job duties.

Forming a brand around your values and your unique gifts allows you to live by it 24/7, not just put it on during your business hours. Talking to clients, writing marketing copy and content, speaking on the stage and updating your social media channels requires less effort and overthinking—the right words and actions come to you naturally.

Even large brands can benefit from more authenticity. In the classic book *Designing Brand Identity*, Alina Wheeler states:

> *"Organizations who know who they are, and what they stand for, start the identity process from a position of strength. They create brands that are sustainable and genuine. Brand expression must be appropriate to the organization's unique mission, history, culture, values and personality."* *

---

\*   *"Designing Brand Identity"* by Alina Wheeler, Wiley (2013).

If you no longer want to wear a mask in front of your audience and clients, the Human Centered Brand approach will help you find ease, and enable you to relax into your own essence more.

## 2. YOUR BRAND ATTRACTS THE BEST PEOPLE TO YOUR BUSINESS

When your brand is broadcasting your personal values, and how you're different from your competitors, it will attract the type of audience that shares those values and appreciates your individuality. Your client relationships will become deeper and more harmonious. Talented people who look up to your brand will inquire about job opportunities, and leave behind even well-paid corporate jobs to be around colleagues they get along with better.

People who *belong* in your community will get your 'Bat-Signal' and come towards it. You won't need to sell hard, because it will be obvious from your website, social media and other marketing materials what you're all about.

## 3. YOUR BUSINESS BECOMES EASY TO RECOMMEND

Some ideas are forgettable, while others are memorable. Researchers have found that people have brain structures that help them decide whether an idea is interesting and useful for others, and hypothesize that this is because communication of ideas is one of humans' evolutionary advantages.[*]

What this means for your business is: people are constantly on the lookout for things to recommend and talk about with their friends. If you make it relevant, your business could become the subject of their conversation. In the upcoming chapters, I'll share some techniques that will help you establish relevance for your target audience, and find what's unique about your business, so that it attracts people's interest.

## 4. YOUR BRAND DRIVES A HEALTHY COMPANY CULTURE

When your values are clearly defined, finding the right people for the job will be easier than ever. When we're stuck in a workplace where other people don't share our values, and don't appreciate our unique gifts, our job feels

---

[*]   *"How the brain creates the 'buzz' that helps ideas spread"* by Stuart Wolpert, Science Daily (5 July 2013).

unfulfilling. We feel like we don't belong in our team, and that the other team members will never accept us for who we are.

When you're starting your own business, you need to draw a line in the sand and say: *"This is what we stand for."* This is something we would never compromise on. This is what all our employees and clients need to get on board with, or else we cannot collaborate. There are lots of people with the skills you need who could fit in that job description, but few of them could fit in your *team*.

## 5. YOUR BRAND FORCES YOU TO ADOPT HIGHER ETHICAL STANDARDS

When you create a brand rooted in your values, you'll often find that manipulative and pushy business tactics are *incompatible* with it. It will become obvious how certain language and actions can harm your brand because they may sour the relationship you've built with your audience.

Your personality reflects on your brand, and your brand reflects on your personality. You cannot use *"it's just business"* as a shield anymore—you're directly responsible for every action your business does. If your business does something unethical, it means *you're* doing something unethical, and there's no weaseling your way out of it.

Reviewing the notes you've made about your brand before making any business decisions, no matter how big or small, will help you stay aligned to your true north. This will allow you to only bring the values and qualities you want to see more of into the world.

## 6. YOUR POSITIVE IMPACT REACHES FAR BEYOND YOUR SMALL BUSINESS

Here's a fact: you have absolutely no idea about all the ways your business helps other people. You may *assume* about specific ways, like the value your clients and your blog readers get, but the truth is there's so much happening around you that you never see or hear about.

Your impact doesn't only concern your services and the free content you provide—you're modeling a new way of doing business by example. Examples and role-models are extremely important, especially for children and youth. They encourage people to take risks and act on their ambitious ideas. People aren't interested in listening to those who just claim to be an authority, they want to see you walk your walk. We can't help but think *"If this worked for this other person, it might work for me too."* (This is the very reason why social proof, testimonials, and rags to riches stories are so effective.)

When you become more authentic, vulnerable and ethical in your business, you're not only directly affecting your clients, vendors, contractors, and employees. Anyone who sees you and your business gets the message that this is a possibility for them as well. At the moment of writing this book, this concept that you can be more free and authentic in a business context is only gaining momentum, and there's lots of people who still haven't gotten the memo. People are afraid that being more human will cost them their livelihood. We can show them that this isn't the case. We can help more people to liberate themselves from the struggle of trying to fit into environments they don't belong in. You don't have to do it by yelling through a megaphone—just being yourself fully and unapologetically is enough. Humans learn through observation. If they can see you, you are teaching them.

## Human Centered Brand Is Not a Personal Brand

On a more superficial level, the Human Centered Brand may appear the same as its cousin, the personal brand. This isn't the case, and I'll explain the difference.

**Personal branding** is applied to a single human being, regardless of the company they work for. The practical application of personal branding can look like:

- Taking professional photos.
- Polishing your LinkedIn profile and Facebook page.
- Publishing articles in relevant publications.
- Speaking at events.
- Becoming a spokesperson for a cause or an organization.

A personal brand follows people around from company to company. CEOs have their own personal brands irrespective of their companies, as do their employees. People with strong personal brands do not only bring their skills to their workplace, they also bring their **social influence**. This is why companies hire celebrities in their advertising campaigns: they're piggybacking on the personal brands the celebrities possess.

Human Centered Brands can take on the form of a personal brand for freelancers and artists operating under their own name. For other business entities, they're applied at the organization level, while each individual still retains their own personal brand.

**You can use the principles in this book to boost both your personal brand, and the brand of your organization.** You can share this information with your team members, and do the exercises together, so that the company brand reflects what you all have in common. Instead of only putting your own photo on your website (which reflects your personal brand), the Human Centered Brand approach encourages you to put photos and bios of all your employees, especially the client-facing ones. The Human Centered Brand is not just about you—it's focused on how you relate to your clients, and your team members.

## Human Centered Branding Is Not for Wimps

Many business owners hide behind their business entity because they feel safer that way. They use corporate speak as a shield from deeper human interactions. **Having a Human Centered Brand requires a great deal of vulnerability and courage to form deep, authentic connections with our clients.** We need to put our guard down enough to let ourselves be seen by fellow humans. The majority of businesses are failing at this. What you typically see on the average About Us page is something along the lines of *"We're a team of highly skilled experts dedicated to the success of your business."* That's corporate-speak designed to obscure the people who work in that company. It's smoke and mirrors they project in an effort to hide their humanity.

Human Centered Brands get to the core of who we are, and display it *prominently*. It doesn't require you to plaster your face all over your website, unless that's what you want to do. But every aspect of your brand—your words, your visuals, your actions, and the requests you make of your clients—tell a piece of your story.

If you prefer to be isolated from your clients, to keep things sterile and stick to the *"It's just business"* motto, this approach is not what you're looking for. The questions I'm asking you to answer in this book are intimate, and you might find them intrusive at times. The steps I'm asking you to take in crafting a brand that's uniquely yours may feel risky and bold. This work is not for everyone, but if you decide to stick with the exercises and give your best effort, the results will trump every other exploratory branding work you've tried before.

## When Is the Right Time to Create Your Brand?

The internet is overflowing with advice about what a new business owner should be doing. Blogging! SEO! Facebook ads! Webinars! Branding! Speaking! Self-publishing! Wherever you turn, you'll be inundated with suggestions on what your next business-building project should be.

I'm in favor of doing the right thing at the right time. While all of the methods above may be effective, they may be less effective if you do them too early in your journey. And yes, it can be too early for branding as well. Each business is unique, and your path may differ from the paths of other people. That said, all businesses go through certain phases in their development, and here's where branding fits in.

### 1. CONCEPTION

You've gotten an idea for your business: you've decided what services to offer, and developed a basic business plan. You've ran the numbers and figured out if you charge this much, with this many clients per month, you'll be able to recover (or exceed) your day job salary. This phase can last for weeks, months, or years—it's not uncommon for people to daydream about their future business for a *long* time until they feel ready to take concrete steps.

### 2. PREPARATION

You're acquiring all the necessary licenses and completing the paperwork that your country or state requires you to have in order to be a legit business. You're creating pricing sheets and sales letters. You're making changes to your home to create an office space, or you're on the lookout for offices to rent. Things are moving, excitement is running high, but sometimes the excessive bureaucracy can cause frustration.

### 3. FINDING INITIAL CLIENTS

Now it's time to start talking to prospective clients about how you can help them. These initial clients typically come from your immediate network: acquaintances, extended family, work colleagues, people you've met at the book club etc. A method that worked for me and other folks I know is posting an announcement on your personal Facebook profile, or sending a personal individual email to people you know. (It can be as simple as *"I've started to offer XYZ services. Please message me if you're interested, or know anyone else who needs this. Thanks!"*)

This is a good time to create a simple, basic website with the details of your services spelled out, so you have a place where you can forward people to find out more information. Some folks offer their services for free to a few clients to test their offering and gather testimonials. However, offering services for free (or bartering) doesn't provide proof that people are willing to pay for your services. The testing phase isn't over until you've acquired several *paying* clients who are happy with the results.

### 4. BRANDING

Once your business idea is validated in the real world, it's time to prepare for expansion. Branding needs to happen *before* any serious marketing efforts, to ensure that your marketing materials and all promotion channels tell a consistent, alluring story and make a great and lasting impression.

There are two approaches to branding: the bootstrapping do-it-yourself approach which I cover in great detail in this book, and hiring a professional brand designer to take care of all your needs. Some businesses go with a professional designer right out the gate, and some do their own design for years before they decide to make the switch. I'll explain the benefits of each approach in this chapter.

## 5. MARKETING

Up until this point, your only source of clients was direct outreach and word of mouth. Once you decide to expand so that even people outside your immediate social circle hear about you, it's time to roll up your sleeves and get serious about marketing.

Most small businesses opt for inexpensive online marketing, while large brands dominate billboards and TV commercials. We won't cover the how's and why's of marketing in this book, but I provide some information on how to apply your brand strategy to your marketing materials in chapter nine.

## 6. PIVOTING (OPTIONAL)

Some businesses remain the same from the day they were conceived. My dad has had a house painting and tile installation business for 15 years, and never changed a thing—he doesn't even have a website. On the other hand, his fickle artist daughter has been pivoting and adjusting her business regularly, and each change brought a website renovation and new marketing copy.* Pivoting can be brought on by different causes:

- You've lost interest in your current business.
- Change in your personal life doesn't align with your current business (health issues, new baby, relocation, etc.).
- Changes in the marketplace are affecting your income.
- Too much competition makes it hard to differentiate.

Your shift may be a huge one where you start from scratch with a completely new business idea, so you need to do the entire process over again. The pivot may also be gradual, where you slightly adjust your offers and either expand your audience, or niche down to a narrower audience. Each of these changes calls for examining your brand before you go investing in a big marketing campaign. Speaking of branding, let's examine the two approaches to it.

---

\*    "Copy" is another term for text. In the context of websites, we differ content that offers free information (articles, videos, podcasts, etc.) from copy that is designed to sell services (sales pages, landing pages, opt-in forms, etc.)

## Bootstrapping versus Outsourcing

I believe that as soon as you decide to start your business—even if it's just a side gig you do in the evenings—you need start thinking about how your business communicates with your clients, and what kind of impression it leaves them with. Even if you're still experimenting and perhaps aren't sure who your clients are yet, make some assumptions and see how they hold up against real life. The branding process is slow and iterative, and you'll know more about yourself and your audience as you gain more work experience.

Often at the very start, new business owners don't have a lot of money to invest, and hiring a designer to create a fancy logo and visual brand can seem unreasonably expensive. This is certainly the case for many business owners I know. I would never advise business owners to hire designers before they can afford it. In the very beginning, most of your efforts should be directed at meeting potential clients in person or online and **improving your sales skills** so you can pay your expenses, save up some money for future investments, and gather testimonials. The do-it-yourself approach has many benefits for a bootstrapping entrepreneur:

- It's as cheap as it gets.
- You can do it at your own pace.
- You can put in as much or as little work as you're able to.
- You retain full creative control over your copy and visuals.
- You can change it at a moment's notice if your business shifts.

In the beginning, when money is scarce and you're still figuring out your offers and your pricing, it's good to be flexible with your branding. Sometimes you might get an idea to revamp your website home page at one in the morning, and you can jump straight in without having to coordinate with a designer or web developer. You can make things happen faster, and it also saves you money in case your new direction doesn't pan out and you need to pivot yet again.

When your business grows and you start getting more and more clients that require your full attention (and there are many other things in business to take care of), holding the reins of design projects can become counter-productive. After all, graphic design is a specialized skill that requires knowledge, skill and experience to do right. You might also consider hiring a brand strategist to help you with setting the foundations of your brand, and enlisting help from experienced copywriters to write engaging content and sales materials that are aligned with your brand. I can't speak for writers, but I know that in order to create a brand strategy and design the visuals that will stand the test of time, there are a few prerequisites you need:

1. A solid business model that has proven to work.
2. Understanding of your clients and their needs.
3. Enough income to ensure a healthy budget for branding.

A **business model** that is bringing in money regularly is a must before you can even think about investing in a brand. Many people have great business ideas all the time, but these ideas need to be put to the test before you pour your entire savings into them. As a rule, I don't work with clients who haven't monetized their business yet, and who don't have proof that there is a demand for their services. I think it's unethical to take someone's money, if they don't have a reasonable chance of earning it back within a few months.

You might wonder then, how come that some businesses seem to come out with a professional brand right out the gate? I'll tell you a little secret, because I work with such businesses often. Before they come out publicly with their fancy consulting company, they have already done this work on the side for months or years, either as a subcontractor for a larger agency or on their own, but without any advertising and online presence. They were quietly growing their work experience and client list, and only launched their business formally when they were 99% sure they could pull this off. (That's when they called me.) If a minimum of three people—at least one of whom is not your friend, relative or an acquaintance—has bought your service at a price that made the deal profitable for you, your business model appears to be in working order.

This book does not deal with business models and profitability, so for that you'll need to get another book or a class. I recommend the Business

Model Canvas framework (it also comes in the form of a book *Business Model Generation*) which I've used for many of my new business initiatives, including this book. Another great resource for creative business owners is Jennifer Lee's book and home-study course *The Right-Brained Business Plan*. (It's not just a cute scrapbook, it also provides spreadsheets.)

Your **clients** are an important part of the equation, and you need to know them *very* well before you bring your project to a designer. The aim of the brand is to communicate with your right clients, and in order to do that, we need to know who they are as a person, as a professional, and why they buy from you. We need to know their needs and desires, both the ones they are aware of, and even those they may not be conscious of. Chapter six of this book is dedicated to this topic, and will help you get clarity about your target audience.

And then there's the **budget**—the topic most creatives hate talking about. You can get a logo for less than a 100 dollars, sure. But *great* brands don't come cheap, because they require lots of time and expertise. After you read this book (especially chapters which concern design), you'll be able to appreciate the work that goes into branding. I firmly believe that your branding budget should only come from your savings, not from credit. I'm not a fan of people spending more money than they can afford. An alternative to using your savings is to get a small grant which some governments and organizations offer to startups, new businesses, growing businesses, eco initiatives, women business owners etc. Ask your local chamber of commerce about any sources of funding that may be available in your area.

Once you have all of the three elements in place, you're ready to start looking for your designer. Ideally, it will be a person who:

- Understands you.
- Appreciates your audience.
- Is responsive and professional.
- Demonstrates an ability to perform high quality design work.
- Has an affinity for the aesthetic that would be appropriate for your brand.

Luckily for you, there are *so many* designers on the planet you can choose from, that you never have to settle for less than your business deserves.

If you find yourself nodding your head as you're reading this, and feel like you're ready to hire a designer right this minute, wait—you'll still benefit greatly from this book. Apart from the few chapters that go into the details of creating a visual identity, the rest of the book is all the stuff that's good to know before approaching a designer. It can prepare you so that you can get the most out of your hard earned money, and it will also help you maintain the high standards that you and your brand designer have set as you go about your everyday work.

## chapter II

# Your Brand Needs a Healthy Foundation

As I've mentioned in the introduction, your brand is a collection of *other people's* impressions about you: what your business is about, what you do and how you do it, what you sound like, what you look like, and what their experiences with you have been.

If you don't do anything about your brand, people will create a story of their own about your business, as they're engaging with you through your website, social media, e-mail, or in person. If you're not consciously crafting your own brand story, you risk being misunderstood—people might not get what you're really about.

When you create your brand *consciously*, you weave your story through all the steps your clients take on their journey with you:

- First impression as they land on your website.
- Learning from you through your articles or videos.
- Getting to know you better as they regularly consume your content and follow you on social media.
- Deciding to finally buy something from you.
- Their buying experience.
- The way you deliver your service or a product.
- The 'big reveal' as they're opening the box or excitedly refreshing their inbox.

- Telling about their purchase to their friends.
- The way you treat them if something went wrong.

All of these moments in your client's journey form an impression of your business in their mind—that is, your brand.

When you create your brand *consciously*, you're making sure that the story other people are telling about you is the one you want them to tell, not just any random story. I'm sure that you're a good and honest person who really wants to help their clients, so you want this story to be *true*. You don't want to put up any facades that we're so used to seeing in marketing. What we're creating here is something that helps you connect with your right people on a personal level, because the kind of marketing that is working right now, and the marketing of the future, is all about being personal and personalized.

Branding not only helps you attract your right people, it also encourages those people to spread the word about you. It's a sustainable and organic way to grow your business, rooted in integrity. Defining the elements of your brand will enable you to make decisions like: what offers to create, how to position and market your offers, how to communicate with your clients, what your visuals should look like, what promotional channels to use and how, and so much more.

You don't have a huge advertising budget for TV, billboards and viral awareness campaigns, so you need to make the best of every single interaction with a person who sees your work. These people don't have a lot of time, and will use the cues you give them to quickly judge whether your business is right for them or not.

This book teaches you the process of creating a foundation for your brand that you'll keep using for years to come, as your business grows with you.

But before we go into the nuts and bolts of my branding framework, we need to discuss another important prerequisite to doing this work: a healthy **emotional foundation**.

As I've mentioned in the previous chapter, adhering to the Human Centered Brand framework is not for the faint of heart. Our culture has spent a lot of time and advertising money to convince us that we're not good enough, smart enough, beautiful enough, funny enough, successful enough, thin enough, healthy enough... all in an effort to make us spend more on the solutions they provide.

Even worse, if you grew up in a family or a community that has chastised you or punished you for your 'unusual' interests and personality traits, you may still be carrying beliefs that are actively holding you back from being authentic. The very idea of saying something or publishing something may cause you to recoil in fear and give up.

Unfortunately, this book can't provide you with the healing you need to not feel fearful anymore. For some of us it may take years of therapy to get there. What I can do is give you some techniques that have helped me to deal with my own limiting beliefs and blocks.

## Dealing with Emotional Blocks That Prevent Your Authentic Self-Expression

On this journey of self-discovery you may encounter some mindset traps, and I want to offer you tools to manage them if they come up. There will be moments when thoughts like this appear in your mind as you're writing down insights about your brand:

- This is stupid.
- Who cares?
- This is embarrassing.
- I couldn't possibly say this publicly.
- My team members would laugh at this.
- My current clients would dump me if they saw this.
- [Famous influencer] will think I'm copying them.
- My peers will think I'm a hack.
- This would never work.
- This might work for someone else, but I don't have what it takes.

It's very rare that a truly new idea will show up for you without any push-back from the basement crew of inner critics, who are working non-stop on undermining your optimism. What do you do when these voices show up? Here are some tips from my wealthy experience of dealing with bouts of inspiration and enthusiasm, immediately followed by crippling self-doubt and anxiety. This is intended as a list of steps you can do in order to get the greatest benefit, but you can skip those that don't resonate with you, or replace them with another practice that suits you better.

## 1. ACKNOWLEDGE THAT THINGS ARE GOING ACCORDING TO PLAN

You're not the only person who has these doubts. Even the most brilliant, successful people doubt themselves and their ideas. You're not broken, and you're not beyond help. The fact that these fears are rearing their ugly head is proof you're *changing* something. That's a good sign.

Give your discomfort and fear some space and simply be with it. Too often we try to suppress our emotions with unhealthy habits like workaholism, substance abuse (including sugar), getting lost in excessive reading, video games or social media. Suppressing emotions doesn't make them go away, they just remain unresolved. By releasing our emotions in a safe way, they get weaker, and no longer hold us in a grip. This may look like crying in the privacy of your room, punching a pillow, walking it off, or whatever method you like that doesn't damage other people or anyone's property.

You don't have to *do* anything to your emotions. They're not bad or wrong, and willing them to go away won't work. It's OK to feel however you feel. This temporary hiccup is not indicative of what your life is really like. It doesn't mean anything about you or your ability to succeed. We all have bad days, and *that's all this is*. The biggest lie our insecurities try to sell us is that this is permanent. It's not. Try to remember a time in your life when you felt similar as you do right now. What happened after that? Did you manage to get your inspiration and drive back? If you have proof that this has happened once before, it *can* happen again—no, it *will* most definitely happen again because that is how life works.

## 2. WRITE DOWN YOUR FEARS

Writing has many benefits. First, it places a thought outside of you, so you can examine it more objectively. Second, the fact that you have it written down means you don't have to keep it top of mind, and you can say to yourself: *"See, it's written down, I'm well aware of it. No need to think about it anymore."*

Another benefit is you can refute your negative thoughts in writing using proof—for example, the kind words your clients, friends or total strangers have said about your work. When the same thought comes up again, look up the proof you've gathered, and that alone will diffuse a lot of that pressure. Many psychological studies have found the benefits of expressive writing both in the cases of severe traumatic experiences, or everyday issues. One study that focused on engineers who have recently lost their jobs found the following:

*"In an experiment with 63 recently unemployed professionals, those assigned to write about the thoughts and emotions surrounding their job loss were reemployed more quickly than those who wrote about non-traumatic topics or who did not write at all. Expressive writing appeared to influence individuals' attitudes about their old jobs and about finding new employment rather than their motivation to seek employment."* *

Simple as it may seem, writing is a very powerful tool. Use it.

### 3. QUESTION THE SOURCE

Our inner monologue originated from somewhere. Often it's a disappointing childhood experience, like other kids ridiculing us when we did something 'weird', or our parents chastising or even punishing us for a mistake we've made. Some of our negative conditioning comes from education or the corporate world.

Very rarely do your critical thoughts come from true wisdom and foresight. More often than not, it's just a reflex that we've developed way back when, in a situation when we couldn't stand up for ourselves.

Yoga teacher, coach and writer Havi Brooks has a saying *"Now is not then."* The painful memories are just that, memories. Those bullies that laughed

---

\* *"Expressive Writing and Coping with Job Loss"*, Stefanie P. Spera, Eric D. Buhrfeind, James W. Pennebaker, Academy of Management Journal (1994), Vol. 37, No. 3.

at you because you wore mismatched socks to the gym class or whatever, are not relevant predictors of the success of your business. You from today are smarter and more well-informed than any of the naysayers were when they said those hurtful things.

### 4. WHAT'S THE WORST THING THAT CAN HAPPEN?

Counter to the "think positive" advice, I encourage you to examine your greatest fears in detail. I've found that knowing what you fear *specifically* helps you with preparing contingency plans in the event that things really do go wrong. You might also find that your fears are unfounded. I recommend picking up your journal again, and answering the following questions:

- What's the worst thing that could happen?
- What would this mean about me?
- Why would that be so bad?

Continue with the question *"Why would that be so bad?"* until you can't find an answer anymore. The final statement you arrive to is likely your **core fear**.

For each of those statements, and especially the last one, repeat the third step of this process: question the source. Your core fears may have originated from real events in your past, but your future doesn't depend on them. You can move past them.

Examining your fears is not the same as inviting them. They are already here, whether you want them to be or not. Repressing and ignoring your fears isn't the same as overcoming them. The power lies in conscious acceptance of your fearful side, and deciding that you're not going to allow it to limit you. Visualizing your fearful aspect as a child-version of yourself may help you see your fears with compassion, and find the courage you need to take responsibility for your adult life. What the afraid child-you needs is acceptance and reassurance, not neglect and judgment.

### 5. FACE YOUR EMOTIONS

When you scratch beneath the surface of an issue, this may open up a huge can of worms you didn't expect. The previous step may have revealed some nasty lifelong fears that have kept you paralyzed whenever you wanted to reach for the next level of your business growth. In my experience, these uncovered emotions can come on even stronger than those initial nagging annoyances from the first step. For this reason, I advise that you do this exploratory work in the privacy of your own home or office when you're not going to be disturbed by anyone, so you can be fully present with whatever comes up. It's difficult to explain this work to colleagues and family members, especially when you're upset.

People in our culture have been trained to run away from strong emotions, and to see them as a weakness that should be eradicated. Psychiatrists like Sigmund Freud and Carl Gustav Jung have argued that repression is the source of psychological disturbances, and many thinkers that followed their lead developed tools that allow people to discharge repressed emotions and truly integrate them, instead of just burying them.

**The simplest method for integrating an emotion as it appears is to stay present with it without trying to change anything about it, and breathing deeply.** While this method seems deceptively simple, it's the exact opposite of what we reflexively do: we typically switch to shallow, constricted breathing and try to take our mind away from our emotion, sometimes by engaging in an imaginary monologue. Try to pause any thoughts and just focus on the felt emotional experience without judging it or making it mean something. Whenever your mind wanders, focus on your breath and get back to feeling the emotion until the feeling dissipates. This process may take a few seconds, or a few minutes.

The benefits of deep breathing have been documented in literature, and a recent 2017 study illustrated *"the potential for diaphragmatic breathing practice to improve cognitive performance and reduce negative subjective and physiological consequences of stress in healthy adults."*[*] Just changing your breathing pattern can trigger physiological processes in your body that lead to a calmer and more focused state.

There are also advanced methods for dealing with strong emotions—here

---

[*] *"The Effect of Diaphragmatic Breathing on Attention, Negative Affect and Stress in Healthy Adults"*, Xiao Ma, Zi-Qi Yue, Zhu-Qing Gong, Hong Zhang, Nai-Yue Duan, Yu-Tong Shi, Gao-Xia Wei, You-Fa. Frontiers in Psychology (2017).

are some sources which I have found helpful:

- *The Presence Process* by Michael Brown
- *Return to Oneness: Principles and Practice of Spiritual Technology* by Živorad Mihajlović Slavinski
- *Integra Protocol: How to integrate internal conflicts* by Vladimir Stojaković
- EFT videos on YouTube

I understand that this might be a bit too weird for the more skeptical folk among us. If you don't like this approach and don't want to even give it a try, that's fine—I won't try to change your mind. In any case, I credit these emotional healing tools for my ability to do the stressful work of putting myself out there in the public eye, despite being a highly sensitive and introverted person. I treat my high sensitivity as a gift and not a flaw to be fixed, so these tools enable me to enjoy all the benefits of open-hearted vulnerability, while being able to quickly get back on my feet when things don't go the way I planned.

### 6. GIVE YOURSELF A BREAK

If the emotions this work stirs up for you become too intense to handle, be gentle with yourself. **You don't need to resolve all your emotional blocks at once**. Taking a short break isn't the same as giving up.

Switch to a pleasurable activity and get some distance from the problem you're facing. Often in those moments that look like you're not doing anything useful, a flash of realization will appear seemingly out of nowhere. Your subconscious mind is working even when you're not. Once you give it a task, like figuring out why you always freeze when you need to introduce yourself to someone at an event, it will dig up the information and the insight you need when you're ready to access it.

We cannot be 'on' one hundred percent of the time. Our bodies, minds, and our businesses need periods of rest to be able to function optimally. Give yourself more time to rest than you think you need. Resist the initial itch to go back to your problem, and wait a bit longer before you indulge it.

## 7. ACCESS YOUR INSPIRATION

The one thing that is always stronger than your fears is your **devotion to your work**. There are reasons why you love the things you do. There are reasons why you want your business to be more successful. Maybe you want to work on more fulfilling projects. Maybe you have a passion project that requires time and funding. Maybe you really want to travel with your partner. Whatever this thing is that causes warmth in your chest and infuses you with energy, bring it into focus and stay with this vision for a while. Fill up on this vision until you feel like you're bursting with energy, and can't wait to get to work on bringing it to life.

Word of warning, though... Do not do this one first. Go through at least one or two (ideally, all) of the previous steps first, because often when we're in a bad mood, our inspiration is gone and the vision appears lifeless and deflated. You can't jump straight from feeling bad about yourself to feeling excited—the change is gradual. Still, it can happen in a very short time.

## 8. TEAM UP

If you've been spinning in circles for a while, it's healing and validating to hear another person say: *"You're not crazy. This is great stuff."*

If you have a business buddy or a mastermind group, you can suggest going through this book and the accompanying workbook together, each working on your own business. You can discuss your findings during weekly in-person or video meetings, and get feedback from others. Your **community support** will quickly lay those critical inner voices to rest. If they realize something about your branding doesn't work, they'll let you know.

Every business owner should have at least one such community to confide in. If you don't have one in your neighborhood, you can find it online. Which community you choose depends on what kind of people and topics you're attracted to. There are communities for ambitious go-getters, start-up owners, artists, writers, wellness professionals, spiritual people, social justice activists, women, people of color, and many other types of business owners. Some are free, and some have low-cost membership. Ask around and you will certainly find a group to your liking.

Intimate communities provide a safe space for you to test your ideas without risking public humiliation (let's face it, that's what many of us fear the most). It's like an incubator where your ideas meet the world for the first time, but in a way that allows you to gather feedback and evolve them before fully committing to them. You can ask people to comment on your biography, tagline, sales pages, book covers or any other new creation. You don't need to implement all the changes people suggest if you don't agree with them, but at least this will give you a preview of what kind of comments you can expect once you launch your thing to the public.

There's another great way to boost your mood that you can access at any time (besides watching cute baby animal videos, obviously). Years ago I read a blog post by a career coach Michelle Ward on creating your own Win Book: a record of all the compliments given to you by your clients and your audience.* To make your own win book, collect all the kind messages, comments, and testimonials into a single place where you can look through them when you need a confidence boost. I started mine immediately after reading that post as a Google Drive document, and I still keep adding to it. If you have a sort of a self-care first aid kit, this is an excellent item to put in it.

## 9. EMPATHIZE WITH YOUR CLIENTS

We often believe that other people expect us to be a certain way, for example to wear a certain style of clothing to meetings, or to be very impersonal on a business website. But do they really? Is it something potential clients consciously think about at all, or is it just what we've been used to because few people step outside of the mold?

What about you—do you expect people to be a certain way, or would you gladly work with a tattooed website developer wearing a Mastodon T-shirt, or an online advertising specialist who posted a photo with her four dogs on her about page? You might find that you're more tolerant to other people's display of humanity than to your own. When they do it, it feels refreshing. When you do it, you fear it looks dumb.

Think about a person who comes to your website in search for someone to *get them* and give them exactly what they need. They might be bored,

---

*   *"Your Win Book: What It Is, Why It Rocks, and How to Make Your Own"* by Michelle Ward (February 21, 2011).

nervous, or even frustrated if they've been looking for a while, and didn't find anything useful. They encounter your site, and suddenly you and your team appear like really nice, approachable folks they can talk to. They chuckle at a nerdy pun in your blog post, and they notice that cheeky P.S. at the bottom of the footer. Would they mind that you don't wear a sharp suit, prefer dogs over cats, or watch Star Trek? Would it really be a deal breaker for them not to work with you?

The things you might worry about may be totally irrelevant for your clients at worst, or at best, be the very thing they love about you. We are desperate to find an honest, true relationship these days when everything is transactional, and people pretend to be just about anything to get money. Authenticity is refreshing.

## 10. TAKE SMALL STEPS & BUILD YOUR CONFIDENCE

If the concepts in this book are completely new to you, and you've spent years adhering to the corporate practices, you can't expect to be able to switch completely in a short amount of time. It will take time to build up the courage to make bold statements and draw more explicit boundaries.

It took me years to develop the confidence in my own self-expression and my ideas. Hearing encouraging feedback from my friends, colleagues, clients, and readers is what made this possible. It wasn't just one instance, either—I've had to get compliments and 'thank you' emails *repeatedly* to start believing that people actually mean it, and it's not a fluke. A community that believes in you can help you grow your confidence faster.

Sending the first newsletter is always a challenge. Pressing the 'Publish' button on an article where you mention your chronic illness for the first time can be nerve-wracking. Declining a client that isn't the right fit for the first time can cause a meltdown. But the second time gets easier. The third time even easier. By the tenth time, you've grown your tolerance so much, you can make an even bigger risk. You don't have to jump out of your comfort zone—*expand* it gradually instead.

Now that we have a contingency plan in place for those potential triggering moments, we can finally dive into the core work of this book—the Human Centered Brand framework.

## The Human Centered Brand Discovery Pyramid

The process of developing your brand can be compared to building a pyramid. You need to build the **foundation** first, before you can move on with the other levels. The pyramid can't balance on its top—it has to be turned the correct way up so that the foundations are supporting its weight. Each element of a Human Centered Brand framework is represented by one level of the pyramid, as we can see on the graphic below.

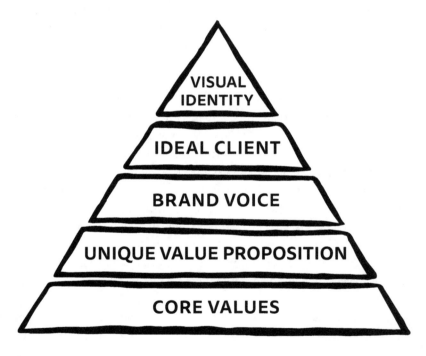

At the foundation of the brand pyramid are your **core values**—they determine what you most care about, the 'big why' behind your business, and how your approach to your work.

Your core values inspire your **unique value proposition**, which is your distinguishing factor—how your particular business is different from all the others who may be offering similar services.

Your core values and your unique value proposition influence your **brand voice**—the topics you write about, how you express yourself, and what kind of a relationship you're forming with your audience.

The next level are your **ideal clients**—the people who share your core values, who are attracted to your brand voice, and who need exactly the kind of unique value that you provide.

Finally, at the very top your core values, unique value proposition, and brand voice are translated into the **visual identity**, in a way that is appealing to your ideal clients.

This book, and the accompanying workbook, are formatted to follow the framework in this exact order. The top levels of the pyramid require the bottom levels to be in place before we can work on them. This is why I don't recommend jumping straight to the chapters on ideal clients and visual brand, no matter how enticing it may seem. The foundational elements of the brand are the most difficult ones to define, but after you accomplish that, the elements higher up on the pyramid will be so much easier.

What I commonly see in small business brands is what I call the 'patchwork approach' to branding: bits and pieces of inspiration from Pinterest, customizing free or purchased templates, and then tacking on a professionally designed logo like a cherry on top. The combination of all that is a confusing mess of mixed messages that you're sending to your potential clients. This type of brand pyramid is attempting to balance on its tip—the poor logo has too much weight on its hands—and it's bound to tumble over.

**A strong brand is cohesive, harmonious, and aligned with your core values.** No matter what touch point your clients see first, they always get a great experience that primes them for buying your services. There is no confusion about who you work with, and what kind of value you deliver— your clients know they're your right clients from the start, and those that aren't are aware of that too. A strong brand is able to answer these essential questions:

1. Who are we?
2. What do we stand for?
3. What value do we provide?

4. How do we express ourselves?
5. Who do we work with?
6. How are we communicating these answers visually?

If you're not able to answer these questions at the moment, that means the foundations of your brand are a bit shaky, but don't worry—by the end of the book you'll be able to answer them with clarity and ease.

The upcoming chapters in this book describe each step in the process of discovering the levels your own Human Centered Brand Pyramid, and bringing it all together to create a visual brand that has your essence at the core.

## Where the Framework Meets Real Life

I did my first branding project ever at my first full-time job. Before that, I only designed logos. Nobody taught me how to do branding, but I was pretty much self-taught in most of the other skills I had, so I was used to learning from books and tutorials. I've read a couple of books and examined dozens of corporate brand style guides from multinational corporations to see how it's supposed to be done.

After completing that first branding project, I knew I wanted to do more of them in the future. As time went on, I did a couple more and my clients were very happy. When I started my own business in 2013, I decided to switch my focus from web design to branding, and the rest is history. Well, not really. I felt that something was missing that would make my work even more meaningful and impactful, but I couldn't quite put my finger on it yet.

Over the course of my design career I became very good at understanding what makes people tick, and learned how to translate their uniqueness into a visual medium. I knew it was one of my biggest strengths. The problem was, I was doing it all based on a *gut feeling*. I didn't have the words to explain what I was doing, and I couldn't teach others how to do it themselves.

As I was going through many self-discovery processes like core values exercises, future visioning, and the like, trying to find what my own purpose was, one thing kept coming up for me. I felt that my larger purpose in life was to **empower people to be true to themselves, and connect with those**

**who love them as they are.** That sounded like something life coaches do, and I wasn't eager to become a life coach—I loved branding and design, and wanted to keep doing it.

But what if branding was really about telling the world who you are, loud and proud? No faking, no acting, just finding out what your best and most unique qualities are, and turning up the dial? It made sense to me on a visceral level, but I needed to *understand* it conceptually so that I could explain it to others. This process of research, testing, and clarifying my message took a while, but slowly the dots started connecting.

I've noticed that for the majority of service based businesses, most clients came to them through word of mouth, from personal acquaintances and former clients. This was true even for me, despite having a pretty active online presence, and getting in touch with people all over the world. I've had a few clients that I've met online, but the majority of them I knew from *way back when*, or we've met at some social event. At first it was bugging me that despite all the hard work I put into my digital marketing, most of my clients—and my *best* clients at that—hired me simply because they knew me.

I thought this was a sign of my personal failure as a digital marketer. If I couldn't make my services appealing to people who don't know the first thing about me, this must mean I didn't do a good enough copywriting job. Or that I didn't write enough blog posts explaining the details of my services. Or that my email subject lines are bad. Or that my website isn't attracting enough traffic. Or maybe my oh-so-professional visual identity wasn't as hot as I thought it was. In fact, the opposite was true: my marketing *was* working, but not in the way I expected it to.

Clients decided to work with me mainly because I was a person they knew they could trust, and they'd enjoy working with. **My main selling point wasn't that I was a great designer—it was that I was *me*.** Being great at your job is a prerequisite that goes without saying, but it's the other parts of the business relationship that make or break a deal, like your communication style and professionalism. My acquaintances had time to get to know me as a person in a relaxed setting, and I left an impression of a capable person who is generally nice and has an interesting artistic style. Those folks knew what they were getting into when hiring me.

When I realized that my personality was attracting great clients in a non-business setting, I started wondering, *"How do I use it in a business setting?"* This is where the puzzle pieces started to fit together, and I got an inkling of what was missing from the corporate branding approach that I previously learned. It dawned on me why corporate branding practices aren't suitable for small, service based businesses: they lack the human personality. A light bulb went on: *"This is what I'm supposed to do."* Now my people-reading skill made a lot of sense. I started working on this framework, which was called Authentic Branding at the time.

I observed people who had a business full of personality, and other people who were scrambling and didn't know what to do. Some of us seemed to have a natural inclination to being bolder, more vocal, out there... Others have a more difficult time. I wanted to create a step-by-step guide to help those people become better at expressing themselves clearly in their business, even if they have no prior experience.

The Human Centered Brand framework cuts down the elements of branding to the most important ones that apply to service based businesses, and show you how to highlight aspects of your personality through them. **Each element of the pyramid corresponds to how you naturally act and communicate** in person and online.

You may find that you naturally excel at one or two elements, but have difficulty with others. For writers and teachers, their strongest suit is their brand voice, while their visual identity may pose a challenge. Visual artists are all about their visual identity, but many of them *hate* talking about their work, and they don't enjoy writing or speaking publicly. Inventors and engineers can have the best unique value proposition on the planet, but nobody gets just how awesome it is because they don't know how to express it in a *relatable* way. Helping professions such as therapists, consultants, and healers may be focused so much on the needs of their ideal clients that they force themselves to be whatever their clients want them to be. Spiritual people may have a very good grasp on their core values, but they may not see how to weave it into the rest of their brand. **The Human Centered Brand framework can help you solidify and highlight your strengths, while empowering you to improve the weaker aspects of your brand.**

Once I got a better grasp of my own Human Centered Brand, I was able to translate my personality *better* to the online world. I became braver in speaking and writing about the things that I only used to express through my visual art. I stopped trying to be all things to all people, and placed stronger boundaries on my business. I stopped censoring myself because of fear that I would be misunderstood or ridiculed by my audience, because I knew not everyone was meant to get it. I wanted my website to become an accurate representation of who I was as a person, and based on the feedback I've gotten, I feel like I've succeeded in that.

Since then, I've seen a rise in interest from clients who have only ever met me online, and haven't even heard of me before stumbling onto my website. When I asked these clients why they hired me instead of some other designer, nearly all of them said that in addition to appearing competent I *"seemed like a really nice person,"* and that they felt like they could trust me. Hearing this from other people's mouths confirmed my assumption that **people choose who to hire based on how trustworthy and likeable they seem, and that authenticity and transparency helps us grow that trust.**

The five elements of the Human Centered Brand framework go from more abstract and 'soft' toward the more practical. You can invest as much effort as you want in each of these, based on where your natural preferences lie. Nobody's brand needs to be perfect. What we aim to do is to patch the holes and inconsistencies in the elements that are a little more challenging for us, and then double-down on the elements that are the most enjoyable.

Instead of the haphazard spaghetti-at-the-wall approach, what we need to do is to decide what our brand is going to be going forward, and then pour everything we've got into this direction. Changing your mind every day isn't going to result in a very appealing brand.

## Consistency, Consistency, Consistency

Branding is, at its most technical level, a **system that enables you to share your message consistently** throughout all the media you use. The act of creating a brand is sometimes a long, involved process that requires deep thinking and high creativity. The result of the branding process is a set of resources that you can use in your business for years to come. Every single time you set out to publish a blog post, design a presentation, or get your business cards printed, you have building blocks at your disposal that you can arrange into any combination and come up with something beautiful, professional and classy.

Reading this, you might ask yourself *"But wouldn't it be boring to do the same things over and over again?"* That's a fair question, and as a creative spirit that thrives on novelty, I get it. Here's a couple of reasons why consistency in branding is better than trying to reinvent the wheel every time.

## CONSISTENCY IMPROVES YOUR CLIENTS' MEMORY

When your clients are in a discovery phase, they're shopping around, signing up to newsletters and social media channels left and right, trying to figure out who is worth listening to. The people who follow you online also follow dozens of others, some of whom do the same, or very similar things to what you're doing. Faced with an avalanche of posts every single day, they're having a difficult time differentiating one voice from another. It's a jungle out there.

This is where having a consistent writing and visual voice pays off. If your graphics are all set in the same layout, use the same colors and fonts, and have a consistent style of photography, after seeing them a couple of times, your online follower will think *"Hey, I've seen this before. I think I know who this is."* After a couple of weeks of following your updates, when this person next sees *your* inspirational quote on their Instagram feed, they know it's you before they even notice your smiling profile photo.

People just love familiar things—which brings us to the next point.

## WHAT IS FAMILIAR IS PERCEIVED AS MORE BEAUTIFUL

The question of what humans find beautiful—from other humans, to environments, animals, etc.—has inspired many studies in the field of psychology. One phenomenon studies have discovered is that **people generally prefer what is familiar to them.** They favor the 'average' faces made up from the members of their own population, much more than faces with non-average features, or faces of people from populations they are not regularly exposed to.* When we're used to something, it becomes more attractive to us. This also explains why there's a big fuss whenever someone starts a new art movement, and why it takes a long time for the audience to catch onto the new aesthetic. It's strange and unfamiliar, and we don't even know how to evaluate it. As we're exposed to a certain style more and more, we develop appreciation for it.

You can use this mechanism to your advantage—stay consistent with your communication. Keep it up even if some people find it a bit strange at first. The ones who stick around will appreciate you all the more for it.

## SYSTEMS CREATE EASE & SAVE TIME

At the moment, you may feel like you want to "get creative" with every single thing you publish because it sounds like the most fun thing in the world, but real life can sap that enthusiasm very quickly. Ask any small business owner, and they'll tell you there just aren't enough hours in the day for everything they want to accomplish. When your to-do list requires you to hop on client calls, deliver your services, publish a new blog post and newsletter, schedule social media posts for the upcoming month, and work on your new workshop materials, it's easy to see which ones will fall to the bottom of the priority list—it's typically content creation.

Creativity takes time and mental resources, and you may not always have a fresh supply of it to pour into your projects. The very least you can do to make your life easier is to **systematize your content creation through the use of branded templates**. Just by switching a photo and replacing the text, you can get a fresh batch of social media posts, ebook covers and keynote presentations ready in minutes. Your audience won't think you're lazy, I promise. Save your precious energy for when it counts—don't get bogged down with the details that yield a low return.

## CONSISTENCY IS A SIGN OF PROFESSIONALISM

Imagine you're visiting a small business fair. There are two booths right

---

* *"Facial attractiveness: evolutionary based research"*, Anthony C. Little, Benedict C. Jones and Lisa M. DeBruine. Philosophical Transactions of the Royal Society B: Biological Sciences (2011, 366(1571): 1638–1659).

next to each other offering handmade cosmetics. Both have natural, organic ingredients. Both offer a wide variety of options for different skin types, featuring different fragrances etc. The only difference is how they present themselves.

Booth A has a large banner featuring their shop name, set in an elegant font. All their packaging and labels share the same general style, with different colors for different lines of products. Their flyers and business cards are professionally printed on quality recycled paper stock. When you buy an item, you get a paper bag with a nice elegant pattern surrounding the shop name. They even offer postcard-sized gift vouchers that follow the same style, and the owner will stamp each envelope with a seal-type monogram, so that if the gift recipient is familiar with the shop, they can already anticipate what's inside.

Booth B has a hand-painted shop sign in the owner's handwriting. Their labels are all different from one another, like they're not from the same shop. Their business cards are elegant and printed on thick white paper, but their flyers are printed on mint green paper. They use plain paper bags. Gift vouchers are printed on standard printing paper, signed and stamped by the owner.

Which of these two shops looks like a legitimate business, and which one seems more like a hobby?

I'm totally for supporting small businesses who sell handmade goods, and their branding is not in any way indicative of the quality of the product. Shop B might be doing the best freaking orange-scented lip balm in the known universe, green flyers be damned. But the level of *professionalism* they bring to their business is so obviously different, that we can't help but wonder. You may choose the shop B to buy something for yourself, but if you're buying a gift to someone you love, you'd want to impress them, right?

Intellectual and creative services are not cheap commodity goods—they make a direct impact on our client's business and typically require a higher level of investment. If a potential client is comparing two copywriters, one of which follows the booth A approach with consistent graphics, and the other one is patching different styles together like the booth B, which one will they be more likely to trust with their business? Which one speaks *"I'm a professional"* through their actions, not just their words? I bet you know the answer to that one.

## PREDICTABILITY MAKES PEOPLE FEEL SAFER

In her book 100 *Things Every Presenter Needs to Know About People*, Susan Weinschenk states:

> *"When people know what to expect, and they know what comes next, they will feel calmer and they will trust you. If they don't know what is going on or what happens next, they might get nervous and become emotionally uncomfortable."* \*

People like pleasant surprises, but too many surprises might cause more harm than good. In a highly charged situation, such as looking for a reliable and trusted service provider that will help their business grow, clients are looking for **signs of stability and predictability**. If you design your client onboarding process in a way that is easy for your client to follow and expect what comes next, and that uses the same verbal and visual style throughout all the steps, this will help them feel safer and calmer.

Service providers sell future results that cannot be seen before the project is done. This is a high-risk situation for a client, so anything you can do to calm their fears and anxieties about working with you, will help you sell more services and maintain better relationships with the people you help.

If these arguments in favor of consistency still haven't changed your mind, let's address another question that might be popping up at this point.

## Are We Ever Allowed to Step Away from Our Brand?

What if the very feature of your brand is that it's always changing? What if you're an artist who comes up with new projects and styles all the time, and you can't even imagine how this might be systematized? I happen to know

---

\*   *"100 Things Every Presenter Needs to Know About People"*, Susan Weinschenk, New Riders (2012).

a thing or two about that challenge.

No matter how much your work varies, there will be threads that connect all of your work. If your visuals change all the time and that is your unique trait, that's not a huge deal. Remember, the Human Centered Brand Pyramid has five levels, only the top of which is the visual identity. Your core values will remain the same no matter how your business changes over the years.

If you have several businesses, they may have independent unique value propositions, different ideal clients, their brand voice may be slightly different, and their visual identities may be completely different. But in order for a single business to gain momentum, it's best not to step away too far from your brand elements.

If your brand works for you, then you won't have the need to step away from it. Of course, this doesn't mean that you're not allowed to introduce a new element to your marketing campaign, or add a new color that you don't have in your palette. Your system can evolve, and you can add the things that were missing later on.

**If your brand strategy and your brand identity are too limiting and don't enable you to express yourself to the fullest, then this is not the right brand for you.** If you find yourself in the situation when the branding decisions you've made in the past no longer apply to your business, it's time to change your brand.

## The Rebranding Process

As your business grows and you discover new things about yourself, your offers, and your clients, you may need to change your brand so that it reflects these insights. In the beginning of your business this may happen more often so it can look like you're never done. As things get stable, these changes will need to happen less and less frequently—maybe once every 5 or 10 years.

Having an old brand that doesn't work can teach you a lot about your business needs, and this information can help you create a new brand that works better. The rebranding process is almost the same as developing the brand from scratch and follows the same steps, but it has one key advantage: years of experience and data that can help you make better assumptions about the future of your business. If you've been in business for a long time, and have a brand that you want to evolve, you're way ahead of new businesses who are starting out fresh.

You can use this book whether you're creating a new brand, or evolving an existing brand. If you have any notes, brand strategy documents, and brand style guides, it's good to have them handy as you're going through the workbook so you can check if you still want to keep some of those things. Rebranding is very common in the business world. People do it for various reasons, such as:

- The business has created new, or significantly changed their offers.
- The target audience focus has changed.
- The market has changed, and new technologies require the business to adapt.
- The old brand followed trends of the past, and needs to be refreshed.
- The old brand hasn't satisfied the needs of the business.

Sometimes our desire for a rebrand may be masked with a more tactical task, such as *"I need a new website."* People may *think* they only need a new website, but then they realize what they actually need to do is to revise all of their content, and come up with a completely new design direction. This exact thing has happened to me. What was supposed to be a quick and easy process, turned into almost a year-long mammoth project that had me changing everything from my logo, website, illustrations, documentation, social media graphics, as well as changing a lot of the website content.

If you're the sort of person who is constantly growing and evolving through new experiences, you're going to find after a while that a logo or a website that used to fit like a glove no longer does. You might get annoyed by some things. This is a sign that you've overgrown the shell of your current brand, and that you need more space to keep growing.

Rebranding projects often follow transformational experiences that we then wish to integrate in our everyday lives. I would not advise to go into a rebranding project if you're in the *middle* of a transformation. This experience is often described like a caterpillar turning into a butterfly—in the chrysalis stage, the caterpillar is dissolved into mush, and is restructured into an organism with a completely different anatomy.

When you're a transformational goo, you'll question everything—your values, your clients, even if you should be in this business at all... So many things will be up in the air, and you need to *wait* until it all settles. Once your situation is stabilized, the truth will be obvious. This is when you're ready to take the next step.

I'd suggest that you make an appointment with your own business to take stock over the current state of your brand. Perhaps you'll need more than one session to go over everything. Once you've done the initial work by yourself, you can involve your team so they can offer their thoughts. If you think you'll need more help, consider hiring a branding strategist to guide you through the rebranding process.

For your initial appointment, take The Human Centered Brand Workbook you've filled out previously. (If you've filled it out digitally, print it so it will be easier to scribble over it with a pen.) If this is your first time reading this book and you don't have a filled out workbook, look up any other workbooks or class notes you may have done based on other people's teachings, as well as your existing brand strategy, and brand style guide documents. Get out of your office—sit on your porch, in a park, by the sea, or in your favorite coffee shop. You want to allow your mind to leave all the day-to-day tasks behind, and to focus on the big picture of your business. Take a pen and go over your own answers and notes. For every statement you've written earlier, ask yourself: *"Is this still true?"*

- If it's no longer true, cross it off.
- If it's slightly off, think about how you might tweak it to align it with your current truth and write notes on the margins.
- If it's still spot on, put a checkmark next to it and move on.

At the end of this review, you might realize that few things have shifted, and you'll be fine with making only small tweaks. On the other hand, you might realize that a lot has changed, and perhaps it would be a good idea to go through the fresh workbook once again.

As I've said before, this is a process that never ends. We are creatures of nature, and nature is forever changing. There are seasons of the year and stages of life. Accept change as natural, and open yourself up to new possibilities. With this in mind, let's roll up our sleeves and finally do some *real* work. In the next chapter, we'll talk about the key concept that your entire brand is hanging on: your core values.

*chapter III*

# It's All about You

In the previous chapter I've laid out the elements of the Human Centered Brand framework, and how they're organized into a pyramid with five levels. The bottom, foundational level of the pyramid are the core values. Our first step in discovering the essence of your brand is determining your own core values, and examining how they affect your life and business.

I've seen some literature on branding and marketing starting with the unique value proposition or your target audience, but that's putting the cart before the horse. If you start from the pure service perspective, without addressing your own needs first, your brand is going to be missing a key element: **you.** You are the most important component of your business. Yes, your clients are important—but you could have a thousand clients tomorrow, and if you ended up incapacitated in some way and unable to perform your service, you couldn't help all these clients. That's one of the big differences between corporations, product based businesses, freelancers, agencies, and artists: how much are you *needed*? If you run an agency, you might have a team of people who serve clients directly, but you're needed for developing new offers, forming strategic partnerships, creating yearly and quarterly plans etc. You could be gone for a few months without your business taking a hit. More than that though? For some folks it might be impossible. Those of us who work alone don't have anyone to fill in for us. Without us, the business is doomed.

There are thousands of potential clients in the world, and there's only one you. Your priority is to treat yourself with care and respect, and to make sure you're getting what *you* need out of your business. **One of the needs we have is to live a fulfilling life**. In this chapter, we'll dive into those needs and identify the foundation of your business: your core values.

## Business is Personal

Some people may be thinking that the personal dimension has no place in business, but that's simply not true. If there was nothing personal in business, you wouldn't be doing what you're doing—instead of starting your own thing, you would have stayed at your last job until retirement.

We decide to change direction in our career because something feels off on a deep level. Maybe you're not able to articulate what it is, but it's constantly present until you move away from the situation. One of the reasons why people feel so dissatisfied, even if they have a "good job" is a core value mismatch.

When your career is not aligned with your core values, a well-paid job can feel unfulfilling. No matter how much we earn, it can never seem enough because our need for meaning is not met. You may feel like your work isn't making a positive impact. Maybe you feel like you don't belong in your team, and they'll never accept you for who you are. In your own business, it can look like working on projects that cause you to feel bored and disengaged, or with clients that make you uncomfortable.

**I want to make sure that the business and the brand that you're building is the one that will fulfill you for years to come**. After a while, typical worldly success just isn't enough—even if you meet all of your financial goals, if the work you're doing isn't satisfying on a deeper level, it's all in vain. There's no point in fabricating a brand that will attract clients you resent working with, and not contribute to your personal fulfillment. Being honest with yourself about what you really, really, *really* want is of utmost importance.

## What Are Core Values?

Values are our strongest and most intimate qualities and principles that govern our choices. They are typically high-level concepts like: freedom, connection, growth, justice, truth, family, or faith. They are what you most want to experience in the world, and what you want to share with other people.

Živorad Mihajlović Slavinski, Serbian psychologist and metaphysicist, describes values like this:

*"Values are guideposts that guide our life, and forces that attract us towards
certain actions that lead to their realization.*

    *[...] it's important to note that not all of our Values have the same gravity.
In other words, not all of our Values are equally valuable. There is a specific
hierarchy of Values within us, which we're usually unaware of until we focus
our attention to it with the explicit goal of making it conscious."* *

While our entire value system may have dozens or hundreds of values with
varying degrees of importance, only the top most important values can be
considered our core values. These core values have the biggest impact on
our decisions.

I can't credit one source in particular for revealing the concept of core
values to me. I've heard about them repeatedly at different times from different people, and it took me a long time to realize and accept their importance in my life and business. I believe that I've first heard about core
values on Steve Pavlina's blog, but it didn't stick with me at the time. Later
I've encountered them in the book *Kreaton* by Živorad Mihajlović Slavinski.
This book featured a card sorting exercise for discovering your value system,
which I'll describe later.

A year or two after that, when I was in the throes of starting my own business, I took an online class by Amanda Aitken that helped people find their
true purpose, and tailor their business according to that. (Unfortunately, the
class is no longer available.) That class shared a core values discovery exercise
in the first lesson, and that's how I settled on my own top core values. Soon
after that, I stumbled upon them once again in Tara Gentile's course *Build
a Stand-Out Business*, which demonstrated how your core values can help
you make business decisions that are best for you. I'll share everything I've
learned about core values in this chapter—from others, my own experience,
and that of my clients.

If you're not aware of your own personal core values, it's easy to wander
off the path that leads to your personal and professional fulfillment. If we
don't know what we want in life, there's little chance we'll get it. Your core

---

\*    *"Kreaton"*, Živorad Mihajlović Slavinski (1995).

values are a compass that guides you throughout your life, and they've been lurking in the background of all the decisions you've been making, no matter how big or small. Steve Pavlina takes this statement even further:

> *"When you know a person's values hierarchy, you should have a fair chance of predicting their behavior."* *

Most people don't consciously think about their core values. If you asked someone what their core values are, they might say something that societal pressure makes them feel they *ought* to value, but their actions would show you a different picture. It's important that you get completely honest with yourself and identify what *your* values are, not what your spouse, parents, teachers, ex-boss or your spiritual guru think your values should be. You're allowed to have any values you want to.

If you dig into the 'why' behind the things you're doing, and how you're doing them, you'll discover what's most important to you, and what drives you forward. This is one of those things that nobody else can teach you, because your personal core values are unique to you. Each of us values different things, and this is the main reason why we have different definitions of success, different desires, and make different choices. Because of this, our world is such a diverse, interesting place—if we all valued the same things, we wouldn't have nearly as much variety.

Other people can assist you in uncovering your values, but what you do with this information is up to you. I'd recommend that you use this self-knowledge to your advantage, because values are more important than most branding and marketing sources give them credit for.

## CORE VALUES ARE AT THE FOUNDATION OF YOUR BUSINESS

Each of us has a number of values—some more important, and some less so. As we grow and change, we identify new values, and let go of others that lose meaning for us. At the very center of our identity are values that are permanent. Core values affect how you see the world and interact with

---

* *"Living Your Values, Part 1"* by Steve Pavlina (December 21, 2004).

other people, your interests and quirks, your dreams and aspirations... all the way down to the very mundane things: the way you talk, walk, dress yourself, the books and TV shows your enjoy, etc.

You've probably met some people who share your core values. When you meet them, you 'click' immediately and form a deep friendship that can only emerge from knowing the other person on an intimate level—because in a way, you do. When you meet people who don't share any of your core values, you quickly realize you'd prefer if you didn't have to talk to them ever again.

When you start thinking about core values consciously, you can't miss them. They're everywhere. The very desire to start your own business stems from them. Your inability to live according to your values while being an employee is likely what pushed you to gather the courage and go out on your own. Your values are what was nagging you during the years when you were still thinking about whether or not to make the jump.

Your business is the brainchild of your core values—or at least, it's supposed to be. If you haven't been paying attention to them, you may have made some decisions that were influenced by other people. Because of decisions like these, your business evolved into a tangle of conflicting values—your own, and those belonging to everyone else who had a say in your choices, whether that's your clients, your coach, online gurus, friends, or family members.

If your business is built on conflicting values, you may be doing the type of work you don't enjoy, or you're following a marketing strategy that's exhausting and feels sleazy. Maybe you have a hard time deciding what you should focus on building next. Conflicting values pull us in different directions, and because of that, we can barely move. The first step to fixing that is to identify which of those values are actually yours, and which ones you've picked up from others, and are ready to let go of.

## Can Our Core Values Change?

Are we dealt our hand of core values and expected to live with them, or can we change them into values that we may like better? I've wondered this myself, and looked up what other authors had to say. Unsurprisingly, the authors who write on the topic of values disagree: some claim that your core values are permanent, and others claim that they're not. Some say both is possible: there are values that can be changed, and those that never change. Those who claim that your core values can be changed, quote two reasons why that may happen:

1.  New life circumstances may shift your core value hierarchy.
2.  You may consciously decide to change your own core values.

Examples of events that may spontaneously change your value hierarchy are starting a family, retiring, surviving a life-threatening illness or accident, losing a loved one, a dramatic career change, etc.

Those that promote the idea of personal control over core values, claim that you can tailor your values so that they better serve your goals. (Both Slavinski and Pavlina have expressed this stance.) What these authors propose is to focus on the goals that you want to achieve, and then commit to a new value hierarchy that will allow for this to happen.

My experience leans more towards the permanent core values. I do believe there is a difference between our most intimate values that are long lasting, and the more transient values that may be affected by our surroundings, or our goals. I don't believe that goal achievement is the golden standard for the quality of life. I find that as a culture, we're a little too obsessed by it. What matters more to me are our experiences. I'd rather choose a goal that's aligned with my values, than force different values on myself to fuel an arbitrary goal.

Marc Alan Schelske, author of the book *Discovering Your Authentic Core Values*, makes the distinction between "aspirational core values" and "authentic core values":

> *"An aspirational core value isn't a bad thing; it's a great tool for casting vision. But without clarity an aspirational value can mask the real values that are driving you or your organization. [...]*
>
> *Authentic core values are (unfortunately) the more powerful kind. Why? Because these are the values that really, truly motivate your current behavior. Sometimes these values lead to really wonderful, noble acts. Other times they*

*lead to choices that we're ashamed of. They represent what is authentically*
*true about us; both what is great and inspiring, as well as what is shadow."* \*

He argues that our core values push us not only towards the 'good' decisions,
but also the decisions which may not be in our best interest. This reminds
me of Slavinski's claim from *Kreaton* that 'freedom' is not a good value to
have within the top of your hierarchy, because for many people it leads to
less happiness and harmony. Funnily enough, his own motto is *"Omnia*
*sacrificabo praeter libertatem"* (*"I will sacrifice everything before freedom"*), so I
take it that he knows something about that. Whether this is true or not, in
any case it's better to be aware of your values than not to be aware of them.

As for the values that arise because of a change in circumstances, some
people who share their stories of how their life has changed after such an
event actually claim their life has improved, and that they felt more fulfilled
in the new circumstances. Could this mean that they've always had these
'hidden' core values they were ignoring, that only got to be fulfilled in the
new circumstances?

I can't speak for others, but I did recognize this in my own life. During
the times I was unfulfilled and depressed, my life did not reflect my core
values. However, as I got in touch with them more and more, and aligned
my personal and professional life with them, I felt like this was what I was
always meant to do. While the details of my dreams and aspirations changed
since I was a child, I can recognize that even my earliest desires were fueled
by the same values that fuel me today. As an adult I have completely different
priorities than I had as a child, but I can see the continuity and can point to
the moments where I've made the decisions that were informed by my values, and the decisions I've made against them because of outside pressure.

The process of discovering your core values that I offer here is based
on the assumption that they are permanent—your only job is to find out
what they are.

---

\*   *"Are Your Core Values Real or Aspirational?"* by Marc Alan Schelske (March 29, 2015).

## Your Transformation Story: The Key to Your Core Values

If all this talk of values is still a bit too abstract for you, let's get more practical. Core values are rather easy to identify, if you know where to look for: your most defining life experiences.

When we live according to our core values, we feel content with our life. Work is pleasurable, even when it's challenging. Our relationships are mostly harmonious. We can look ourselves in the mirror and fully stand in our integrity.

When our life is in conflict with our core values, we have a nagging feeling of dissatisfaction, though everything might look fine on the surface. Our work drains us, even on days when we aren't so busy. We pick fights with loved ones, and enhance disagreements with our clients and colleagues. We're burdened by doubt and regret about decisions made long ago. *"If only I've made a different choice, my life would be so much better right now."*

We all have a mix of the former and the latter, depending on which value we live by and which value we ignore in each area of life. Core values can be seen in our everyday life, but it's on such a subtle level that most people don't even notice. It's easier with the big things, something that smacks you over the head and you cannot possibly ignore: **your transformation stories**.

Every person in the world, no matter how ordinary and mundane their life is, has lived through several defining life experiences. Every one of us has had their own version of 'The Hero's Journey' (as described by Joseph Campbell in his book *The Hero With A Thousand Faces*). We're inspired by moving stories of transformation in books and movies, because they reflect our own challenges and transformations. We may not be fighting dragons, evil masterminds or aliens, but we've all faced our own fear, self-doubt, unsupportive environment, or physical challenges at some point. Replace the supernatural monster from the blockbuster story with a typical life difficulty, and you get a very familiar narrative: your life.

Transformative life experiences shake our very foundations and bring our core values into question. Should you make this choice, or that one? What have you based this choice on? Even people who try their best to rely on facts to make their decision, like jury members and judges, are prone to biases and making emotional decisions.*

These extreme situations that change the course of your life signify how at a certain point you felt the discord with your core values, and then you've made a change toward alignment with your core values. In this very clear 'before and after' snapshot, you can pinpoint what was missing in your earlier choices, and what became present in your subsequent choices.

If you can't remember any single life defining event, try this one on for size: the story of how you started your own business, or found your calling. This is a typical pattern that I've seen in many creatives' lives who grew into their art later in life. At first, their life is dull and mechanical—they have a difficult time fitting in their immediate community, but they don't know why. Suddenly, they discover a new creative skill that becomes the center of their world, and opens up new possibilities for them. This skill helps them meet other people who share their passion, so they finally find a community of people who understand them and accept them for who they are—something they've been desperate to find for so long. This skill unlocks new potential for supporting themselves, and expressing their unique gifts. It brings joy and fulfillment to their life, and the people around them.

The other type of story is what the designer and entrepreneur Amy Hoy calls the "'Fuck This!' Moment"†: the exact moment when you realize that the life you've been living has become so painful, there is no alternative but to make a bold risk. This can be starting your own business, or a project that you've been postponing for years.

What compelled you to start your business? Why did you leave your job behind? What need were you trying to fulfill with your own venture that you weren't able to fulfill in a job? What circumstances in the old job were the most annoying for you? What are you *so elated* to never have to experience again? The answers to these questions all point to your values.

---

*  "Emotion in the Behavior and Decision Making of Jurors and Judges" by Terry A. Maroney, Emotion Researcher (October 2016).

†  "How Your 'Fuck This!' Moment Changes Everything" by Amy Hoy (August 19, 2014).

## HOW I DISCOVERED THE RELATIONSHIP BETWEEN MY OWN CORE VALUES & MY WORK

I started my own business in 2013. Before that, I was employed as a lead designer in a web development agency, where I worked for several years. On the outside, the job looked perfect: I worked with a great team of people who were all top experts in their field. I had a reasonable salary, and a casual office atmosphere. However, this didn't feel 'enough'. I disliked the clients we worked with, and the projects I got to work on most of the time weren't very creative. I had no control or any say in who we worked with, or how we worked.

Despite supposedly doing what I loved, I was losing passion for design: in my free time, I was desperate to do *anything but design*. While I was creating my personal surreal and fantasy artworks, or sketching local landscapes and cityscapes while I was out and about, I was daydreaming about becoming a freelance illustrator. I felt like my design skills were getting worse over time, instead of getting better. I didn't know what to do, so I didn't do anything until I was forced to make a choice.

The agency was going to shut down, and we were all to go our separate ways. I had to make a decision: do I find another job, or do I finally dare to start freelancing full-time? I chose freelancing.

My first year in business was the *worst*. My very next freelancing gig resembled employment, but without any of the benefits. I went through project after project, still not feeling like I was making anything worthwhile. It took me a long time to regain the lost confidence in my design skills, and I slowly start rebuilding my professional life, almost from scratch. I relied on personal connections I'd made years ago to get clients, and this gave me hope that there were better things ahead.

Things started turning for the better when I became more selective about the clients and the projects I was taking on. I became more attuned to what I really wanted from my work, and I looked for opportunities to bring in more of that. I found that what I really don't want to compromise on are my values. I used the self-reflective processes I mentioned earlier to discover that my most important and meaningful core values are **creativity**, **freedom**, **individuality**, **brilliance** and **compassion**. I vowed that I would honor these values in my business by:

- Crafting original content with love and care, that expresses my unique point of view.
- Encouraging others to express themselves creatively.
- Respecting everyone's freedom of choice and sovereignty.
- Refusing to limit my own freedom, or the freedoms of my clients and partners.
- Refusing to use manipulative marketing practices that impede people's freedom of choice.
- Encouraging my clients to express their individuality through their business.
- Refusing to conform to the cultural expectations.
- Cultivating an atmosphere conducive to deep thought and creative problem solving.
- Refusing to force the creative process and stifle innovative thinking in order to push things out faster.
- Creating conditions for authentic sharing and connecting with my audience and clients.
- Refusing to avoid difficult conversations and gloss over uncomfortable topics because of shame.

As you might expect, not everyone I've met has welcomed this approach. It's rubbing many people the wrong way, as it should be—if I choose to live the life I was meant to live, I can't live a life other people want me to. Sometimes you have to make a choice: do I want to commit to my own fulfillment, or other people's expectations? Conforming to other people's expectations does not necessarily lead to *their* happiness, nor does refusing to conform do any real damage to other people in most cases.

A lot of us have been raised (women especially) to make other people happy: our parents, our teachers, our friends, our partners. Maybe your social operating system is calibrated towards people-pleasing, and neglecting your own needs and desires. The very idea that you could live the life that *you* want, instead of following a neat set of 'reasonable' steps can sound downright selfish—until you realize that pleasing others, never attending to your own needs, and making yourself smaller than you are, isn't doing anyone a favor.

It's a crushing realization to see how we've not been living according to our own values, but instead scrambling to make everyone around us respect us by tending to their values. In my old life, I was trying to conform to my boss' and colleagues' ideas on what a designer should be and do in order to have harmonious relationships with them. On the inside, I was unhappy and resentful, and didn't give 100% percent in the workplace. Right when I began working for myself, I replaced the boss figure with the client figure—conforming to their needs, desires and sometimes unreasonable demands, in the interest of looking like a professional. Little did I know that this approach would not earn me respect, nor the money I deserved.

My new life is very much a work in progress. While I try to live up to my values, it isn't always easy, and I often slip back into my old ways (and then bang my head because I should know better by now). What's different now is that I'm conscious of what my values are, and when something goes wrong, I can pinpoint what went wrong much quicker, and course-correct. I've become more outspoken about the things that matter to me. I stand firm behind my line in the sand even in the face of criticism, and I don't let other people's opinions shake my world. For every one person who complained about the fact that I talk about personal growth almost as much as I talk about branding and marketing, there are dozens who wrote back to thank me precisely for writing about the deeper work we need to do.

Even if things aren't always easy, and my business brings on all sorts of challenges, I enjoy my life much more than I did before. I work out of a small studio in my apartment that's filled to the brim with books and art supplies. Yoga pants are my work uniform. I get to start my day with a personal creative practice, and begin working at a time when I'm most focused, instead of crawling out of bed at dawn. If I want to shift my career to include more teaching or writing, I can do it without asking anyone for permission. I'm not even considering going back to work for an agency, because I can't imagine a workplace that would bring me as much fulfillment and joy as my current business does. I don't think entrepreneurship is for everyone, but it certainly is the right path for me.

## Your Most Defining Core Value

Some people can easily recognize one value or quality that is way above the rest in its importance. It's as if a person is an archetype for the value itself. My top value is creativity, and this is probably true for many other artists (although there are most certainly many artists who have a different top core value). Business consultant and Sufi Master Teacher Mark Silver calls this most important quality your Jewel:

> *"Your Jewel is the unique quality in your heart that makes you, and your business, magnetically attractive."* *

The reason I mention this is that different people use different terminology for what may be the same thing. The science isn't in yet, and we're all trying to use words to describe something intangible that can be better understood through experience. When I first heard Mark's explanation of the jewel, I realized that this was entirely compatible with my understanding of core values. If there's one value that's jumping at you more so than the others, this may be your Jewel. This value can have a disproportionate effect on your decisions and your brand, and you can use it as a leverage to differentiate yourself from your peers.

If you can't quite pinpoint 'the one' core value, don't worry—I'm only putting this out there for those who may already be aware of it, and are wondering if it's relevant. Some examples I mention in this book are focused on the most important core value, while others hold all core values as equally important.

---

* *"Why Marketing Often Feels Sleazy (and How to Avoid It)"* by Mark Silver (November 16, 2005).

## How Core Values Ripple through Your Business & Brand

When you know what your core values are, you're able to weave them into your work. You start recognizing all the ways in which your profession has been missing them, and this gives you the opportunity to make a difference. One of my friends and clients has done this so clearly that I felt compelled to share her story.

Mihaela Marija Perković is a communication specialist whose extensive experience includes fiction writing, copywriting, digital marketing, PR, and crisis communication. She started her business with the intention to help her corporate clients communicate better with their audience and their employees, because she noticed that many people find communicating difficult, despite it seemingly being something all people know how to do. When thinking about what it is that *she* brings into this work, she realized it was the qualities of playfulness and humor, which are rooted in her core value of **fun**. Specifically in her clients' example, fun has the ability to transform how teams approach their internal communication, which results with improved mood and increased mutual understanding. Here's how she describes this effect:

> *"Nothing promotes effective communication like a good story, and the best stories are conceived and told when in a good mood. When I introduced this to the internal communications of companies whose employees work in large, distributed teams across the world, it turned out that the cheerfulness of the person who communicates is a key part of communication skills. Grumpy people read everything in the negative tone, have less patience and understanding, and are less intelligible when communicating."*

The obvious ways to use this insight is to add more fun and playfulness to her writing, and to teach her client's employees how to use it in their everyday work, but she took it a step further. She didn't want to do *"boring presentations about communication"* which is typical for corporate training. Instead, she approached it by teaching storytelling and comic writing workshops, with the specific aim to learn better communication skills.

Mihaela and I met years ago at a sci-fi convention (where else?). When she brought her own company Savarakatini back from hiatus, she hired me to design its logo and visual brand identity. When I was exploring what makes her unique compared to other agencies in her market, she explained her fun-driven approach, and I went wild with this angle. I came up with a fresh visual identity that communicates this core value of fun, but in a way that is feminine, elegant, and quirky, without any childish connotations. Mihaela's core value of fun is evident in all the facets of her business:

- The methods she uses in her offers.
- Her writing voice.
- Her company name.*
- The names of her offers (*Geek Whisperers*, *Creative Troublemakers*)
- Her visual brand identity.
- Her presence.

When you meet her in person, it's clear from her loud laugh, bright green hair, and colorful clothes that she simply *radiates* fun, and that's what people love about her.

Core values are most effective in branding when emphasized to the extreme. Find out what yours are, and go *all out* on them—this will make your brand remarkable. And if your core value happens to be 'balance', well then go all out on balance. Not everyone needs to be loud and boisterous, that's precisely what makes this work so beautiful. There are no shoulds, only possibilities. Now that we've seen a few examples of how core values work in business, I'll share techniques and prompts to help you find yours.

## How to Identify Your Core Values

The easiest way to identify your values is to examine your interests, motivations, past decisions, passions, and pains, and find out what all of them have

---

\*    "Savarakatini" is a word from a children's counting rhyme.

in common. I recommend getting a journal or a piece of paper to answer the questions below (you can also use the bonus workbook). Some of them may speak to you more than others. There's no right or wrong way to do this, just write what comes to mind.

### WHAT DO YOU MOST ENJOY DOING?

Think both in terms of business and personal life. List all of your active hobbies, and even those you haven't done in a while, but were meaning to get back to. There's a reason why you enjoy those things—they help you experience your core values.

If there was ever a time when you neglected one of your interests or hobbies, and felt like a part of you was missing or dormant because of that, it's likely that you were actually lacking the values it was giving you. This activity may provide a key to what you need in your life to be content.

### WHAT INSPIRES YOU TO DO THOSE THINGS?

What are you getting out of your professional activities, hobbies, and other interests? Think about *why* you enjoy them so much? What makes these activities different from other things you have to do? How do you feel when you do them? How do you feel when you *don't* do them? What is the opposite of that feeling—what is it that you crave for?

### WHAT MADE YOU START YOUR BUSINESS OR CREATIVE PROJECT?

Think of this like your own superhero origin story. What was your life like before you started your business, and what was the moment when you realized you had to turn a new page? Did you experience a life-changing event? Or did you perhaps meet someone who 'infected' you with their creative bug? Or did you just get tired of your life being as is and wanted a change?

Your journey might have been evolving for years, and still is—but that moment when you *knew* that you had to take this path was a turning point. Try to identify what the quality of this impulse was. Don't worry if it was a seemingly negative one, like *"I got sick of my boring old life,"* or *"I got divorced,"* or *"I was envious of all my creative friends and wanted to prove to myself that I could do it too,"* etc. Often people's transformation stories include challenges, but it's what you make of that challenge that counts.

## WHAT DO YOU STAND FOR?

Each of us puts a priority on certain things, and when these values are threatened, we're ready to fight for it (even if we're normally a very agreeable person). Whether you're naturally calm or have a short fuse, think back at moments when some person, organization or event deeply offended you, and you felt the need to say or do something about it. Here are some examples of what I mean:

- Human rights (women, children, minorities, refugees...)
- Animal rights.
- Protecting the environment.
- Preserving a cultural identity.
- Achieving economic equality.
- Finding an effective cure for a disease.
- Equal access to health care/education/technology/arts.
- Changing the public perception about arts/entertainment/etc.

These are broad, but you can also stand for a local cause. In fact, the closer to home it is, the more motivated you'll be to take part in the change.

## WHAT DO YOU GEEK OUT ABOUT?

This can be related to your field of work, or completely random. A *geek* is a person who is deeply interested in a specific topic, and knows information that isn't common knowledge. It can be a science, history, art, or a pop-culture thing—something reasonably well known (like Star Wars) or more obscure (like LARP).* The things you geek out about also carry elements of your core values, which is what makes them so attractive to you. Better yet, these interests can help you connect on a deeper level with the members of your audience who share these interests.

---

\* Live action role play: a type of game similar to pen and paper role playing games, in which players wear costumes and act out the actions of their imaginary characters.

## WHAT ANNOYS YOU IN YOUR PROFESSIONAL WORLD?

Let your inner meanie go wild with this one. What do people in your industry do or say that makes you wonder *"What the Hell are they thinking? Is this where our profession is going now?"* You may have great respect for your colleagues, but perhaps there are little things that you repeatedly see others do, that you would never allow yourself.

If you were elected to be the chairman of a professional association and had unlimited executive power, what changes would you initiate during your mandate? How do you want to see your profession change in the future?

## IF YOU HAD ALL THE MONEY YOU NEEDED, HOW WOULD YOU TRANSFORM YOUR BUSINESS?

Would you do the same things you do now? Or would you quit and do something else entirely? Maybe you would change some aspects of your business while keeping others?

If money wasn't an issue, how would you spend your time? (Besides binging on TV shows and sipping cocktails on a beach, obviously.)

## WHAT DO YOU WANT TO ACHIEVE THROUGH YOUR BUSINESS— FOR YOURSELF AND FOR YOUR CLIENTS?

Think of your business as a vehicle, or a tool. It's not here just so you could create things and sell them for money. When a business is profitable, it can be used to achieve greater goals. Some CEOs start a foundation that's funded by their profits. Others create programs within their business that enable them to help people who otherwise wouldn't be able to afford their services, like a scholarship fund, or a free community project.

Your clients have much bigger visions for their life than what you help them achieve. Your work is just one step on their journey, but if you know where their journey leads to, you can position yourself to help them even more.

What is your big vision? What do you see yourself doing ten years from now? What kind of legacy do you expect your business to leave behind when you're gone?

## FIND THE CONNECTING THREAD

Go back through your previous answers and see which words and phrases you keep repeating, and which values may be at the core of your answers. Write down what stands out for you. Distill the above answer down to 4–5 values that are the most important for you. Try out different synonyms for each one, until you find a word that just vibrates with life and meaning for you.

These exploratory questions, along with a list of examples of personal values that can spark ideas for you, are available in the bonus book resources. If you're still having trouble pinpointing your core values even after going through these questions, here's another exercise you can try.

## DISCOVER YOUR CORE VALUES WITH THE CARD SORTING METHOD

The following exercise is described in the book *Kreaton* by Živorad Mihajlović Slavinski. If the previous writing prompts haven't given results, try this—you may find it suits you better.

For this exercise, you'll need around 50 small pieces of paper, about the size of a business card or a playing card. On each piece of paper, write one of the things that is most important to you in your life. If you don't know where to start, look over the Core Values List in the bonus materials and write down those that jump at you as most important. Keep writing your values down until you run out of paper. If you end up with less than 50 cards and have no more ideas, that's fine too.

Next, gather all those cards into a deck and put them on the table. Take two cards from the top of the deck and **compare them: which one is more important to you?** If they seem like they're equally important, think of a scenario where you'd be required to choose between the two. Allow the decision to surface without effort. Don't overthink this—your first answer is the right one. Place the one that is more important to you above the other one, and now you have a new deck with your value hierarchy. Take another card from the other deck, and compare it with the first card in your value hierarchy deck. If it's more important, put it on the top. If it's less important, compare it with the second card in the deck. If it's more important than the second one, it goes above that card. If it's less important, it goes to the bottom of the deck. Repeat this process for each remaining card in the other deck.

As you're comparing these cards, it's important how you intuitively *feel*, and not what you think is morally or spiritually 'right'. You don't have to share the results of this exercise with anyone. If 'family' or 'truth' falls further down your values list than you'd like, so be it. There's no reason to be ashamed of that. Your values are your own, and the best way to honor them is to be honest with yourself about them.

After you're done comparing each individual card with every other card, you'll know the exact ranking of each value in your value system. The first five or so cards at the top are your top core values. Other values are also important, but they will have less of an impact the further down the list you go. Focusing on just the top three to five will make the biggest difference.

## How to Use Core Values in Your Business

Now that you know what your core values are, what do you do with them? You didn't go through all this trouble for nothing. Your core values will inform the other elements of your Human Centered Brand Discovery Pyramid, which we'll explore in the upcoming chapters, but they also bring certain benefits on their own.

One way you can use your core values is to make decisions based on them. You can start by making small decisions, like what and where to eat, which style and color of clothing to wear, which books to buy... After you get some practice with small and simple decisions, you'll be ready for bigger decisions like:

- Which services or products to offer?
- How to market your work?
- Which business consultant to hire?
- Which conferences and events to go to?
- Where to publish your work?

- In which publications to advertise?
- Which colors and fonts to choose for your website?

To answer questions like these, ask yourself *"What would a person who has these core values choose to do in this situation?"*

If there's a conflict between two of your values, answering these questions will reveal which of them is more important to you. One of the choices will feel obviously more appealing to you, which means that this core value is stronger.

Another way to use your core values is to **publish them**. Some organizations disclose their core values on their websites, to show to their clients and potential employees who they are, and to help them determine whether they would fit in.

Paul Zelizer, the founder of the community and podcast for conscious entrepreneurs Awarepreneurs has published their core values on their About page, and explained how each of these values impacts their work. Their core values are listed as: *"social entrepreneurship, awareness, community, transparency, social justice, awareness & self-care."* Knowing about these values upfront has helped me decide to join the community. Because of the group's core value of social justice, members have taken part in many challenging conversations, which aren't as welcome in the other business-oriented communities. This dedication to conversations concerning social justice is probably the key differentiating factor for Awarepreneurs.

Once you go public with your core values, there's no shuffling about. If you claim to stand for something greater than yourself, and then you make a misstep, people will call you out on it. I've seen it happen to several prominent names in the conscious entrepreneurship space in the past year alone, and it gets ugly when people don't know how to handle the fallout.

If you claim to hold a core value and then act out of integrity, you need to be able to accept feedback with grace. Being called out for doing something out of integrity is different from being called out for doing something that other people simply don't *like*. What other people like or dislike is not your

---

*   *awarepreneurs.com*

problem. Your core values are what you should be concerned with. Making your core values public isn't just a beacon for your right people, it's also an invitation to be held accountable. If your audience is aware of your intentions, they can help you stay the course.

Owning your values is challenging, especially if society as a whole considers them irrelevant, trivial, or dangerous. That's the difficult work of being ourselves in the world that may not always appreciate our uniqueness. It's not easy to live according to your values, but the alternative is missing out on fulfillment and happiness than can only come from living in alignment with your true essence. It's not easy to do business according to your values, but that may be the only way you'll ever *feel* truly successful.

How many stories have you heard where someone had a 6-figure corporate job, a house in a great neighborhood, a nice car, a loving family, and still they felt like something was missing? Then they've decided to leave the cushy job behind and start from the ground, and built a business that brought them a different kind of success—one that isn't often featured on the covers of glossy magazines.

Living true to your values is profoundly subversive. It's not what *normal* people do. Most people tend to accept the values of the majority because they want to fit in. They don't like standing out and attracting attention—they just want to live their comfortable lives, and not cause too much trouble.

If you're still reading this book, I'm guessing it's because you're not that kind of person. (Those people don't appreciate the things I have to say, and call me an idealist and a dreamer like it's a *bad* thing.) You may not consider yourself an idealist or a dreamer, but here you are, doing your thing. You're dangerously close to living aligned with your authentic core values, or maybe you're already doing it. Maybe you swing back and forth between living true to your values, and hiding behind other people's values.

You're not better or worse than anyone else because of this. Living true to your values is a spectrum, not a clear destination you can easily reach. It can take a lifetime to learn how to live in 100% alignment with your essence. It's not a game you're supposed to "win". But you can still take the next step. You can look at the answers you wrote and paint a picture of a future you want to have. You can write your values on a post-it and put it on your desk, so you can ask yourself every single morning when you get to work, *"How can I live according to my values today?"*

Nobody expects you to make a 180 degree turn in one day, and it would be a stressful thing to do. One small decision every day, and soon enough you'll be back on the path, living your values. This is not a goal, it's a practice. Every day gives us a chance to test our commitment to what's most important to us.

## chapter IV

# It's All about Them

You sell something that people (at least theoretically) want to buy. No matter what shape or form of the things you sell is—whether it's services, digital products or physical items, the same rule of commerce applies: what you're really selling is a solution to a problem.

Your clients don't really want to hear about how awesome your service or product is, they want to know how it can help them solve a problem they have. **Your unique value proposition is a statement of how your business solves your client's problem in a unique way.** It's what differentiates your business from thousands of other businesses in the world who are attempting to do the same, and it's the second level of your Human Centered Brand Pyramid.

Some authors claim that the unique value proposition (or UVP) is the single most important part of a brand, and that without it you don't have a brand. If we're talking about commodity goods with lots of competition, than this is true. If we're talking about services though, you don't need to come up with something crazy. As we've already established, clients who buy your services are more concerned with trustworthiness and the quality of your relationship. Where unique value proposition comes very handy is attracting people's attention. If you can position yourself as the *only* business within a certain category, you can benefit from that "only cobbler in town" effect.

You can have one general unique value proposition for your company, and more specific ones for each service or product you sell. Ideally, your unique value proposition is a short sentence that can be distilled into a tagline, but you can also expand on it a bit to create a short introduction to people you meet in person.

Formulating a good unique value proposition that doesn't sound too contrived, cliché, or full of meaningless buzzwords is hard. Often you don't get it right the first time you try to do it, but it evolves over time, as you get clearer on what differentiates you from everyone else. I'll offer some tips on how you can shorten that path as much as possible, and create a unique value proposition that clearly communicates the value you offer to your clients, so that more of them recognize you as the right choice.

## Your Unique Value Proposition Is a Promise of Client's Transformation

Through it, you're promising to the client that after they've experienced working with you, they'll become the person they want to be. Products and services *change* us—they equip us with the skills, abilities, or resources that we need in order to have a different perception of ourselves.

A hungry person buys a sandwich at a stall, and is no longer hungry. For most people, this change may be enough (those whose only goal is to fill their stomach with the least expenses). Another hungry person buys an organic vegan tofu tortilla wrap and is not only full, but feels good about their impact on the environment, and their health. Buying a fast food meal seems like such a trivial transaction, and yet there's so much identity stuff wrapped into it.

It's no different with other services. If you ask yourself the question *why* someone would want to buy what you sell, and you keep asking the question *why that is*, eventually you'll get to the real value people are getting from your work. Let's see how someone might answer your questions on an example of copywriting services.

- *Why would you want my services?* Because our website copy is bad.
- *Why is that?* It doesn't convert our website visitors into buyers.
- *And why do you want that?* Because we want to make more money, duh.

We've found the main reason: the transformation the client wants is to *earn more money*. (Writing is just one possible method of achieving it.) Let's check another example: wedding photography.

- *Why would you want to buy that?* Because we want a memento of our big day.

- *Why is that?* Because we'll never be this young and beautiful again, and we want to remember how handsome, happy, and in love we were when we're old, wrinkled, and weary.

- *And why is that?* Because memories are priceless.

The main value that clients get is not photography, it's *memories*. Well that, and to see themselves as breathtakingly gorgeous, because you'll pick the most flattering lighting and angle.

This isn't about the features. The technical specifics of your offer and your method don't matter to the clients as much as you'd think. If you could get the same results with cardboard and duct tape, they'd buy it. Clients care about the *transformation*. They need your help to become a better version of themselves. Here's what business strategist Tara Gentile, author of *The Quiet Power Strategy* says about it:

> *"Value is transformation. If the transformation isn't clear, neither is the value of what you're offering. 'Life coaching' isn't value. 'Website design' isn't value. 'Jewelry' isn't value.*
>
> *Value is telling someone how their idea of themselves, their environment, their relationships, their skills, or their behavior will change as a result of using your product. Value is making it clear that there's a Before and an After and making that story come alive on the page, on the call, or in the conversation."* \*

To get to the bottom of the value your clients want to buy, ask yourself:

- What does your business achieve for your clients?

- How are your clients transformed through the process of working with you?

- What do they have now that they didn't have before?

---

\* *"It's Not You: 3 Things to Consider in the Face of Failure"* by Tara Gentile (October 28, 2015).

- What can they do now, that they couldn't do before?
- What do they feel like now, that they weren't able to feel before?

**The value you offer can be described in terms of new skills and abilities, profits, time saved, or effects on health and satisfaction.** That's what ultimately matters to people, and that is what you sell. Positioning your service as a unique solution for their problem will set you up as a *helping* brand, instead of a self-centered brand, and this will increase your sales.

Let's take custom hand-crafted jewelry as an example. On the surface, it may not look like a problem-solving item, but it is. The actual reasons why people might buy jewelry can be:

- A birthday gift for their partner, friend, or family member (value: connection).
- An accessory that will lift their boring outfit for an important event (value: confidence).
- A luxury item that will broadcast their wealth and social status in a tasteful way (value: belonging).
- Specific crystals or a picture of a saint that will remind them of the unseen forces that support them through difficult times (value: faith).

If you're wondering why people always compliment your work, and yet rarely pull out their wallets, this is why: they don't see how your services are relevant for their problem. Either they don't know they have one (or maybe they really don't have it), or you haven't done a good enough job of explaining how you can help them solve it. Explain the value clearly, and you'll see those wallets coming out way more often.

Unfortunately sometimes, no matter how well you explain your value, people are simply not going to be interested. Either they don't have a problem that your service can address, or they are not aware of it. The client's readiness to buy is expressed in the concept of the buyer cycle.

## The Role of the Buyer Cycle

The **buyer cycle** consists of 4 phases that people go through on their quest to solve their problem:

1. **Unaware**: people who are oblivious to the fact they have a problem.
2. **Problem-aware**: people who know they have a problem, and are actively looking for a solution.
3. **Solution-aware**: people who know about the available solutions, and are in the process of choosing the best one for their situation.
4. **Prospects**: people who know that your solution is the best one, and are ready to buy.

The farther along a person is in the buyer cycle, the easier it is to sell to them. It's not wise to focus primarily on the people in the earlier phases of the cycle where you have to spend more energy, while your chances of making a sale are low. This is why methods like cold-calling have such a low rate of success: you're trying to push a person through several phases of the buying cycle at once, which doesn't work. It's only when you encounter someone by chance who was already thinking about buying what you sell, that you'll be able to make a sale on the first call.

Since your time is limited, it's best to use it on those people who are only a step away from buying. This doesn't mean you'll forget about the people in other phases: you can capture them with your free content like blog posts, conference talks, videos, podcasts, etc. and gently nudge them toward the next phase. Once they become convinced that your solution is the best, all you need to do is *ask*.

**Design your unique value proposition for those who are ready to make a buying decision.** Solution-aware people don't need to be educated about the benefits of solving their problem, because they already know that. They need to understand how your service solves their problem *better* than the other potential solutions they're comparing it to. This way, you'll be able to capture the attention of those who are most likely to spend money with you *soon*.

Nurturing the audience that may become buyers months or years in the future will ensure the long-term sustainability of your business. You can also simply give value through your writing and speaking with no strings attached. But if you only have a few seconds to get someone's attention, and you need to make a sale, make sure your unique value proposition speaks to the people who are eager to hire someone like you, right now.

## The Real Challenge: Making It Unique

Finding the value part is relatively easy—you just need to put yourself in your client's shoes for long enough to learn what they care about, and highlight that. Maybe you've already done this, and are wondering where the good stuff is? We're getting to it.

The problem with your value proposition is that you're certainly not the only person in the world who has figured out that good website content leads to more money, or that memories are priceless, or that jewelry brings confidence. When everybody is saying the same things, how are the clients supposed to know who is right for them? You're in a moderately better position than you were before, but you can do better.

The uniqueness comes from something that only you can offer—something nobody else has figured out how to do and articulate it yet. Or at least, few people have figured it out, but nobody has heard of them, so for all practical purposes, you're as good as being the only one. Common unique value propositions that companies use are:

- **Innovation**: being the only one, or the first in the category.
- **Production quality**: being the best.
- **Convenience**: having a wide distribution.
- **Price**: being the cheapest.
- **Aesthetics**: having the best design.
- **Reliability**: being the most durable, offering guarantees, best customer service.
- **Exclusivity**: available in a limited edition.
- **User experience**: being the easiest to use.

- **Ethical benefit**: using means of production that do less harm to people, animals, and the environment.
- **Story**: having a long tradition, or supporting a charitable cause.

Some of these are contradictory: higher quality, reliability, aesthetics, and ethical means of production often make the price higher. Boosting convenience can mean scrimping on other features. You can't have all the bases covered—you'll need to *choose*. If you have to make a choice between offering a better service or cutting corners, I always recommend the former. Premium brands inspire more loyalty and word-of-mouth marketing than cheap commodity brands.

If you can't have the highest quality, the cheapest price, the most innovative product, or the best convenience, you can always create a story. Stories are a powerful way to talk about your business, because people connect to them. Find a story within your business that is worthy of highlighting. If there is none, create one—what can you *do* that would make a great story in the future?

If you find a unique twist to your business, clients will have a difficult time comparing you to other service providers. Even if they try, you will be able to say *"But here is what I provide that they don't"* and effectively end the comparison there. Here are some ways to find your unique twist that will make it worth it for your clients.

## 1. CREATE A GROUNDBREAKING, INNOVATIVE PRODUCT OR SERVICE

The first person to ever build a copywriting e-course cashed in on the amount that most copywriters will never get to earn. The first freelancer to create a monthly website conversion optimization service opened up the possibilities for every other freelancer who wanted to create a recurring revenue stream.

Being the first person who did something is noteworthy in itself. You can get **free press** solely based on the fact that nobody else has done it before. Even if your product or service is imperfect, there's nothing else to compare it to, at least until the competition catches up. By the time they do catch up, you'll already have built a loyal fan base and a ton of organic buzz.

Your innovative thing doesn't have to be your only product or service, or even your most profitable one. Whatever you're selling now, keep selling it—but think of another way you can add value that will attract the attention in a saturated market.

## 2. NARROW DOWN YOUR NICHE

Sometimes focusing on a specific underserved market is the way to become the go-to expert in that field. Even if your skills are applicable in multiple industries, choosing a niche where your unique skills come into the spotlight will, paradoxically, help you get *more* clients.

The reason why narrowing down works is because it makes standing out and staying memorable easier. Generalists are quickly forgotten, while experts remain top of mind whenever their field of expertise is mentioned in conversation. Those who recognize themselves in your value proposition will think: *"This is perfect for me!"*, and those that don't will think of *someone else* who fits the niche. Even people outside of your niche can help you promote your business by recommending you to the people they know.

A designer that's focused on serving legal professionals has skills that can be applied in other fields just as well, but clients generally assume that if you're specialized in a certain client demographic, you're going to be much better at it than generalists. This isn't far from the truth, either. Legal professionals have specific needs, and if you're focused on catering to them, then you truly are better equipped to serve those clients than those designers who also serve cafés, hairdressers, and florists.

## 3. FIND A NEW ANGLE

Maybe your competitors are typically serving people in a certain role (like a CEO or a marketing manager), but you can focus on helping the HR department. While most wedding professionals cater to brides, you can find an angle that puts equal emphasis on the groom's priorities and desires. Maybe you can make your car wash service kids-friendly, to appeal to busy parents who don't have a babysitter.

Here's an idea I'd like to see someone do: a hairstylist for the science nerds. You could buy National Geographic, Science, and Wired magazine subscriptions for your salon, and entertain your clientele with intellectual conversation instead of celebrity gossip and sports.

In other words, do what you normally do, but *with a twist.* See how fast you can get people talking about you.

## 4. FIND AN UNLIKELY COMBINATION

Maybe there's really nothing new under the Sun, but a new blend or a remix still counts as original. Years ago when I was designing jewelry, I invented a technique that was a combination of miniature paintings on canvas and wire-wrapping. I've never seen anything like this before or since, and maybe I really am the first person who did it. Neither wire-wrapping nor miniature paintings were in and of themselves original, and many people I know do one or the other—but there was not a single artist that I know of that combined the two. If I had pursued my hobby into a career, my unique value proposition could have been something like: original wearable framed paintings. This approach is very easy if you have multiple interests or skills:

1.  Take one skill you do exceptionally well.
2.  Connect it to another skill you do exceptionally well.
3.  Now you have a recipe that is less common than either of the skills on their own.

If you're struggling to find the second thing to combine with your core service, think about the skills and talents other people have complimented you for. Maybe it's something you're not even aware you do so well, or you don't think you could monetize—but this could transform your ordinary offering into a secret weapon.

## 5. HIGHLIGHT YOUR PERSONALITY & YOUR CORE VALUES

If nothing else works, focus on what makes your business unique above all else—*you.* Your core values influence all the other elements of your brand, including your unique value proposition.

There may be many people in the world who do the same things you do, but they are not *you.* Your ideal clients will like you for who you are as a person, not just because you can help them with their problem. If you form a genuine relationship with your audience, they will reward you with loyalty, and do a big part of your marketing for you.

So, who are you? What's your story? Why should your audience care? You don't have to offer the best quality, the cheapest price, or the most widgets in order to be the first person someone will recommend to their friend. Sometimes, it pays to just be yourself.

## DOES IT PASS THE ONLYNESS TEST?

"Onlyness" is what a brand strategist and author Marty Neumeier calls *"by far the most powerful test of a strategic position"*.* It's what makes your brand unique in its category. When you're the only one offering something, you have an immense advantage over your peers who are wallowing in sameness. The fill-in-the-blank onlyness statement Neumeier offers is:

### *"Our [offering] is the only [category] that [benefit]."*

The offering can be a product, a service, an event, a business, or a non-profit organization. The category can include similar products, services, business-es, and can be limited to a geographic region. The benefit is your unique value proposition: the thing your clients can only get from you. Here's a couple of statements based on earlier examples:

- *"Our salon is the only one in Berlin that lets you enjoy intellectual conversation while getting your haircut."*
- *"Our business is the only design studio based in Ireland that caters specifically to the needs of lawyers."*
- *"Our business is the only car wash service in Zagreb County that your kids will love spending time at."*

Your onlyness should be derived from the core of your business, not tacked on like a bow to make your marketing sound better. Since your business is based on your skills, expertise, and personal history, there must be some-thing that only you can provide to your clients that others are not able to

---

* *"The Onlyness Test"* by Marty Neumeier (October 3, 2016).

do. Find what that is, and you've solved half of your branding problems.

## How to Identify Your Unique Value Proposition

After you've established what makes your business unique from all the others, you need to express it in a compelling way, that's easy for clients to understand. Even if your clients are highly intelligent people, they are probably very busy, and have many worries on their minds. They can't devote all their time to deciphering what you meant to say when you used some clever and esoteric statement.

It's your job to make it *easy* for your clients to say "Yes" to your offer. A compelling message that presents your business as relevant, valuable, and interesting will attract more attention, and make it easier for people to recommend your business. To help you to formulate your unique value proposition, here are some questions to answer. (They're also available in The Human Centered Brand Workbook.)

### WHAT PROBLEM ARE YOU MOTIVATED TO SOLVE FOR YOUR CLIENTS?

People likely come to you asking to solve a problem they believe they need to solve—but more often than not, what they think they want is only the surface problem that may not feel that exciting to you. We can't blame clients for that—they're the experts in their own domain, not ours. What kind of a challenge *does* excite you? What's the underlying problem underneath the ones your clients come to you for? Explain the connection between what they want, and what you offer.

Maybe their dream is too small. Show them an expanded vision of what their life or their business could be like if they worked with you, as opposed to putting a band-aid on a problem they think they have.

### HOW ARE YOUR CLIENT'S LIVES IMPROVED AFTER THEY'VE USED YOUR SERVICE?

There's no better way to describe the benefits of your work, than using your own client's words. Ideally, you'll want to stay in contact with your clients for long after you've delivered your services so you can follow their progress. Collecting feedback immediately after the project is concluded is recommended, but usually the real results come months later. Check in with your clients, follow their social media updates, and celebrate their successes. Some of that success may not have happened if it weren't for your work.

## HOW DO YOUR CORE VALUES MAKE YOU AND YOUR BUSINESS DIFFERENT FROM YOUR PEERS?

How do your values play out in how you perform your services? What real, tangible effects do your core values have on your philosophy and your method? If your core values are not a part of your unique approach to your work yet, how can you make them a part of it?

If you have a process that you follow in your work, I recommend going step-by-step through that process: from answering the initial client email or phone call, through delivering the service, to wrapping up the project. For each step in the process, examine: what values influence this step? How could I bring even more of my core values into it?

Two service professionals that have a different set of core values will have a different approach to their craft. **Copying what other professionals do, without examining how it reflects on your core values, can harm your business.** Don't let your peers pressure you into conforming. Own your values, and grow your business around them.

## HOW IS YOUR METHOD DIFFERENT FROM ALL THE OTHER POTENTIAL SOLUTIONS?

What do you bring to the table that the other solutions don't? Keep in mind that the other solutions are not necessarily only your direct competitors— think about all the other solutions that a person may turn to.

A psychotherapist's direct competitors may be other therapists of different branches (cognitive-behavioral therapy, Gestalt, cybernetics, art therapy, expressive therapy etc.) But what might your potential clients try before they even think about therapy? It could be talking to friends, confiding in a spiritual leader, reading self-help books, over-the-counter medication, medication prescribed by a family doctor... What are the benefits of your method over all the other potential methods a client may have tried before that didn't work? Address this directly in your website copy and conversations.

## WHAT MAKES YOUR OFFER IMPOSSIBLE TO DUPLICATE OR IMITATE?

For some service providers, this may mean that they have a unique blend of education and experience that few other people in the world (or their local area) have. Others may have developed a special technique, and use materials that are difficult to obtain.

What would a competitor who wanted to imitate your work have to go through in order to do it right? Sometimes, the time and money investment is a barrier for others. Highlight this barrier, and show that you weren't deterred by it.

## WHAT UNIQUE PERSPECTIVE DO YOU BRING TO YOUR FIELD OF WORK?

How do your interests play into your offerings? Refer to your answers from the previous chapter on core values. Maybe your hobbies and interests make you a really good candidate for working within a certain client niche.

Another way your interests might influence your work is to make it a part of your process—either the method, or the presentation. Gamers might want to use certain gaming vocabulary in their marketing, or form their method around game mechanics. Even 'boring' accounting or virtual assistance work can become interesting to clients if you put a unique spin on it.

Julie Wolk, a former environmental activist and non-profit director turned business coach, uses plant and nature models and metaphors extensively in her work. Her educational background and passion for nature enabled her to come up with offerings and marketing language that highlight this connection between business and nature. One of her services, *Networking in Nature*, is exactly what it sounds like: organized hikes for conscious entrepreneurs who want to get away from the computer, move their body, and enjoy the fresh air in the company of like-minded people. This approach makes hers one of the best examples of branding for coaches that I've ever seen.

What passion of yours could you bring forward through your work? Is there a way to weave your entire business around this passion, so that people who share it can feel like they're in the *best* place for them to be?

### FORMULATE YOUR UNIQUE VALUE PROPOSITION

Looking back to these answers, give a compelling reason why someone would need and want exactly your solution to their problem, instead of other people's. This is your unique value proposition.

Try to distill your unique value proposition into a **short sentence** that you could use on your website, or when meeting new people. Don't worry about the exact wording yet, we'll get to that in the next chapter. Feel free to refine it until you come up with a sentence that sounds good. You're not running for any awards here—the important thing is that it communicates the value you provide *clearly* to people who would appreciate it the most. It's OK if your grandma wouldn't understand it, as long as your intended audience does.

## How to Use Your Unique Value Proposition

Once you've gone through the hard work of figuring out what makes your business unique, you need to share it with the world. Here's a couple of variations of unique value proposition you might need, depending on how you meet clients.

### THE SHORT & CATCHY TAGLINE

We'll talk more about taglines in the sixth chapter, but what you need to consider now is how to make your unique value proposition as short as possible, so that it can be included in your tagline without it getting overly complex. The ideal places for your short tagline are:

- Website homepage.
- Email signature.
- Social media profiles bios.
- Social media cover photos.

- Business cards.
- Search engine, banner, and social media advertisements.
- Headlines of advertising materials, press releases, sponsored articles etc.

When there's only a short time and a small physical space to talk about your business, lead with a short and catchy tagline that puts your unique value proposition front and center.

## THE SIMPLE SENTENCE

Short taglines work great in a written format, but they don't sound very natural when you speak them out loud. For this reason, you may come up with a slightly different wording that you can say when you introduce yourself. This wording may be less precise than ideal, but you have the opportunity to clarify it in the conversation if the other person is interested. Since you don't have a character limit, you can use several simple words instead of one complex one.

Our imaginary hair salon owner might say *"I run a hair salon for geeky folks who want to talk about science and technology while getting their haircut."* It's clear, it shows the unique value, and it's unpretentious—just what a good verbal introduction is supposed to be.

Write this sentence down, and practice saying it until you can say it without any excess "Umms" and "Ahs" in any situation, no matter how stressful. If you stumble over a certain word, find a different way to say it to minimize the chance of making a mistake.

## THE DETAILED PARAGRAPH

Once you capture the interest of your audience, you can go into more detail, and specify what makes it possible for you to achieve this unique value. You can do this on your website 'About us' page, your services page, brochures, and other marketing materials that allow for more space.

This is the place where you can go into your personal interests, passions, and credentials that make you the perfect person to deliver this value. On top of that you can describe your unique methodology, or mention any special equipment or materials you use that helps you deliver this value. This is not the time to be modest and hide your brilliance. Let your clients know why you're the right professional for them.

For now, all of these statements and paragraphs are *rough drafts* that you'll keep working on and improving over time. Don't let perfectionism stop you from writing your ideas down.

Before you go on to write your actual marketing copy, you may need to figure out how you naturally communicate with people—what your brand voice is like. The next chapter will show you how to do that, and with this knowledge you'll be able to make your unique value proposition sound even more compelling and engaging.

*chapter V*

# Talk the Talk & Walk the Walk

Being in business requires communicating with clients, prospective clients, business partners, contractors, and your audience. No matter what kind of services you provide, you can't avoid it. You share your ideas via email, on your website, on video, during in-person meetings, in interviews, in articles, on social media... Most of us communicate spontaneously, and don't give it too much thought—that is until we need to write something that's going to be seen by many people, or speak in front of an audience. That's usually when we become self-conscious about how we sound. In this chapter, you'll learn how to identify your natural communication style, so that you can always present your ideas in a manner that is 'on brand'.

**Your brand voice is the way you communicate across all the written or spoken media**, and it's the third element on the Human Centered Brand Discovery Pyramid. My definitions may differ a bit from other sources. For the purposes of this book, brand voice covers both the **topics** you're covering with your content (what you're giving your voice to), and your **voice qualities**, that is your style of verbal expression.

For groups, organizations, or businesses with more than one team member, brand voice is synthetic, and most of the communication to the public is done by one or several people who are trained for this job, like copywriters, public relations specialists, social media managers, or customer support staff. The employees or contractors that work in these positions take on the business's brand voice, not their own personal voice.

For solo business owners, their brand voice is very similar to their own personal voice. I wouldn't recommend that you steer away from your natural personality, because it's difficult to maintain a consistent voice if you need to act the entire time. You can choose to what extent you want your personal voice to align with your brand voice. Some people commit to 100% of their personal voice and don't censor themselves at all, while others put on a slight filter so they don't come out too vulgar or too intense. Choose what feels right for you, and take your time to allow your voice to evolve.

When you show up consistently with a brand voice that sounds like an actual human being instead of a trained parrot, people trust you more because you appear genuine.

Even if you're the only person working in your business, it's good to have your brand voice qualities documented. That way, whenever you're producing an important piece of content, or need to write a difficult email, you can check whether you sound like yourself.

## How to Discover Your Authentic Brand Voice

People who are not professional writers can be intimidated by the difficult quest of "finding your voice". The questions in this chapter are designed to give you a starting point in identifying your dominant voice qualities, and to focus your writing and speaking on the topics that matter to you. I can't promise that you'll find your writing voice overnight, but you'll be one step closer than you were yesterday.

The best way to find your authentic brand voice is to *write a lot*. You don't need to publish everything you write—treat it as a practice. If you write a little bit every day, even in your journal, you'll find a voice that's grounded in your personality much faster than trying to think your way through it. Keep producing content, and you'll develop a voice that is natural, consistent, and appealing to your right people pretty soon.

Sometimes if we're exposed to someone's voice for a long time, we start sounding like them, and lose touch with our own voice. In my case it's so pronounced, it's ridiculous. I'm a verbal chameleon—I easily accept not only the vocabulary of the community I find myself in, but their accent too. One time, I was talking to a group of Irish folks, and after a couple of minutes

I started unconsciously picking up on their accent and talking more like them. When I realized what I was doing, I had to make a conscious effort to get back to my usual American English accent. This also happens to me in writing. While I was binge-reading old posts by one of my favorite bloggers Havi Brooks of The Fluent Self, who has a terrific and unique brand voice, I started picking up on her style of writing, and it became evident in my own blog posts.

If you're easily influenced by other people, perhaps it would help if you went on a media fast for a while to discover what you sound like when there's no one around you to imitate. A week-long stay-at-home writing retreat could do wonders for your brand voice. If you feel brave, you could do a full month. I once did that, and came out of it with some of my best writing to date.

The following questions will help you look critically at your own style of expression, and to create a guideline for future communication with your clients and your audience.

## WHAT KIND OF TOPICS DO YOU MOST ENJOY TALKING OR WRITING ABOUT?

What matters the most to you? You might be surprised to find that you don't really enjoy writing or talking about the subjects that would be expected from someone with your expertise.

As a graphic designer, people expect me to write about the rules of good design, image editing, Photoshop and Illustrator tutorials, and so on. To be completely honest, these topics do not inspire me at all. I wrote about them at length a decade ago. There are many people talking about these subjects today, better than I could. Instead, I want to talk about the fringe subjects, where design meets art, business, meaning, and the human psychology. This is where I feel I can create the most impact. It's the reason why most of this book doesn't focus on graphic design. (There will be some graphic design in the chapters that follow.)

The topics you focus on will be influenced by your core values, so refer back to your answers to previous questions to help you with this. The better you can express your core values through your communications, the more you will connect with your right audience.

Your topics also need to back up your unique value proposition, so you can create interest for your offerings through your content. You're allowed to write on topics that aren't the core of your business, but the whole story needs to make sense for your audience. They don't know you as well as your friends do, they only see your dispersed announcements and articles, and try to piece them together to form an image of you. Switching from topic to topic may confuse them if they don't see a connecting thread.

### IF YOU HAD TO PICK ONE THING YOU WANT TO BE KNOWN FOR, WHAT WOULD IT BE?

This one is more difficult. We're all complex and multifaceted creatures, and picking *one thing* can feel like going against our nature. This is where your brand voice takes a slight turn from your personal voice.

In your personal life, you're going to talk about different subjects to different people, depending on their interests. (I assume that your family, friends, and acquaintances are not all interested in the very same things.) In your professional life, you assume that your clients are interested in what happens to be your most important interest. This isn't the only thing you'll talk about to them, but it's *the* thing you want to be *known* for.

If you have many things going on at the same time, you can choose an 'umbrella topic' that covers all of your offerings and projects. This is not your unique value proposition, which should be specific. Your umbrella topic is a lens through which you focus your work, and help people understand how it all connects. As a mixed media artist, brand designer, consultant, writer, and teacher, the umbrella topic that I want to be known for is *authentic self-expression*. It encompasses all the projects I've worked on, and will work on in the future, even if I decide to shift my career over time. This book plays right into that. Knowing what my one thing is helps me focus on what matters the most in my writing.

### WHAT DO OTHER PEOPLE COMPLIMENT YOU ON?

If you have a blog, a podcast, or have done lots of public speaking in the past, then you've probably received some feedback. If you have a place where you store all of your positive feedback (like the Win Book that I've mentioned in the second chapter), this should be easy. If you don't, then your homework is to go through your emails, blog comments, testimonials, reviews, feedback forms, social media replies, media mentions, and any other places where people have talked about your writing and presentation skills. Write down the key terms that people use to describe your way of expressing yourself.

Other people's comments may offer clarity and perspective that you can't get yourself seeing it from the inside. I had no idea I was funny until a couple of my readers told me so. (My jokes and puns didn't land well with other kids in school.) Now that I'm surrounded by nerds, they do tend to appreciate my sense of humor much better. I'm still not comedy material, but it helps break the tension when I teach.

If you don't have many (or any) written feedback, you can always simply ask people who know you to tell you what aspect of your personality they enjoy or find most attractive. What are the keywords that pop up again and again in the feedback and compliments you've received? Do any of them explain certain situations in your past when you've felt self-conscious about the way you talk?

## WHICH VOICE QUALITIES BEST DESCRIBE YOUR STYLE OF EXPRESSION?

In order to complete this exercise, keep a couple of your best content pieces handy. It could be your articles, heartfelt letters, interviews, presentation transcripts etc. Interviews are particularly interesting because they force you to think on your feet. What comes out of your mouth is more authentic than a piece of text that went through three rounds of editing. As you're thinking about the qualities that describe your voice, try to find evidence for it or against it in your own content.

I define voice qualities using a list of extremes. When viewing two extremes side by side, you may get the one of following impressions:

1. Your brand voice leans towards one quality more than the other.
2. Your brand voice is somewhere in the middle of the two extreme qualities.

3.  Your brand voice encompasses both qualities in different situations.
4.  This pair of qualities is irrelevant for your brand voice.

Write down those voice qualities which are relevant for your voice. We're not interested in the middle-of-the-road balance, because it doesn't affect your voice as much as the ones that are near the extremes.

When trying to describe your style of self-expression through qualities, consider not only your written and spoken words, but other mediums as well: visual art, music, performance, etc. After you've noted all the qualities, **trim your list down to a maximum of ten most important brand voice qualities**. Keep these qualities close to hand whenever you're writing any kind of content, to make sure that what you create is aligned with your brand voice. Here is a list of brand voice qualities that I've collected, and you can add your own qualities to this list in the workbook.

| | | |
|---|---|---|
| • Formal | • Emotional | • Objective |
| • Conversational | • Serious | • Meditative |
| • Gentle | • Humorous | • Active |
| • Harsh | • Cheerful | • Introverted |
| • Simplistic | • Poignant | • Extroverted |
| • Complex | • Sensual | • Agreeable |
| • Feminine | • Cerebral | • Contrarian |
| • Masculine | • Transparent | • Moderate |
| • Sophisticated | • Enigmatic | • Extreme |
| • Plain | • Mysterious | • Quiet |
| • Assertive | • Clear | • Loud |
| • Shy | • Cryptic | • Passionate |
| • Bold | • Exposed | • Cool |
| • Mild | • Closed | • Technical |
| • Intellectual | • Subjective | • Humanistic |

- Raw
- Refined
- Common
- Extraordinary
- Intimate
- Reserved
- Expert
- Beginner
- Detached
- Compassionate
- Calm
- Excited
- Ethereal
- Grounded
- Esoteric
- Common sense
- Friendly

- Professional
- Theoretical
- Practical
- Mature
- Childish
- Playful
- Geeky
- Extravagant
- Glamorous
- Idealistic
- Cynical
- Rational
- Imaginative
- Creative
- Verbose
- Concise
- Metaphoric

- Mystical
- Unconventional
- Whimsical
- Natural
- Literal
- Fun
- Expressive
- Laid-back
- Dramatic
- Comedic
- Sensational
- Ordinary
- Informative
- Focused
- Expansive

## WHAT IS YOUR RELATIONSHIP TO YOUR CLIENTS?

When talking to your clients in person, in writing, or your free content, what role are you taking on? Here is a list of some potential roles:

- Teacher
- Mentor
- Advisor
- Friend

- Leader
- Confidant
- Sports coach
- Cheerleader

- Guru
- Celebrity
- Muse

This is different from what you actually do in your business—it's about your approach with your clients. Some professionals like to be in a hierarchical position to their clients, while others don't feel comfortable in positions of perceived authority. Other experts or coaches may enjoy their mentor or guru status and looking like they know all the answers, but it doesn't mean you have to keep that image as well. There are many clients who detest authority figures, and will prefer working with someone they see as an equal.

Your role in your client's and you audience's life affects your language. If you claim a position of authority, then you'll need to reference literature, studies, your education, and professional experience in your writing. If you want to be seen as a friend, you can share your personal experiences instead. If you see yourself more as a confidant, instead of sharing your own stories, you can share intimate stories of your clients (with permission or anonymized, of course).

Sports coach types have tough-love attitudes and expect everyone to be at their best all the time. Celebrities like to keep their fans at arm's length, and create an image that their audience aspires to. Cheerleaders want to inspire through positive messages directed at their audience. Muses don't care much about what their audience does—they're here to inspire others through their own creations. Teachers try to educate as many people as they can, and always turn personal mistakes into lessons. Mentors on the other hand like to invest in a smaller number of people, and tailor their advice. Advisors like to look at the facts, and tell their clients what the best course of action is. Gurus seem to think they know what's best, even without knowing the details of their audience's situation.

You might find your own style is a mix of two or more, but try to pinpoint the dominant one—the one that happens without pretense, when you're not trying to impress anyone. What are you like with your best clients, ones you've worked with for a couple of years and you can feel relaxed with them? Start treating people that way from the start.

## How to Use Your Brand Voice

Your topics, your unique combination of voice qualities, and your role all define your distinct brand voice. Once you know what your brand voice is like, you can get intentional about using it in all your public appearances, and in your personal communication as well. Here are some tips on how you can start implementing it.

## THE DIFFERENCE BETWEEN VOICE & TONE

Your brand voice is a consistent set of qualities that doesn't change, no matter what you're writing or talking about. It's simply how you write and talk.

The **tone** of your voice changes based on the subject. When you talk, it's literally the volume and pitch of your voice. It may be lower and more quiet when talking about serious and sad topics, and higher pitched and perky when you talk about happy topics. This isn't something you consciously think about, because we're socialized to use the tone that's most appropriate.

The tone is slightly more difficult to identity in writing, which is why we've made smileys and emojis. It's a lot easier to communicate the full meaning of a message with visual aids or sounds, than through words alone. We do what we can by trying to set the mood with our writing.

You might want to reduce the humor and flowery adjectives in your contracts, in order to keep the meaning clear, and with no chance of misunderstanding or double meaning. (No emojis, either.) On the other hand, positive events require a bit of celebratory language and exclamation marks! Thank you letters, success messages, greeting cards, and other good news could use more joy in them, to the extent that your natural brand voice allows. If you're responding to a client complaint, or are communicating an error message, pepper it with a bit of empathy. People are more willing to forgive you if they believe that you honestly care and want to help.

When writing a new piece of content or a system message, identify the mood of this message. (You can draw a happy face, a sad face, or a frowning face on your draft.) Then think about how you can rephrase your message so that it reflects the mood the reader is likely experiencing.

## PERSONALIZE YOUR CORRESPONDENCE

When writing an email, I spend the most time thinking about the opening and closing greeting. If I write *"Dear"* am I assuming too much about our relationship? Is *"Love"* too intimate? Is *"Best regards"* too cold? For these reasons, my go-to greetings for everyone are *"Hi"* and *"Cheers"*, unless I receive cues from the other person that we can graduate to *"Dear"* and *"Love"*. These greetings are pretty vanilla, and I admit I could think of something more unique, but I haven't gotten around to it yet.

Some people have signature greetings. Feminist marketer and writer Kelly Diels signs her newsletters with *"love + justice,"* which obviously refers to her core values. Entrepreneur Leonie Dawson used to have newsletters and video intros starting with *"Hola gorgeous soul"* which tells you in about 2 seconds whether you want to stick around or press the close button. Creativity coach Andrea Schroeder of Creative Dream Incubator rotates hers, but they always start with *"Wishing you the magic of..."* and what follows is usually related to the topic of her newsletter.

If you can come up with an original greeting that makes sense for your brand, go for it. If not, simply make a decision on what your go to salutations will be from now on, so that you don't have to overthink it every time.

Emails are not formal letters, and you can relax about them. Try to keep them short, and write like your speak. Check your writing for spelling errors, because that leaves a bad impression. I use smiley faces in email liberally, but your mileage may vary.

## ENHANCE YOUR MARKETING

If your audience enjoys your unique brand voice, they will *want* to receive your messages, even if they're not ready to buy from you yet. Imagine if people signed up for your newsletter *just because*—you didn't have to bribe them with a free PDF or anything. Sounds improbable? It's not. When you have a unique point of view, and a focused brand voice that people like, they welcome the opportunity to receive more of your content.

Your website is the first thing to review because it can create the most impact for your business. Go through **every single page** of your website that your prospective client sees when they research you. Check whether the language you're using on this page is aligned with your brand voice. If it's not, rewrite the content until it does. Pay special attention to headlines and calls to action. Your website is often the first thing people see, and you want to make the best possible first impression. The more your natural voice comes through your website, the better it prepares your clients for working with you.

Sounds like too much work? You have no idea. There are pages on my website that I've rewritten over ten times, and keep rewriting them. You don't have to do it all at once. Small progress counts! When you're done with the most important pages of your website, look up the blog posts that receive the most traffic, and check if you need to fix those too. Identify what content best portrays your brand voice, and highlight it by either linking it in the sidebar, or adding a 'best of' page. Do this for all the other marketing methods you're currently using: brochures, flyers, social media posts, social media bios, newsletters, email auto-responders, etc. When all of these different channels use the same consistent brand voice, your audience trusts you more, because you sound like a real human.

## CUSTOMIZE YOUR TEMPLATES

You're probably using at least some downloaded templates in your work. People sell ready-made contracts, terms and conditions documents, sales letters, and even offer email generators (like Jessica Hische's *Client Email Helper*). None of these templates sound like you. If you use several different ones in your business, it becomes a mess of conflicting messages.

I'm not against templates per se, but recommend that you always, always customize them so they sound like you. Contracts are difficult because we need to use precise language, but even those can be written in a more easily digestible manner. Designer Andy Clarke has released his own *Contract Killer* to the public, and it sounds remarkably different from the typical thick legal document. You have more freedom when customizing templates than you might think. (Disclaimer: this is not legal advice.)

## BUILD YOUR PHRASEBOOK

If you speak and teach a lot in front of different audiences, you'll notice when something you say deeply resonates with your listeners. Write these sentences down, and *keep using them*. Perhaps you've found a great analogy to explain a concept relating to your work, and now not only you can use this explanation again, but make it your *thing*. You can write about it on your blog, or record a video, and then reference this resource in your other content. Sometimes this concept of yours can be so powerful, that other people start referring to it. An example that comes to mind is the boat metaphor that Tad Hargrave uses for marketing:

*"(...) no one is buying what you sell. They're always buying the result it offers them. It's like a boat that takes them from Island A to Island B. They don't actually care about your boat. They just want to know it can take them where they want to go."* *

He mentions the boat and the islands metaphor in numerous places. Is it repetitive? Sure. But is it useful? Absolutely. Why keep coming up with more metaphors when this one works great? (Tad also provides a guide on how to come up with your own in his article *Metaphors in Marketing: The Power of Uncovering Your Core Metaphor*.) The more you write and speak, the more of these tidbits you'll come up with. Don't wait until you get home to write them down because by then, they might be gone. Record them immediately on a phone, scrawl them on a receipt, whatever you need to do, just please—save your pearls of wisdom so you can share them with more people.

Own your authentic way of expression, and try not to worry too much about some people who may not like it. I happen to not like Gary Vaynerchuk and Tony Robbins, but they're doing just fine regardless. On the other hand, I could listen to John Oliver go on for hours, and not just because of his accent. You can't make everyone like you, and you don't have to. Your own voice is just fine.

## Naming Your Business

Your business name is a part of your verbal brand—one that appears on literally *every* piece of official business communication. Coming up with a name that is fitting, original, memorable, and conveys the right message isn't easy. Naming experts have a detailed research, ideation, testing, and legal verification process to ensure the name can be trademarked. In the book *Designing Brand Identity*, Alina Wheeler states:

*"The wrong name for a company, product, or service can hinder marketing efforts through miscommunication or because people cannot pronounce it or*

---

* *"No One Cares About Your Project"* by Tad Hargrave (September 19, 2012).

*remember it. It can subject a company to unnecessary legal risks or alienate a market segment. Finding the right name that is legally available is a gargantuan challenge."* \*

We may imagine a business owner coming up with a name in a zap of inspiration, but more often than not choosing the company name is the step that takes people the longest when registering a new company. It pays off to spend some time exploring different options to avoid potential problems later on. Sometimes a name that isn't built for growth can force a business to change it. It's not the end of the world when it happens, but you could save yourself a lot of work if you start with the right name.

Many small businesses choose the **founder's name** as their own name—either the full name or the last name. This is common in the creative industries (like design, fashion, and architecture) and the law industry. Personal names are often the most original, although perhaps not as easy to remember as generic names. On the other hand, they are flexible and allow the business to expand into any niche. Examples include: Dolce & Gabbana, Martha Stewart, Preston Bailey, Vukmir and Associates, Danielle LaPorte, and Allison Crow.

Descriptive names use a term that's relevant for the industry they're in. These names may be more memorable since they lean on the associations people already have with a given term, but it's difficult to come up with a combination that doesn't already exist. Another drawback is that if you choose a name that is connected with a certain niche, it will be difficult to change your business model, or expand into another industry without having to come up with a new name. Examples of descriptive names include: Win Without Pitching, Enter Arkitektur, Algebra, Heart of Business, Sorry Mom Tattoo, Marketing for Hippies, Art Biz Coach, Creative Genius Law, and The Naughty Nutritionists.

**Metaphoric names** don't have anything to do with the business or services, but speak to the spirit, core values, and the inspiration behind the business. This type of name is powerful, memorable, and flexible, but it's

---

\*  *"Designing Brand Identity"* by Alina Wheeler, Wiley (2013).

difficult to find a name that's short, easy to pronounce and not already taken. Examples include: Nike, Mount Sinai, Five, Lateral Action, and Lemon & Lime.

**Acronyms** are common among large and well-known corporations, but rarer in the small business space because they require a certain amount of success and confidence. Some businesses choose an acronym in order to "mask" the founder's name to make it more growth-proof, and less like a personal brand. Examples include: IBM, DKNY, LKR Social Media, and MNIB Consulting.

Another option is **made up names** that don't reference any existing words, which makes them easy to trademark and purchase domains for (like Pinterest and Kodak). On the other hand, these names may be more difficult to remember, as they don't carry any associations until the companies themselves become famous. In an effort to create short domain names, many startups resorted to misspelling of common words, which was a trend that boomed in the early 2000s (Google, Tumblr, etc.).

Combining two different types of names into one can give you the best of both worlds—originality, memorability and relevance. You can combine the name into a single made-up word, or have multiple words. Test this name with others to make sure it's easy to pronounce, spell and doesn't have any negative connotations. Examine what the words look like when the words are separated by a space, or compressed into a single word (like in a domain name). Some names drastically change meanings when viewed in different contexts, and you should account for all of them before you register your company. To make sure you can use your business name, do the following:

- Check in your country's business database if there's a company with the same name that's already registered.
- Search for the name on Google and see if similarly named businesses already exist in other countries.
- Look up the terms in your country's trademark databases, and other trademark databases if you want to operate internationally.
- Look up available domain names on Name Mesh.

If all these searches come up with no results, you should be able to register and use the name with no problem. (Disclaimer: I'm not a lawyer, and this is not legal advice. Different countries have different regulations. Check your local laws before registering a name.)

## Authentic Connection or TMI?*

One of the ways we connect with our audience is through shared experiences. People have a habit of idealizing others, while seeing only flaws in themselves. This unrealistic perception of self and others creates a disconnect. We don't think the other person could ever understand us from their platform of perfection.

Sharing about experiences that paint you in a more real, human light helps people see that you're a person that knows what it feels like to be imperfect and uncertain, like them. For a moment, they see you step down from the platform and extend your hand towards them. For a moment, *they feel like they know you.*

This is one of the reasons why people enjoy hearing about other people's transformation stories. They provide something we can relate to (before), and something to aspire towards (after). It helps us feel as though we're able to achieve what other people have achieved as well, despite our shortcomings. We're enchanted by people who can make us feel this way. This technique is to be wielded with caution, because it can bring people to a very tender place. We shouldn't make unrealistic promises about what our clients can achieve with our help.

How much should you share? This is something that every person needs to answer for themselves. Some people like to share every little intimate detail of their personal lives (like bloggers, columnists, and memoir writers). Others like to keep personal things personal. My choice is somewhere in the middle: I choose to share aspects of my personal life that I believe my readers and clients could relate to, and that have an impact on my career. As it turns out, many things have an impact on your career—your health

---

* Too much information

being at the top of the list. I'm publicly open about my depression, because it has both impacted and had been impacted by my professional life. This doesn't mean I talk about it all the time, but whenever there's a conversation about productivity, positive thinking, healthy work habits etc. I highlight the specific needs of people with chronic health issues, since it can change how we approach business significantly.

I don't discuss my personal relationships online, but there are aspects to our relationships that do affect how we conduct our business, like balancing family roles, receiving emotional and financial support from your partner and your family, creating a pleasant work environment at home etc.

Personal history is a touchy subject since it typically involves other people, like family members, who may not appreciate us talking behind their back. I don't think we necessarily need to get permission from others to share *our* story, especially about events that have happened years ago. If the conversation or an event that you want to share happened in private, asking people if they want to be mentioned by name is a courteous thing to do. Otherwise, you can use a non-specific descriptor like *"a friend of mine," "one of my clients," "a colleague," "my cousin."* If the story requires mentioning the person multiple times, inventing a name can make writing simpler, for example: *"The other day I was talking to a client of mine, let's call him Mark."*

Sharing a personal story publicly for the first time is awkward. You might get the urge to delete what you wrote, and fear clicking the publish button. That is totally normal, and definitely not a sign that you shouldn't share it. If anything, it's the stories that you feel most afraid to share that your audience responds to most powerfully.

A rule I've made for myself is not to publish things in the heat of the moment. I used to do that back when I was a teenager and had just started blogging. I'd realize later that it was not an appropriate story to share, and delete the post. Now I let every post sit for at least a few days, but usually for a few weeks, before publishing. This gives me the opportunity to read it again with a clear head and decide if I should share it or not.

Some folks advise sharing your challenge only after you've overcome it—that way you won't only talk about the challenge, but also about the lessons you've learned. I don't think that's a must. Sometimes sharing a challenge while you're still inside it is powerful. But just because you're still experiencing the challenge, it doesn't mean you need to let *all* of your raw emotions show in your writing. You can write while you're affected by the challenge to explore your own experience, and also add another perspective before publishing once you feel more at peace.

Creating a set of guidelines for yourself in advance on how much you're prepared to share will help you decide whether to tell a certain story, or keep it private. Here's a quick recap of the questions that I use to make a decision:

- Can my audience relate to this story?
- Did this event or issue influence my career in a meaningful way?
- Is this story anonymized enough, or have I received permission from people to mention them?
- Am I able to look at this event or issue objectively, not only emotionally?

Your decision-making questions may be different. You'll probably make some mistakes along the way, but that's fine, as long as you learn from them.

## Is Swearing Ever Acceptable?

Swearing in a professional context is a topic people disagree on. There are business owners who include a great deal of swearing and emotion in their writing and speaking, and this is a part of their brand. Then there are people who think swearing is immature and distasteful, and are openly against it. I personally don't mind when people swear, and I have occasionally used swear words in my blog posts. I've edited them out of this book (with the exception of Amy Hoy's "Fuck This! moment"), because I see this as a more formal form of writing. I don't think I've ever dropped an F-bomb in a client meeting, unless the client has dropped it first. My rule of thumb is: if I'd have to censor it with an asterisk, I'd rather just not use the word because I find the whole censoring thing tacky. Everyone knows what you wanted to say anyway, and the asterisk doesn't make it any more polite. If I'm comfortable saying it, I'll just say it or type it explicitly.

This is, again, a very personal decision only you can make. Whatever decision you make, try to stick with it and only change your expression moderately depending on the situation. If you opt for no swearing in public at all, then simply don't. You can leave some "bleep" noises in the video bloopers or something like that, which can be viewed as funny and endearing.

There's one thing I sincerely ask you not to do: don't tell other people how to communicate on *their own* platforms. I've heard so many stories from bloggers and business owners who receive emails chastising them for swearing. You're not their mom, so just leave them be. If swearing bothers you so much, find someone else to follow whose language is more to your liking.

You are also not required to change your communication style based on your individual audience members' preferences. If your brand voice doesn't match that of a certain audience member, this means they're not your right person. You can't please everyone with your style of speaking and writing, and trying to do that may frustrate you. It's fine if certain people don't like it. As long as you are attracting an audience that responds well to your content, it's working out fine. In the next chapter, we'll talk about how to find out who you're actually talking to—your ideal clients.

*chapter VI*

# Who Are You Serving?

I've talked at length in the beginning of this book why it's so important to be able to attract the *right people* to your business, and why the *wrong people* actively harm your business. We've established that the purpose of your brand is to connect you with your right people—to create resonance with your target audience. There are questions we've left unanswered until now: Who are these people? Where do you find them? How do you get them to buy from you? Finally, we're getting closer to answering them.

**Your ideal client is a mental model that describes the people you're trying to reach.** If you did even a little bit of reading about marketing, you've probably heard about it already, or perhaps even done an exercise to identify your ideal client. Some of the information that's floating out there is helpful, but a lot of it isn't. Try to set aside what you've heard about ideal clients until we get to the end of the chapter, and then decide what approach you like better.

I used to hang out in quite a few Facebook groups for entrepreneurs. Every now and then the question of branding came up. Each time a newbie business owner asked: *"Where do I start with branding my business?"* a fellow designer or marketer answered: *"Start with your ideal client."* Whenever I saw that I'd cringe, because I don't recommend people to start with their ideal client. There's a reason why I've placed the ideal clients at the fourth level of our Human Centered Brand Discovery Pyramid, right next to the top. Focusing your attention on the ideal client too early in the branding process can lead to frustration instead of clarity.

Your ideal clients interact with hundreds of brands, but only one of them is yours. That's why we've dealt with your core values, your unique approach to work, and your brand voice, before touching on the clients you work with.

Your ideal clients share some of your top core values, which is why you're equipped to help them better than anyone else. You know what truly matters to them, and you're dedicated to bringing more of that into their life. Knowing what your core values are is a prerequisite to attracting the sort of people who share them. If you don't know what your core values are, you might attract people who don't appreciate your personality, your approach, and your needs.

Clients have many needs in their life and business, and you're not able to fulfill all of them. What some clients need and want may be in direct opposition to what you're willing to provide—for example, they may need an affordable 'quick fix' solution, when your approach is deep, intense, transformative work that carries a premium price tag. Does this mean you should change your unique value proposition to make it palatable for the largest number of people possible? No, this means you should look for people who need *exactly* the kind of value you're most excited to provide. When you define the unique value of your work first, you can then focus on who is most likely to appreciate the true value enough to pay your prices with enthusiasm.

Some branding strategists propose creating a 'synthetic' brand voice that suits your target audience, and stick to the topics they would find interesting, but I propose a different solution: adapt the target market to people who appreciate your authentic style of expression. Putting on a persona every day that's radically different from yourself is difficult and draining.

If you've followed along with the questions in this book and have identified your core values, your unique value proposition, and the qualities of your brand voice, you're now ready to define who your ideal client is.

## How Narrowing Down Makes You Stand Out

I've explained in the introduction why accepting just about any client who walks by is harmful for service based businesses and may even lead to serious financial issues. You may not yet be entirely convinced. People are often afraid of narrowing down their target market, because they worry they won't be able to sell enough services to make a living. However, the experience of many freelancers and companies has confirmed over and over again that this is usually not the case: it's precisely the feeling of **exclusivity** and **uniqueness** that helps you reach more people. If you try to appeal to everyone, you won't be able to stand out from thousands of others who are offering similar services.

When you define who you most enjoy working with, and who is most likely to want to work with you, you're better equipped for creating a brand that makes a difference. With intense client work, mutual chemistry matters. Clients won't mind about the things you're not so great at, because what they really care about are the things you're awesome at.

When you take the entire world's population and eliminate everyone who doesn't appreciate your unique approach and personality, doesn't need the value you provide, and is not on board with what you stand for, what you're left with is your pool of potential clients.

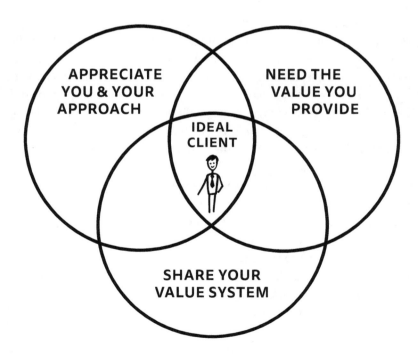

You can further refine them by their current circumstances:

- What stage of business are they in—a startup, or a mature company?
- How much do they earn per year?
- How many employees do they have?
- What are their top goals this year?
- Are they local?

When you specify who you work with, you have a much easier job reaching them: you can craft a visual brand that resonates with them, create content that meets them where they are, and present your service as a means to where they want to go. You can attend events where they hang out and advertise in publications they consume.

Instead of dabbling in a range of offers to cover a wider market, narrowing down your clientele to a specific group of people lets you tailor your service for those people and becoming an expert in the thing that your clients value the most. As an expert, you're able to charge more per each client than you would as a generalist, so you don't need as many clients as you did before. Instead of trying to find 10 new clients every month who each buy a one-off consulting session or hire you for a small project, perhaps all you need is 10 clients *per year*, each of them engaged in a long-term program or a large project that spans months.

Bad clients try to strip down your offers in order to pay the least amount possible to get what they want. Great clients want the value you know they *need* and will be happy to get the full package, as long as you can assure them it will bring them the results they want.

Narrowing down your clientele can paradoxically lead to *more* prospects instead of less, because it makes standing out and staying memorable easier. **Generalists are quickly forgotten, while experts remain top of mind whenever their field of expertise is mentioned in conversation.**

After you've defined who your ideal client or 'right people' are, you'll need to own it and state it on your website, your marketing materials, and as you introduce yourself in social situations. This has a very powerful effect on people. Those who recognize themselves in the description will think to themselves: *"This is perfect for me!"* Those that don't will think of *someone else* who fits the description. Even people who don't fit under the umbrella of your ideal client can help you promote your business by recommending you to people they know.

As you draw a circumference around a specific group of people you help, you become 'that guy/gal' whenever the topic of your skills for this particular group of people comes up. People understand and talk about your business— and you'd love it if people talked about your business more, wouldn't you?

The level of detail you want to employ in your ideal client profile depends on how much demand and competition there is for your service (usually the two go together). Those of us who provide popular services such as design, web development, business training, marketing consulting, copywriting, illustration, etc. need to find a more focused niche. Businesses whose services are highly industry-specific (like repairing medical equipment) or innovative can afford to be a bit more general with their ideal client, since there are typically fewer competitors in their market. However, even if you fall into this group, you can identify that certain types of clients bring you more pleasure and profit than others.

If you produce creative works which people tend to collect or buy regularly such as artworks, jewelry, or novels, keep in mind what kind of works your would-be patrons are currently buying, and how their hobbies, interests, and personalities play into their choices.

## How to Identify Your Ideal Clients

A good way to start finding your right people is identifying everything that's *wrong* with your current clients. Defining your ideal clients consists of drawing a line in the sand between what you're willing to tolerate from your clients, and what you're not. Nice and kind people usually cringe at this, because we want to be accommodating to others and not turn anyone down. Take it from someone who was brought to tears by frustrating client behavior: not turning anyone down will be your demise. We need to turn down everyone who displays the red flags we've noticed in our past clients.

For starters, you can list all of your past frustrating experiences, where you feel you were legitimately doing everything in your power to deliver your service on a professional level, and your client was obstructing the process, or was in any way a pain to deal with. Record all of the signs you've noticed in the beginning of your relationship that you chose to overlook and give them the benefit of the doubt. From now on, be determined not to let these red flags go unchecked. The prospects who display them *cannot* become your clients, as it will only lead to more frustration on both sides.

I recommend doing this as an online document that you can easily reach whenever you're responding to prospective client inquiries, so you can remind yourself what you're *not* tolerating anymore, and reject any inquiry that makes your 'spidey sense' tingle in a bad way.

After you've completed your 'naughty list'—all the things you never want to experience from your clients, it's time to write your 'nice list'. This is a wish list of qualities your ideal clients demonstrate. Again, you can go back to your previous experiences and note which clients you've enjoyed working with the most. List a few of their names and try to identify what they have in common, whether it's their personality traits, or markers relating to their business like income, development stage, etc.

Let's recap: your right people are most likely to:

1. Share your core values.
2. Need the unique value you provide.
3. Appreciate your personality, as communicated through your brand voice.
4. Be enjoyable to work with.
5. Be willing to pay your prices.

Let's look into these factors in more detail.

## YOUR IDEAL CLIENTS NEED THE UNIQUE VALUE YOU PROVIDE

The appreciation for the unique value you provide is determined by their current situation. When offered what you sell, a lot of people will say *"Oh, that's nice."* but won't pull out their wallet—only the people that have been aware of the problem you are solving for some time will be motivated to solve it. Your ideal client is the person on the verge of buying, not someone very early in the buying cycle (as I've explained in more detail in the fourth chapter). While early-stage prospects are welcome to enjoy your free content, the majority of your energy should be spent on reaching people who are ready, willing, and able to buy your core offer. That's why the ideal client's current business and life situation is an essential part of the ideal client profile, much more so than demographic information such as gender, age, level of education, etc.

## YOUR IDEAL CLIENTS SHARE YOUR CORE VALUES

Their core values are often demonstrated through how they approach their business and personal life. It will become easier for you to recognize the core values in other people over time. When a prospect rubs you the wrong way as you're negotiating a new project, but you're not sure why, ask yourself if maybe it's a core values mismatch?

## YOUR IDEAL CLIENTS APPRECIATE YOUR PERSONALITY

People have different perceptions of 'professionalism', and what you've learned in your former workplace may not be relevant anymore. As long as you're in integrity, provide high value for money, and treat your clients with respect, there is no set way of how you must behave.

It's easier to maintain a brand that's aligned with your personality traits, then pretend you're someone else as you're interacting with your clients and writing marketing copy. Your brand voice is the verbal element of your personality, and finding clients who like your natural brand voice is easier than twisting your brand voice to charm a certain type of client.

This doesn't mean you'll dump TMI-bombs on your clients at inopportune moments, and it doesn't mean your clients need to know everything that happens in your personal life—but if an interest or an issue is an important part of your life, there's no shame in letting it be known, at least on your blog or social media.

## YOUR IDEAL CLIENTS ARE ENJOYABLE TO WORK WITH

Since service based businesses collaborate with clients intensely, you want this time to be pleasurable and without any unnecessary stress. If you could have your pick between a kind, funny, and well-organized client, or a grumpy, stuck-up and disorganized one, who would you prefer to work with?

## YOUR IDEAL CLIENTS CAN AFFORD YOUR PRODUCTS OR SERVICES

I know that you want to help as many people is possible, but you're not running a charity—you need to make a **profit** in order to remain in business. Undercharging for your services is not making anyone a favor. If your business becomes unviable and you have to close it, your current clients will be disappointed. If you ever experienced a favorite shop going out of business, you know what I mean.

Your potential clients' current financial situation dictates whether they're able to buy your most valuable offering. You might be tempted to strip down value in order to provide a lower-priced service for those who cannot afford your regular rates. Before doing that, run the numbers and check if this will work out long-term. If you're offering lower-priced services or products, make sure that the difference in the value is clear. Try not to spend more than 20% of your billable hours creating or providing low-priced offers. Put in the majority of your effort toward offers that bring more profit and repeat business.

Now that we've narrowed down your pool of potential clients quite a bit, here are some questions that can help you understand them better and craft marketing content that will gain their attention and trust.

## WHAT IS THEIR CHARACTERISTIC LIFE OR BUSINESS SITUATION?

Look at the list of your best clients (and only your best)—ones that come back for upgrades or repeat services, send you referrals, give compliments for your work, never run late on payment, etc. What do they have in common? Examples may include:

- Specific profession or job description (lawyer, student, fitness coach, CEO of a tech startup)

- Personal life situation (single woman, parent of a large family, same sex couple)
- Demographic group (teenagers, men aged 30–40, women of color)
- Health condition (disability, mental illness, injury)
- Political and religious affiliation (Christian, liberal, Buddhist)

If your clients fall within a certain group, it's easier to make predictions about their needs and challenges, and create offers and marketing tailored to them. If it seems like your people are all over the spectrum, there may be other connecting threads, which the remaining questions can help you find.

## HOW DO THEY DESCRIBE THEMSELVES?

Using the exact words that your ideal clients use to describe themselves, their situation, and their problem is the most powerful copywriting tool you can use. By addressing them in the way they're addressing themselves, you establish **trust** and the sense of **mutual understanding**. People love to be seen and appreciated for who they are, and by describing your ideal client (on your website, content marketing, ads, and in-person conversations) in the terms that reflect their perception of themselves, you immediately earn their attention.

What words does your ideal client use in their Twitter bios, LinkedIn profiles and about pages? (Research the profiles of your best clients, and people you'd love to work with.) How do they perceive themselves in their mind? What title they don't dare to claim for themselves, but secretly they wish to be referred as?

## WHAT ARE THEIR MAIN INTERESTS & HOBBIES?

Knowing other people's personal interests and hobbies helps us to establish a common ground. People are more attracted to those who share similarities with them.* Not only that, but you can use your mutual interests and

---

\* "Birds of a Feather Do Flock Together: Behavior-Based Personality-Assessment Method Reveals Personality Similarity Among Couples and Friends" by Wu Youyou, David Stillwell, H. Andrew Schwartz, and Michal Kosinski, Psychological Science (Vol 28, Issue 3, pp. 276 - 284, January 6, 2017)

hobbies to meet new potential clients in a non-business setting, when they are more likely to be relaxed, open, and authentic.

As a science fiction and fantasy fan, I visit many local conventions every year. Several of my most valued clients are friends and acquaintances that I've first met at conventions. We've kept a completely non-professional pitch-free relationship for years, but I've been the first person they've remembered when they needed a brand designer.

The arts, sports, culture, health, and spirituality can be a powerful catalyst for creating new, deep relationships that may later lead to an exchange of value.

### WHERE DO THEY HANG OUT IN THE REAL WORLD, AND ONLINE?

Marketing takes a lot of time, and there's no point in spending it in places and platforms where your ideal clients don't hang out.

I used to spend a ton of time in Facebook groups for small business owners. I've joined every weekly 'share your blog post' and 'share your offer' thread, answered all the questions as thoughtfully as I could, and I've met some great people there. But I've only gotten *one client* in two years from a Facebook group, so this strategy clearly wasn't working for me. I've realized later that my ideal clients *aren't there*—they're simply too busy for that. They might be running their own Facebook group, or interacting in an exclusive mastermind, but they're not a part of your average free group for entrepreneurs. Since that realization, I've shaved *hours* off of my weekly schedule and was able to use this time for things that made a bigger impact.

So, where *are* your ideal clients appearing regularly? Are there any platforms specific to their area of expertise? Are there any seminars, conferences and other social events they might be attending? Include the venues related to their hobbies, family life, self-care, and other non-business interests.

### WHERE ARE THEY CURRENTLY AT AS IT RELATES TO YOUR SERVICES?

Your ideal clients, being well aware of their problem, have probably tried a few different solutions that hadn't brought them the results they wanted. Perhaps they've tried a do-it-yourself solution that they lacked the knowledge and experience to implement properly. In that case, contrasting the experience and knowledge you *do* have can help you sell your offers more easily.

Maybe they've hired a competitor of yours, but they weren't happy with their work. That makes your job more difficult, because you'll have to convince them than not all service providers are the same, and that your unique skills and approach *will* work better for them. Client testimonials, awards, and media features can go a long way. Perhaps they've considered your type of service before, or something completely different: your job is to prove (through detailed case studies) exactly how your service works, and what makes it different from other potential solutions on the market.

### WHAT TYPE OF CONTENT DO THEY PREFER TO CONSUME?

There are many different technologies you can use for content marketing and paid offers. How do you choose which ones are best for your business? Easy: ask your clients what they prefer. The ideal content you want to create is at the intersection between the type of content you enjoy creating, and the type of content your ideal clients enjoy consuming.

Do your ideal clients prefer text, pictures, audio, or video? Do they like live, in-person experiences, or something they can do at their own pace? Why is that? Their personal life situation can give you many clues: a parent of young children may not have the time to attend events or to watch long videos—they might prefer audio recordings they can listen to as they run errands. Students may enjoy videos and visual social media updates (as opposed to 'boring' books). Before committing to any medium for your content, check in with your clients first. Are they able to consume it without disrupting their life?

## How to Use Your Ideal Client Profile

The answers to the above questions will help you get a clear image of who your clients are as professionals, and as people. When you know who they are, getting their attention will be much easier. Some of the ways we can get the attention of our ideal clients is through a compelling tagline, a short introduction, and a more detailed public client profile.

## CRAFTING YOUR TAGLINE

A tagline is a simple, short sentence used to describe what a business does. It's designed to **capture interest**, so that people who may have just landed on your website for the first time in their life decide to keep browsing to learn more.

Taglines are challenging. There are branding experts and copywriters whose sole job is to create taglines for businesses. Coming up with a clever combination of words that symbolizes your entire business sounds like an impossible task. But it's only impossible if you're trying to get a 'Best Tagline of the Year' award in advertising. Taglines for small businesses are **straightforward** and literal. As the copywriter Nenad Vukušić put it:

> *"Our tagline [...] will grow with us in the beginning. First it will be descriptive, and later it will be more inspirational–aspirational."* [*]

**The purpose of a tagline is to let other people know what you do and whether they're your ideal client in less than two seconds.** You can create a tagline with just two elements: your unique value proposition (UVP), and your audience. A basic formula for that type of tagline looks like this:

### *[UVP] for [ideal client]*

If you haven't come up with a clear unique value proposition, you can use the service you offer for the time being. Use the words that your ideal clients might use, not the expert term. You're aiming for easy recognition. If the service you offer is new or unusual, use the term that most easily explains the nature of your work. You'll have the opportunity to dive deeper in follow-up conversation or content.

The other element of your tagline is your ideal client. If you had to describe them in just two or three words, what would you call them? One of the questions I've had you ask yourself was what words your clients used to refer to themselves, and what words your clients maybe didn't have the courage to own. Make note of these words, because they will grab their attention.

---

[*]  *"Kako smisliti superslogan za firmu ili obrt"* by Nenad Vukušić (November 27, 2017).

You can spin this formula around and perhaps come up with a less clunky and shorter wording. Don't feel constricted by the formula—its purpose is just to get you started somewhere. Here are a few examples of taglines created using this formula:

- *"Relaxation & replenishment for moms who work too hard"*
- *"Trust-building social media for health professionals"*
- *"Healing sexual trauma through art"*

Fewer people resonate with taglines that are highly specific, but those who do will feel that your business is *perfect* for them.

The tagline you come up with using this formula is a starting point that you can improve further, taking your brand voice qualities into account. If you have writing talent, you'll probably be able to come up with a more interesting solution that's not as formulaic.

It's important to note how your tagline relates to your business name, since they'll be shown next to each other. If your company name already mentions the service, avoid repeating it in the tagline.

The River Valley Health clinic specializes in helping athletes recover from injuries. Their tagline *"We are all athletes."* focuses on their target audience and their goal (to go back to their athletic practice), while also sharing a worldview. Since their business name has the word 'health' in it, it won't be confused for a sports brand.

Some taglines manage to appeal to the businesses' ideal audience even without explicitly mentioning them. The company Heart of Business has the tagline: *"Every act of business can be an act of love."* It speaks to the spiritual, heart-centered person who wants to lead with love in their business. When you read it, you *know* whether you're the intended audience or not. Coming up with such a tagline takes excellent copywriting skills, and a deep understanding of what motivates your ideal client.

Wedding planning business The Plannery, founded by Katie Wannen, currently features the tagline *"Where ideas become events, and sh\*t gets done."* While this language may not appeal to most couples, it attracts those who appreciate the cheeky, no-nonsense attitude in their wedding planner.

## SHORT INTRODUCTIONS

An **introduction** (sometimes called the elevator speech) is a short and simple description of what you do to someone you've just met. We've already discussed them in the fourth chapter, but now we're going to add a new element—your ideal client.

Introductions are spoken (or written in an email), and we don't have to sound poetic or clever. Clarity is the name of the game. Use plain language, without tongue-twisters or buzzwords. Here are the elements to include in your short introduction:

1. Your ideal client.
2. Their biggest problem.
3. The goal you help them achieve.
4. Your method (optional).

If your introduction only refers to your profession, this doesn't give any context to the listener. In their mind, they'll file you in the same box where they've put other colleagues of yours, even if that's not appropriate.

If you include your ideal client in your introduction, people will know who to refer to you. If you let them guess, they may recommend people who aren't the right fit, and then it will fall on you to turn them down.

The purpose of including the problem and the goal is to help the listener connect your work with a real world situation—their own, or of someone they know. The closer this hits to home, the more interested they will be in hearing more about it. You can use this structure to craft your introduction:

### *I help [ideal clients] with a [problem] to achieve [goal] (through [method]).*

Let's see how one of our previous taglines would work as a spoken introduction using this structure: *"I help overworked moms to relax and recover from burnout with massage and aromatherapy."* That's a little long for a single sentence, so we might shift things a bit. If someone asked our business owner what they did for a living, they could reply: *"I'm a massage therapist. I help overworked moms to relax and recover from burnout."*

Mark Silver of Heart of Business recommends that you don't even mention your method in your introduction, because it puts the focus on you, instead of your clients. In their course *How to Say What You Do in One Compelling Sentence* they teach a method that is all about the client's problem and the result they want to achieve. I do agree that it's most important to describe the transformation the clients go through working with you. Also, some folks have a difficult time coming up with a job title that describes what they do accurately. This approach removes the need for a job title. My choice is to include the job title, but then move on to the client-focused language.

Another resource on crafting an intriguing introduction for social situations is *Book Yourself Solid* by Michael Port. In the chapter *How to Talk about What You Do*, he introduces the Book Yourself Solid Dialogue,* which may be adapted based on how much time you have to strike up a conversation. Both of these resources are compatible with the Human Centered Brand approach, so I encourage you to look into it if you need more help.

Independent artists such as painters, fiction writers, and musicians may not solve 'problems' in quite the same way that service professionals do, so if that's you, your introduction might be slightly different. You could use a formulation like *"I [make art/write stories/compose music] inspired by [core values/ topic/tradition] that helps people [feel emotions/get in touch with core values/take action]."* Again, it's not about following a specific formula, but finding a way to connect with the listener and reflect the needs of your clients.

## DETAILED IDEAL CLIENT PROFILE

Now you know who your ideal clients are—but do they know it? You can never be too clear or too explicit when business is concerned. Reflecting your client's needs, professional and personal situation, and worldview in your marketing copy is an effective way to relate to them.

The first step is to make an *internal* ideal client profile. This is the document with all the descriptions, references, and ideas that relate to your ideal client. The purpose of this document is to serve as a resource when

---

* The gist of this technique is explained in the article on their website: *"How to Talk About What You Do"*

you need to write content for your website or marketing materials. You can keep adding, removing, and adjusting things as you learn more about your ideal clients.

You can drop references about your client and their situation anywhere: your blog posts, services pages, social media posts, newsletters, brochures, flyers, etc. If they recognize themselves in your references and stories, they'll trust and respect you even more. If they don't, they'll realize they're not your ideal client and move on.

Many service based business owners have an "Is This You?" or similarly titled page on their website which outlines their ideal client profile in great detail. The purpose of this page is to clarify who your services are aimed for, and who they're not aimed for. (The copywriter Abby Kerr of The Voice Bureau shares a detailed guide on what to include on this page in her article *Do I Really Need an 'Is This You' Page?*)

## CLIENT PERSONAS

While your ideal client is a generic model that represents the totality of what your best clients have in common, the client persona is an individual with a name, profile photo, date of birth, height, weight, hair color, skin color, education, job history, family members, pets, favorite books, Myers–Briggs type,* etc. This persona may be based on an existing or an imaginary person.

I was taught to create invented personas as a part of my user experience training, which supposedly prevents projecting our own ideas about people we know onto the persona. Naomi Dunford, the marketing maven behind IttyBiz, advocates for using profiles of actual people instead. She admits to having developed 15 highly detailed profiles of people important to her business, including her best consulting clients, biggest ebook and course buyers, and people who consistently share her content on social media.† I've switched to this approach and have found it quite helpful. If you already have clients you enjoy working with, try it. If you don't, you can base your

---

\* The Myers–Briggs Type Indicator (MBTI) is a popular personality test that sorts people into 16 types. I'm an INFP, in case you're wondering.

† Naomi has shared this information in her former class *Six-Figure Products*, which is unfortunately no longer available.

personas on people you know that you'd like to become your clients. **Use the persona to imagine yourself in the shoes of your client, and try to look at your business from their perspective.** You can ask them questions, and imagine what their answers would be. Here are some examples of mental exercises you can do with your persona:

- What is their daily routine like?
- Where does your offer or marketing fit in their routine?
- What do they need that they're not getting anywhere?
- What are they already getting too much of?
- How can you make your offers even more valuable to them?
- How can your business make things easier and simpler for them?
- What would they think about this marketing message & imagery?
- What do they see when they visit your website?

Whenever you have any doubts about what kind of offer or marketing campaign to make, look at your client persona sheet and think about what they might say to you. Ideally, you should talk to your actual clients whenever you can, but sometimes that's just not feasible. In that case, the client persona can provide the information you need.

With four levels of your Human Centered Brand Pyramid in place, now we're ready to move on to the final piece. In the next chapter, we'll examine the elements of visual brand identity, and how to use them to communicate with your ideal audience through visual language.

*chapter VII*

# Wrapping It Up with a Bow

People typically associate the word 'brand' with visuals: logos, typography, color palette, packaging, website design, etc. Since we've been working on the first four levels of our Human Centered Brand Discovery Pyramid, you now understand that branding involves many non-visual elements as well. However, visual communications design (also called graphic design) is an essential part of any brand strategy.

Your visual brand identity is the direct extension of the other aspects of your brand that we've defined in the previous chapters. In this chapter, you'll learn some basic design techniques you can use to decide which elements will make up your visual identity.

Design isn't just about making things 'pretty'. The role of design in our society is functional, as well as aesthetic. While design may be seen as a subjective discipline, research supports the idea that **design has a measurable influence on commerce**: businesses that invest in design see an increase in revenue, and faster growth.* For many companies, visual design is their defining point of differentiation.

Perhaps while reading this book you were impatient to finally get to the chapter on design, and may even be a bit disappointed that the majority of it revolves around non-visual themes. There's a reason why I've structured the book this way, and in this chapter it will all become clear. The main

---

*   *"The Economic Effects of Design"* by Danish National Agency for Enterprise and Housing (2003).

purpose of graphic design is **communication**. When we define design this way, one thing becomes clear: in order to fulfill its purpose, design needs to be formed around a **message** that we want to communicate. Aesthetics without a message is mere décor, not design.

The previous chapters of the book were dedicated to exploring and refining the *message*, so that we could use design to communicate it in the most appropriate and appealing manner. In this chapter, we'll examine *how* design communicates, and learn several key design elements that make this possible.

## Beauty Matters

I sometimes hear people say that *"how something looks doesn't matter to them,"* and that they're not easily swayed by shiny visuals. They choose their phones, cars, and home appliances based on utility and specifications, not the product design or packaging. They claim not to care about the colors of this or that website—what's important is the quality of the information presented on it. If it's well written, they will forgive the slightly old-fashioned design. I find these claims amusing, because study after study in the past few decades showed that people are way more biased than we'd like to admit.

Visuals matter, no matter what your skeptic, numbers-driven friends say. We've got some numbers of our own to prove it. (And by that I don't mean the often repeated bogus statistics like *"we process visual information 60.000 times faster than words,"* or that *"90% of the information we perceive is visual,"* which are not supported by any known scientific research.)

In a study comparing verbal presentations that used visual aids with presentation that wasn't supported by any visual aids, presentations using visual aids were found to be 43% more persuasive than unaided presentations.* The study subjects also thought the presentations with a well-balanced amount of colored visuals were more interesting and clear, and presenter who used visuals was perceived to be better prepared and more professional.

---

* *"Persuasion and the Role of Visual Presentation Support: The UM/3M Study"* by Douglas R. Vogel, W L Dickson, and John A. Lehman (2005).

When two speakers with different presenting abilities were compared, a 'typical' quality speaker using visual aids was just as effective as the better speaker without any visuals.

Marcel Just, Director of the Center for Cognitive Brain Imaging at Carnegie Mellon University, offers the reasoning behind the differences in our ability to process written words and visuals:

*"Processing print isn't something the human brain was built for. The printed word is a human artifact. It's very convenient and it's worked very well for us for 5.000 years, but it's an invention of human beings. By contrast Mother Nature has built into our brain our ability to see the visual world and interpret it."* [*]

However, not all visuals are made equal. There's a huge difference in how people will perceive and use a 'beautiful' design, versus an 'ugly' design. We're often told that beauty is in the eye of the beholder, and that may be true to a certain extent: some of us prefer darker clothing over light, red cars over blue, dark-haired people over blonde, or the sound of an electric guitar over accordion. The current trends also affect how we perceive something: the shiny 3D web buttons of the early 2000s now seem old-fashioned. At the time of writing this book, most web and app interfaces are flat, with very subtle occasional drop-shadows so that is what we currently agree is visually appealing. But beauty is not *completely* subjective.

People tend to agree on whether someone or something is attractive or unattractive, even across different cultures.† Not only that, but we judge other people based on their looks. We assume attractive people possess more socially desirable characteristics: professional competence, more money, better marriages, and overall happiness.‡ Judging of how good something

---

[*]   *"Watching the Human Brain Process Information"* by Marcel Just and Melissa Ludtke, Nieman Reports (2010).

[†]   *"Maxims or Myths of Beauty? A Meta-analytic and Theoretical Review"* by Judith H. Langlois et al., Psychological Bulletin (2000, Vol 126 No. 3, 390-423).

[‡]   *"What Is Beautiful Is Good"* by Karen Dion, Ellen Berscheid, Elaine Walster, Journal of Personality and Social Psychology (1972, Vol 24, No. 3, 285-290).

is based on appearance alone does not stop with people. How appealing or unappealing a design is will affect people's ability to use it and elicit more positive or negative emotions. Usability expert Don Norman has found in his research that *"pleasing things work better, are easier to learn, and produce a more harmonious result"*\*. Unattractive design can make us feel more frustrated even before we've started using a website or an app so we tend to judge it unfavorably.

When reviewing how trustworthy a website is, people rely on the site design to eliminate less trustworthy sources. Visually unappealing websites with poor interface design, too bland or too intense color palettes, banner ads, etc. give a poor first impression, and make people less likely to continue browsing them—even if the textual information may be of high quality.†

I can understand that when faced with many overwhelming business decisions, appealing visuals may not be very high on your priority list. However, those who choose to neglect the appearance of their websites, presentations, brochures, or business cards may be leaving a lot on the table. Those who go the extra mile reap the benefits. I hope that with the help of the information in this chapter, you'll become one of them.

## IF IT LOOKS LIKE A DUCK...

People rely on their sight to make a judgment about their environment and the people surrounding them—appearance triggers a certain set of expectations. For example, we might subconsciously expect that an attractive, athletic person we've just met is not very intelligent. Or we might expect from someone who wears eyeglasses to be bookish and introverted. Of course, these expectations have nothing to do with the real truth about these people, but our culture and our previous experiences may get the better of us. Extreme cases of this type of bias lead to sexist and racist behavior. We need to actively work to dismantle the stereotypes we've developed over the years, and it's a constant process.

---

\*    *"Emotion & design: attractive things work better"* by Donald Norman (2002).
†    *"Trust and mistrust of online health sites"* by Elizabeth Sillence, Pam Briggs, Lesley Fishwick, and Peter Harris, Conference on Human Factors in Computing Systems (2004).

We've also developed expectations from places and objects that look a certain way. The packaging gives us clues about the quality, durability, and the pricing of the product. We expect well-designed products to be high-end, and are willing to pay more for them. Products which don't have that high-end *appearance* seem lesser in quality, so we expect them to cost less. Again, this has nothing to do with the actual quality of the product. The one that looks cheaper may in fact be superior in quality, and sometimes it is. But unless someone has specifically recommended this product to you because they were happy with it, you're going to be skeptical of it, and think that the high-end looking one is a safer bet.

**When we lack other verifiable information, we turn to appearance to make a judgment.** Does this make us superficial? Perhaps. But visuals truly do provide us with a lot of useful information, so we've learned to trust these impressions. This mechanism has become so embedded in us, through our evolutionary history and socialization that we cannot escape it without a great deal of effort—so most people don't.

What does this mean for you as a business owner? The way you *appear* to people will affect their expectations of you. If you appear like a person who's good at keeping things together, the trust people place in you as a professional will be greater. If you appear like a bit of a slob, this will impact how they perceive the quality of your work, even if one has nothing to do with the other. Clients are looking for *any* red flag that might disqualify you—as you should look for in them, as well. Only if everything checks out will you be set for a pleasant working relationship.

There's a difference between putting your best foot forward, and keeping an image you can't live up to. The appearance you project should be in line with the quality of the service you provide, so that your potential clients get an accurate idea about what they might expect from your business.

Pleasant surprises might feel good, but if your clients are consistently surprised, you're not doing a good job of communicating how awesome your work is. Disappointing your clients is much worse than exceeding their expectations, but if you fail to make them optimistic and excited about working with you, this means you're not selling nearly as many of your services as you could. For every client that buys from you, there may be one, or five, or ten that were turned away because they didn't see enough evidence that you're that good.

**Use design to your advantage.** Even making small, incremental changes over the course of the next few weeks and months will produce a large, measurable result later on. This is especially true if you services are more high-end. If you're running a business-to-business company, your production quality needs to be at least at the same level that your desired clients have. If you're offering services to consumers, aim for the production quality that matches the level of other services they're buying. If you're aiming for clients who visit fancy hair stylists, make sure your massage or coaching practice looks equally fancy.

Appear 'too good' and you might intimidate your clients—they'll worry they can't afford you. Appear 'not that good', and they won't trust that you're capable enough. The Goldilocks rule applies well to this.

## CHAMPIONING BEAUTY

One thing that can be said about my work is that I go out of my way to make things visually appealing. Whether it's project proposals, conference talk presentations, holiday greeting cards, or self-published books (hello, there!) I take a close look at what other people do, and then find a way to raise the bar. If I didn't have it in my budget to professionally print something, I'd spend days crafting it myself. My guiding question was: *"How can I make this more creative and beautiful?"* Having visuals be the most impactful part of my brand makes perfect sense for a visual artist. This may lead people to believe that the reason my brand is so polished is that I'm a professional designer. It's easy for me to do this for myself, you might think, now that I've done it so many times for my clients, right?

In fact, it's the other way around. I've created the foundations of what is now my brand long before I was a professional designer. I've always had an urge to create visuals, and I've tried my hand at many different mediums, and still continue to experiment. Making ordinary moments extraordinary, by elevating them with visual adornment was something I've been doing all my life. I suppose it was just a matter of time before I'd find a way to turn it into a career.

I rely on my skills of creating appealing visuals most of all, because that's what flows the easiest *for me*. My story is not everyone's story. The way I do branding for myself is different from the way I do it for my clients, and the way you're going to do yours. I'm telling you this so you can set your expectations accordingly. If you're a visual artist, the visual aspect of your brand is likely going to play the most important role in attracting an audience—but you still need to have the solid foundation to back it up. For business owners who are not primarily visual creators, visuals have a *supporting* function. They do matter, but you might find that writing or speaking is more up your alley.

When I work with clients, we spend the majority of our time on crafting their new logo, visual brand identity, and website. Often we create a set of templates that they can use for their documents (like proposals, invoices, email signatures, presentations, newsletter, etc.) and then they're free to do what they do best. Typically, once you create your initial visual brand, the upkeep is very easy. You make the decision on what fonts and colors to use once, and you never have to revisit it again (unless you want to make a change).

The things you see me do are not necessarily the things you should be attempting. I hand-letter and illustrate my blog graphics because I genuinely enjoy the creative process, and specifically look for opportunities when I can do that. Adult business books typically don't have chapter cover illustrations, but my book does, because I asked myself *"How can I make this more creative and beautiful?"* and followed my inspiration. Some people may think it's a silly thing to do, but that's *my way* of doing things. Use this example as a springboard for your own imagination and figure out what *your way* of doing things is. I'm a champion for beauty and creativity. What are you the champion of?

## Design Is a Visual Language

Verbal languages use sounds and letters which form different words, each of them holding a meaning for those who understand that language. Just like verbal languages, design is built up of elements that convey meaning to people who can understand it.

The visual language consists of **the elements and principles of design**:

- Line
- Shape
- Color
- Form
- Motion

- Texture
- Pattern
- Direction
- Orientation
- Scale

- Angle
- Space
- Proportion

You might think that graphic designers are the only ones privy to the meaning of visual language—after all, it takes years of education and practice in order to "speak design" effectively and become proficient in it—but that's not entirely true.

## OUR FIRST LANGUAGE WAS VISUAL

Some species in nature rely mostly on scent. Others rely heavily on sound. Even plants have highly developed senses, which continue to surprise and mystify us the more we learn about them. Humans are one of the species that predominantly rely on vision.

Our vision isn't perfect. We can't see as far as the eagle does. We can see only a fraction of the light spectrum that the bees do. Our night vision sucks. When we can't trust our eyes, we rely on other senses, but vision is still the biggest source of information. (As someone living with very high myopia, I can appreciate how disorienting the world appears to people who don't have a healthy eyesight.)

Nature talks to us through visuals. The colors of berries, animal tracks on the ground, position of the Sun in the sky, the color and texture of clouds—all of this information warned us of available food choices, the approaching nightfall, or a heavy storm.

The Latin alphabet and other writing systems in the world developed from early pictograms and ideograms—drawings that represented concepts and enabled people to record their culture more permanently. Visuals have become even more meaningful in the industrial age. Enter: traffic signalization, map symbols, warning labels... Children are taught the names of animals and how to count using picture books. Nonverbal children use communication aids with pictorial symbols corresponding to different concepts, and are able to interact with others in this way. In his paper on visual language, the scientist and scholar Robert E. Horn noted:

*"People think visually. People think in language. When words and visual elements are closely intertwined, we create something new and we augment our communal intelligence."* *

Horn predicts that our visual-verbal language will keep evolving with the aid of new technologies, and play an even larger role in education, the sciences, and everyday life.

Every human with a healthy vision living in our society understands visual language, whether they're aware of it or not. The limitation of most people is that they're conditioned to *interpret* what's being communicated, but not taught how to *formulate* a message themselves. This is where **graphic designers** differ from other people: we've broken down the language of visual communication into its elements, and know how to use them correctly.

## Who Is a Designer?

What a silly question, right? A designer is a person who graduated from a design school, and/or a person who professionally creates designs for their client or employer. The same way a *lawyer* is a person who graduated from law school and passed the bar exam, and is legally allowed to practice law in a certain jurisdiction. The same way a *psychotherapist* is a person who graduated from any of the schools of psychotherapy, and has the credentials to practice therapy on people.

When you examine a contract before you sign it, you don't fool yourself into thinking you're a lawyer. When a friend comes over in distress and you help them calm down, you don't foster any illusions about being a psychotherapist (even if the conversation may well have been therapeutic

---

* *"Visual Language and Converging Technologies in the Next 10–15 Years (and Beyond)"* by Robert E. Horn (2001).

for your friend). I suppose that when you type your documents, or create a Facebook cover photo, you don't think of yourself as a designer. But here is where you may be wrong—*you are a designer*. Maybe not a professional one, and maybe you don't know all the things experienced designers do, but you use design in your everyday life.

People have been designing things since the dawn of history. Our hands are equipped to manipulate clay, wood, metal, rock, ice, bones, threads... Ever since the first early human thought of the idea of forming raw materials into something usable, we've been making clothing, tools, weapons, adornments, shelters, sacred items... In today's world, few of us make things ourselves. We buy them in stores or online, and most of what we buy today has been created in the People's Republic of China.

For the general public, most of their creations are digital. There's few office jobs that don't require typing paperwork and preparing presentations. Even café and restaurant staff needs to update their 'daily specials' list. Look at any notice-board, and you'll see dozens of public service announcements and ads created by ordinary people. The simple action of *typing an email* carries design decisions with it. How many line-breaks? Which font size? If something is important, do we italicize it, mark it bold, or type it in caps? Smileys, emojis, or keeping it serious? What's the proper signature format? You may not think of these as design decisions, but they're the same decisions I need to make when designing a document for a client.

### THE ROLE OF DESIGNERS

We've established that you're a designer—but don't put that on your CV just yet! There's a lot more to design than most people are aware of. Plenty of training and experience is required for a person to become a *good enough* designer to communicate visually in an effective and appealing way. In my experience, most attempts of non-designers to create a design are random—like a person trying to play a musical instrument they've never seen before by the ear. A professional designer is like an experienced musician: they know exactly where the key for each note is, and in which order to press them to play the music that captivates people.

Designers know how to communicate messages visually fast and with higher precision, because that's a skill they've been perfecting over the years. Someone with 20 years of experience is certainly a lot better at it than someone fresh out of design school. When the stakes are high and you don't want to risk people getting the *wrong* message, you need to hire a designer that has experience *in that domain*.

Situations that most definitely call for a designer are high-traffic websites, marketing campaigns you're investing thousands of dollars in, and packaging for luxury or innovative consumer products. In cases like this, not investing money in design will likely cost you more in the end—the website won't work properly, and it will have to be completely redesigned; the marketing campaign won't convert people; the product won't sell.

I emphasize the need for hiring a person with the appropriate experience. The field of graphic design is wide, and most of us specialize in one or few fields. Specialization leads to greater expertise, so you can be confident that a web designer with hundreds of websites under their belt will know what to do. That said, design is a valuable skill that costs money. Beginner business owners are typically operating on a tight budget, so going all out on a new brand, website, brochures, and magazine ads may not be in the cards at the moment. I don't recommend investing in design before you can afford it. If you can secure a grant to pay for initial branding and marketing expenses, that's great—if you can't, you'll need to bootstrap for now, and save up for a professional rebrand later on, when your cash flow is steadier. This book will provide some pointers on how to do it yourself.

Visual language is not a mystical, innate talent that only the special few possess. There are rules, and there are books (some of them very old) that you can learn from. Everyone has the capacity to learn it, as Josiah Kahane emphasizes in the article for Fast Company:

> *"It seems that human beings have an innate capacity for cognitive modeling and its expression through sketching, drawing, construction, acting out, and so on, that is fundamental to human thought."* *

---

\* *"How Your Brain Understands Visual Language"* by Josiah Kahane, Fast Company (2015).

This is great news for you: no matter what your starting point is, you can improve your design skills just by paying attention to the elements of the visual language, which is what the majority of this chapter is about.

## The Elements of a Visual Brand Identity

This section of the chapter will give you a quick overview of the various design elements, and some general instruction on how you might use them to improve the appearance of your brand. If you'd like to dig in deeper into the subject, there are entire books written on each of the elements. Covering all this information in a single chapter would be impossible, so I've kept the theoretic part light, and limited the technical terms only to those that you might need for everyday use. The elements of the visual brand we'll examine are:

1. Brand mood board
2. Color
3. Typography
4. Logo
5. Photography
6. Illustration

Regardless of whether you decide to design your brand yourself or hire a professional to do it for you, becoming more familiar with these elements will help you make better choices and effectively communicate your vision to creative professionals you collaborate with.

## 1. Brand Mood Board

**A brand mood board is a collage that represents your core values and brand qualities in a visual way.** It's the first step in translating these abstract concepts into visual language. It serves as a source of inspiration, and as a communication aid. When working with a client, I use the mood board to establish mutual understanding about the visual direction of their new brand. Instead of using words to describe what I envisioned for their brand, which can lead to different interpretations, I *show* it to them. Whether you decide to work with a designer or by yourself, creating a mood board is a great exercise in giving your ideas and impressions a more solid form. Your mood board may consist of:

- Photos
- Illustrations
- Words
- Patterns
- Color swatches
- Graphic fragments

Mood boards are typically created using elements found online or in printed media. Since they're only meant for internal use, you're allowed to use copyrighted images—under the condition that you don't use these elements in the final design, and do not publish the mood board. If you use purchased images, or those licensed under creative commons, in that case you're allowed to publish the mood board.

If you're a visual artist, elements from your own work should be a part of your mood board as well. Focus on the details your works have in common, such as color palette, brush strokes, patterns, repeated motifs, etc.

Mood boards can be created using a variety of tools. You could even make a physical collage if you have enough source material on hand. Graphic applications commonly used in mood board design include Adobe Photoshop, Canva, and Pinterest. There are also specialist applications like Moodboard, Adobe Spark, and Sampleboard. The process of creating a mood board is simple.

1. Install the application you wish to use, or register an online account.

2. Create a new document, album, or folder for your project (depending on the app).

3. Open a search engine and enter keywords that include your core values, brand voice qualities, unique value proposition, ideal client, and anything else you feel is important.

4. When you find an image that gives you the *feeling* of your brand, save it to your mood board.

5. When you're done adding images to your mood board, make sure to save it. You might also export it for viewing on other computers, so you can access it at any time, or share it with your team.

You don't have to complete your mood board in one sitting. Feel free to keep adding to it whenever you encounter a visual that makes an impact on you. Keep referring to your mood board when you need to make a choice on the other visual brand identity elements.

The overall look and feel of your brand mood board can offer insight into your **brand qualities**. Brand qualities are all about *how* you express yourself in a non-verbal manner, and what your ideal clients are attracted to and expect from a business like yours. While brand *voice* qualities we've covered previously are verbal, brand qualities in general can apply to any sense. They are often visual and tactile. Examples of different brand qualities may include:

| | | |
|---|---|---|
| • Casual | • Natural | • Bold |
| • Classic | • Feminine | • Minimalist |
| • Healthy | • Masculine | • Modern |
| • Eco-friendly | • Luxurious | • Retro |
| • Artistic | • Mysterious | • Sophisticated |
| • High-tech | • Hand-made | • Progressive |
| • Corporate | • Elegant | • Traditional |
| • Geeky | • Whimsical | • Dynamic |
| • Athletic | • Fun | • Simple |
| • Extravagant | • Glamorous | • Powerful |
| • Mystical | • Playful | • Friendly |

You'll notice that some of them are the same as brand voice qualities, because these qualities apply to multiple senses. When determining other elements of your visual brand identity, keep your chosen brand qualities in mind.

## 2. Color

Color is a physical property of light. It's one of the most significant and memorable elements of the brand. Colors create such an impact on the audience that we start to associate a certain shade of color with a particular notable brand that's been using it (e.g. the Facebook blue, the Starbucks green, or the Coca-Cola red). In graphic design, each color has three properties:

1.  **Hue** tells us where the color is on the light spectrum (e.g. red, blue, lime green).
2.  **Saturation** is the intensity or the vibrancy of the color.
3.  **Lightness** is the tone of the color.

Colors, whether used in isolation or as a part of a wider palette, communicate different **moods**. Light, saturated colors appear fresh and youthful, while duller and darker colors appear mature and conservative. So called 'warm' colors such as red, orange, and yellow appear more outgoing and intense, while 'cool' colors such as blue, green, and violet give the impression of reservation and moderation.

We should also give some consideration to **color symbolism**, but it's not as important as you might think. Color symbolism varies among different cultures. In China, white is the color of death and mourning, and red is a traditional bridal color, associated with celebration. In contrast, in the West the wedding dresses are traditionally white. In some countries, certain colors are powerfully associated to political movements and religions. We should keep these things in mind, but not let them control our choices. As brands become stronger and more visible, they are the ones that lend meaning to certain colors. The table below outlines common symbolic meanings of colors in the Western culture:

| | |
|---|---|
| **Black** | Power, luxury, mystery, elegance, mourning, depth, sophisticated, formal |
| **White** | Peace, purity, innocence, minimalism, perfection, clean, quiet, neutral |
| **Yellow** | Happiness, joy, creativity, warning, intellect, the Sun, optimistic, youthful, energetic |

| | |
|---|---|
| **Orange** | Energy, vitality, adventure, creativity, fun, warmth, confidence, enthusiasm, determination, success, encouragement, exciting, friendly, cheerful |
| **Red** | Passion, energy, action, excitement, love, adventure, strength, power, desire, bold, daring, loud |
| **Pink** | Sweetness, love, nurturing, childhood, delicate, feminine, romantic, passive |
| **Purple** | Luxury, imagination, wisdom, creativity, magic, spirituality, wealth, power, ambition, calm, extravagant |
| **Blue** | Trust, security, reliability, strength, authority, business, fidelity, truth, wisdom, tranquility, sincerity, calm, dependable |
| **Green** | Growth, health, nature, relaxation, regeneration, luck, wealth, fertility, freshness, harmony, safety, hope, organic |
| **Brown** | Nature, stability, comfort, fertility, practicality, the Earth, organic |
| **Gray** | Balance, neutral, calm |
| **Silver** | Prestige, wealth, prosperity, luxury, spirituality, illumination, reflection, the Moon, glamorous, elegant, sophisticated, feminine |
| **Gold** | Success, achievement, triumph, luxury, wealth, prosperity, abundance, quality, extravagance, the Sun, masculine |

Exposure to certain colors can affect human emotions and behavior.[*] For this reason, color is used carefully and intentionally in marketing of specific

---

[*]   *"Environmental Colour Impact upon Human Behaviour: A Review"* by Nurlelawati Ab. Jalil, Rodzyah Mohd Yunus, and Normahdiah S. Said, Procedia – Social and Behavioral Sciences (2012, Issue 35, 54 – 62).

goods and services, but also in hospitals, prisons, and schools. When choosing your color palette, aim for a mood that will be appealing both to you and your ideal clients. Just because you have a 'favorite color', it doesn't mean it's appropriate for your business. These are the questions to ask when selecting colors for your brand:

- Is this color's mood appropriate for my brand?
- Do my ideal clients have any negative associations with this color?
- Is this color distinct from those that my competitors use?

Your brand **color palette** includes the colors that are used in the logo graphic, as well as an expanded selection of colors that offers more flexibility to your designs. The need for many different colors is especially obvious on the web where we need:

1. **Neutral** colors for paragraph text and large surfaces.
2. **Highlight** colors for headings, subheadings, and graphics.
3. **Accent** colors for links and buttons.

This way, website visitors can easily distinguish the most important and clickable elements from the rest of the content.

Tools that can help you with generating a color palette include Adobe Color, ColourLovers, Paletton, Palettable, Coolors, and Material Palette. Many color palette generators rely on the color wheel and color harmonies. The **color wheel** is the most popular way of organizing colors: they're arranged in the shape of a circle, with hues going clockwise from yellow, orange, red, magenta, violet, blue, aqua, green, lime green, and back to yellow. **Color harmonies** utilize the shape of the color wheel to select a range of colors that are either closer in hue (monochromatic and analogous schemes), or contrasting in hue (complementary, triad, and tetrad schemes). I recommend playing with one of the color palette generators to grasp how color harmonies work on a practical level.

You don't have to use color harmonies if you don't like the result. When I create color palettes, I only use the color harmonies as a starting point, but make sure to mix each individual color manually, until I'm pleased with how the colors appear next to each other. This is a skill that you can get better at with practice. If you don't trust your own color choices, you can use one of the pre-generated palettes from the tool's library, though that does mean it may not be unique to your business.

## COLOR SYSTEMS

Color systems are different ways the color is described and reproduced with digital and print technologies. When using color palette generators or graphic design software, you'll notice there are different designations for each shade. The most frequently used are RGB and CMYK, but there are others as well.

**RGB** color system stands for red, green, and blue, and it's a system used on digital displays. Our devices have millions of tiny LED lights (pixels) that light up with red, green, and blue light, which create all the colors we can see on our computer monitors, phones, tablets, and TVs. The individual red, green, and blue channel values range from 1 to 255, giving a total of 256 levels per channel. Each shade of color has its own RGB formula, which can be expressed in several ways:

- R=10 G=100 B=255
- RGB 10/100/255
- #0a64ff

All of these formulas express exactly the same shade of blue. The last formula is called the **HEX code**, which is a shorthand for the RGB color formulas in the first two rows using hexadecimal notation*. Graphic design applications will accept either version of the color formula, through the corresponding input fields. Colors in the RGB color system can also be expressed through the HSB (hue, saturation, brightness) and the HSL (hue, saturation, luminosity) color models, but these are not used as often in color palette notation.

**CMYK** stands for cyan, magenta, yellow, and key (black) and it's a color

---

* Hexadecimal number system uses 16 digits: 0 to 9, and letters A to F. Number A corresponds to the decimal number 10, and F to the decimal number 15.

system used in print—both on your home printer and on professional printing machines. It's also referred to as the four color print. Most full-color prints today are made by printing these 4 base colors on top of each other, and the overlapping of colors results in various shades. CMYK color formulas are expressed in percentages, from 0 to 100. For example, the most intense red formula is C=0 M=100 Y=100 K=0. A shorthand notation for this color would be 0/100/100/0.

Since RGB and CMYK color systems are completely different technologies, the colors from one system don't exactly correspond to the colors in the other. Our blue color from the first RGB example can be expressed in CMYK as C=96 M=61 Y=0 K=0, but if we compared the printed sample with our computer display, there would be notable differences. Even worse, two different samples from two different print shops could look slightly different. These minor discrepancies in colors are to be expected, and typically the printed designs will always look a bit darker and less vibrant than the previews on the screen.

Another color system frequently used in design is the **Pantone** Matching System. Pantone colors are **spot colors**, which means each shade is an individually mixed ink. (Similar to wall paint, artist paints, and nail polish.) By using Pantone inks instead of the conventional CMYK print technology, we can insure that the colors on our printed materials look exactly like the swatches from the Pantone color books. Printing with Pantone inks is more expensive than using classic four color print, so it's only used on larger print runs, and when only few colors are needed. Pantone also has a range of neon, pastel, and metallic inks which are impossible to get with CMYK.

When creating a brand palette, we need to define each color using the RGB and CMYK color formulas, so that the appropriate color is used on screen and in print. Professional designers also provide the corresponding Pantone color names.

## 3. Typography

Since the main role of visual design is communication, most of our designs will use letters and words. The appearance of words influences how the information is perceived. If the information is written in a more classic form, it will appear more 'official' and professional. Messages written in a more expressive and free-form fashion can appear more artistic or juvenile. This is why we must carefully choose the style of letters that is appropriate for the message we want to convey.

**Typography is the art of designing letters.** People who create fonts are called typographic designers. Thanks to their effort, we have thousands of free and commercial fonts to choose from for literally any occasion. This abundance of different fonts makes our choices easier in some ways, but more challenging in others. How do you know which types of fonts are appropriate for your brand? How do you know when you've found the 'winner'? I'll offer some tips on making this process easier—but first, let's introduce some typography terms you might need to know.

A **glyph** is the typographic term used for any alphanumeric character, punctuation mark or special character. 'A', 'b', '$', and '9' are all glyphs. In everyday use, we may simply call it a character.

A set of glyphs that are designed in the same style and share common geometric features, is called a **typeface**. Features of a typeface include the proportions, line angles, roundness of letters, stroke thickness, slant of the characters, letter decorations, etc. Helvetica Neue Italic is the name of one typeface. Helvetica Neue Bold is another one.

All the typefaces that share the same name and only vary in thickness (weight), letter width, or slant, are called a **font family**. Helvetica Neue is the name of the font family that includes the regular, bold, italic, and bold italic variations. Some font families also have additional weights (like light, thin, semi-bold, extra-bold, black) or letter widths (condensed, extended). Examples of free font families with many different typeface variants include Open Sans, Barlow and Fira Sans. (You can look them up on Google Fonts.)

A specific typeface set in a specific size is called a **font**. This term is often used as a synonym for a typeface, although it's not technically accurate. Still, if you say 'font' when you mean a 'typeface', most people will know what you mean.

Each font family has a different personality, and a unique 'voice'—they can appear serious, funny, elegant, fun, sensual, futuristic, rugged, childish, old, modern, or even neutral. Here are some examples of fonts with different personalities:

# Questa Grande
**ELEGANT, FORMAL**

# *Lust Script*
**EXTRAVAGANT, BOLD**

# Orbitron
**FUTURISTIC, TECHNICAL**

# Comic Sans
**CHILDISH, INNOCENT**

The problem arises when you choose a font family whose natural voice doesn't match the written message. A common culprit for this is Comic Sans: I see inappropriate uses of this typeface almost every single day. It has a childish appearance, and is only suitable for comics and perhaps children's birthday party celebrations—it's definitely not intended for any kind of professional use. Similarly, a serious and classic font such as Times New Roman wouldn't be appropriate for a brand aimed at teenagers, as they would perceive it as conservative and boring.

In the fifth chapter, we've talked about your brand voice. When selecting the main font family, or a font pair for your brand, you need to look at the qualities you've chosen for your brand voice, and aim to find fonts that share these qualities. Since there are thousands of different fonts you may choose from, it would be better if you already knew what you're looking for before you start searching, so you can filter and narrow down your choices.

The easiest way to filter fonts is to decide in advance which category your ideal font is most likely to be in. Here are the most common categories defined by typographic designers, based on their dominant characteristics:

| Category | Characteristics | Example |
|---|---|---|
| Serif | Thin 'legs' at the bottom of every letter (called serifs). Circular or angled endings (terminals) at the top of the letters. Often have varying stroke thickness: vertical strokes are thick while horizontal are thin. Most suitable for classic and elegant brands. | Bodoni |
| Slab-serif | Serifs ('legs') are as thick as the letter strokes themselves, and the letters are uniform in thickness all around. More modern-looking than serif fonts, and can look a bit retro if decorative elements are included. | Rokkit |
| Sans-serif | Letters with uniform stroke thickness and no decorations. Can be divided into sub-groups: geometric, humanist, grotesk etc. Very versatile fonts that can be used in just about any brand. Probably the most common type found in logos today. | Helvetica Neue |
| Script | Letter shapes emulate calligraphy. Often features decorative swashes at the letter endings. Suitable for elegant brands, as well as special events. | Parisienne |
| Monospace | Each letter has the same width, which is useful in computer programming, because code appears more organized. In design, they're often used to emulate computer interfaces (like sci-fi shows). | Courier New |

| | | |
|---|---|---|
| Handwritten | Resemble freehand handwriting. Often have a texture of a writing instrument (marker or brush). Suitable for artistic, hand-made, and natural brands, and those aimed at younger audiences. | *Chalky* |
| Blackletter | Also called gothic fonts. Letter shapes resemble the old German calligraphy style. Suitable for metal bands, beer, and alternative fashion brands. | **Amador** |

There are many other special categories such as typewriter, stencil, pixel, or comic. Knowing the general category of the font family you're looking for will help you narrow your choices when looking them up in a font library.

Another trick that can help you find the most appropriate font family is to use the font library's tagging system. For example, the free font website FontSquirrel has a comprehensive list of tags that you can find in the right column of the website. You can select from tags such as 'elegant', 'casual', 'retro', 'high-tech', etc. and the site will display only the typefaces within that category, which will speed up your process of finding the perfect font.

## TIPS FOR SELECTING FONTS FOR YOUR BRAND

Here are some best practices that will ensure the typefaces you've selected will perform well on any design application, whether it's web or print.

**Test your fonts on small sizes.** While the font you like the most may look wonderful on large banners, what happens when you scale down your logo or text to fit the size of a business card? Imagine the smallest size where this text is likely to appear, and print out test samples with your business name and contact information set in that size. Is it still easy to read? Script and handwritten fonts often scale badly, especially if they're overly ornate or thin.

**Select a simple serif or sans-serif for body text.** While unusual fonts such as script or handwriting may look wonderful in logos and headlines, they're not so fun when your clients need to decipher your phone number or the details of your offer. Reserve the funky fonts for large, short text. Use an ordinary-looking secondary typeface for any other text. Your readers will appreciate it.

**Use two different font families at most.** Stick with one font family for your logo and headings, and a second font for smaller text and tagline. That's it. If the font has variants such as bold and italic, that's all you need to create variety in your text. Designs that use too many different font families look messy.

**Use the same fonts throughout all your printed and digital designs.** The only exception is emails, newsletter, scheduling and invoicing apps, and other media where you don't have control over the fonts you use, or the software has a limited selection of available fonts. In that case, use the font that most closely resembles the one you chose for your brand, if possible.

**Always use the same fonts in the same way.** If you selected a thick serif font for headings, always use this font for headings. If you use a sans-serif font for paragraph text and lists, always use it for paragraph text and lists. Don't mix them up. This creates consistency in your designs and appears professional.

**Avoid all caps in longer text.** Capital letters may be used in logos and headings, but when used in long form text, they quickly become tiring to read. Lowercase letters are easier to read, so use them in paragraph text, lists, tables, quotes, fine print, taglines, etc. You can emphasize certain parts of text with **bold** or *italic* style, instead of all caps.

**Avoid special effects on your text.** Effects such as color gradients, textures, beveled edges, glowing letters, strong drop shadows, or outlines can make designs look cheap and juvenile. (Remember WordArt?) Professional designers almost never use these effects. Even when they do, it's either subtle, or done so well that it still retains a classy appearance. I'm not saying don't ever do it, but if you do—be mindful of the thin line that separates 'creative' from 'tacky'.

**'White space' matters just as much as letters themselves.** If you pay attention at the way this book is formatted, you'll notice that there is a gap between each paragraph, and a slightly larger gap above each subheading. If you're reading the ebook version, you can adjust the margins of the page and the line spacing by yourself. In the print version, I've adjusted the margins and line spacing to make reading comfortable. I've noticed in the classes I teach that most beginner designers ignore the empty space between letters, lines, paragraphs, and page edges. This results in crammed text that lacks organization. If your text processor doesn't automatically add space after paragraphs, get familiar with the program settings and add the spacing yourself. Increase the line-spacing from the default value. Add more space before each heading and subheading. This will result in a more professional design, and the text will be easier to read. (Also, entering a new line is not the same as adjusting spacing in the paragraph settings, so try to avoid that lazy method.)

There is so much more that we could talk about, and entire books have been written about typography. If you create a lot of documents in your day-to-day work, I advise that you look into typography a bit more, since it will make a huge difference for how your clients interact with your contracts, proposals, reports, white papers, etc.

Excellent resources for business people include Matthew Butterick's website Practical Typography, and his book *Typography for Lawyers*. Despite its name, it isn't useful just for lawyers, but anyone dealing with a lot of documents. If your aim is to become a better designer, a classic primer on typography is the book *The Elements of Typographic Style* by Robert Bringhurst.

## 4. Logo

**A logo is a unique graphic that represents a business, an organization, or a product through the use of typography, color, and symbols.** We're surrounded by logos in our everyday life: they're on our clothes, electronic devices, cars, food, cosmetics... We see them on billboards, TV advertisements, social media, vehicles... You couldn't go a *day* in the modern world without seeing at least one.

Logos are a staple item of the corporate brand identity, but many small businesses who want to be perceived as more professional and successful create them as well. While you could absolutely have a brand without a logo, there are some clear benefits to using them.

A logo is more than just a decoration—it's a business tool. The benefits that the logo provides to your business are:

- Recognizability
- Differentiation
- Memorability
- Confidence and trust
- Emotional connection
- Status

Having a **recognizable** logo subtly reinforces the sense of familiarity that people have whenever they interact with any type of content you publish. You can place an unobtrusive icon or a monogram on all your social media graphics, your speaker presentation slides, in the corner of your YouTube videos, and your email signature. This is even more important for physical products and brick-and-mortar businesses. There are so many touch points that you can use to strengthen your brand with a prominently placed logo: packaging, gift bags, loyalty cards, shop windows, signage, vehicles, and more.

The strongest **differentiation** is achieved through using a logo that features symbols and colors that are distinct from its competitors. Your logo will often be seen next to other logos, and rarely in isolation. If you put your own logo next to those of your competitors, ideally you'd want it to stand out, so that no client could mistake your business for someone else's.

**Memorability** is achieved when a logo is original enough so that it creates interest, but is also familiar enough so that people can make mental associations. This is a delicate balance that professional designers are trained to achieve. Short company names are more memorable than long ones. Names that relate to a familiar subject are more memorable than those based on people's personal names. Certain types of logos, which we'll explore in this chapter, are more memorable than others.

A business that features a professionally designed logo appears more **trustworthy**, and their clients develop greater **confidence** in their skills and abilities. All other things being equal, the business that *looks* more professional will *seem* more professional.

As people repeatedly buy products or services from a business, they form an **emotional connection** with the brand, and may even proudly display the logos of their favorite brands on their clothing and accessories. Clients and customers may become so attached to the brand's logo, that they take attempts at redesigning logos very seriously. Notable examples of this include the latest change of the Starbucks logo where they've dropped the rounded 'Starbucks Coffee' ring and only kept the green mermaid symbol. Their audience was strongly divided on this change, and many preferred the older variation with the name*. The latest Gap logo change was met with protests on social media, and after only a week they went back to the previous version.†

A logo can be used to communicate the brand's premium **status**. Typically, brands that feature carefully crafted logos give the appearance of a higher value, whereas less appealing logos may give the appearance of a budget business that caters to a budget-conscious audience. People today are trained through repeated media exposure to expect a certain level of service from a business simply by observing what it looks like. If you wish to see a real life example of this, just visit the wine shelf of your local grocery store: the premium, more expensive wines will often feature well-designed minimalist labels, while the cheaper wines will cram as much information on their label as possible, and the designs will appear a bit old-fashioned and tacky, with realistic grape illustrations, faux-old-paper textures, and script fonts.

### SYMBOLIC MESSAGE OF A LOGO

A logo is a **communication device** that expresses your brand message. This message can be as simple and superficial, or as deep and layered as you'd like. I categorize it into four different levels: the function or content, the benefits, the brand qualities, and the core values.

The most basic message, and one that is quite common and most immediately recognized by people, is one where the logo depicts a **literal function or content** of a service or product. Examples of this include:

---

\*   *"Starbucks' New Logo: A Risky Move"* by Nigel Hollis, Harvard Business Review (January 7, 2011).

†   *"Filling in the Gap of a Rebranding Disaster"* by Natalie Zmuda, AdAge (October 18, 2010).

- Scissors for a hairdresser.
- Tooth for a dentist.
- House for a real estate agent.
- Dog for a pet groomer.
- Flower for a florist.

This type of logo is most common for physical products, or services that use a recognizable tool. This practice is very old, and was used on medieval store signs. They are also the most obvious, cliché, and overused visuals, which is why I advise that you avoid them in your own logo. The brand message they communicate is simple: *"We write your website copy," "We cut hair," "We serve coffee."* I'm sure you can come up with something better than that.

The next level of your brand message are the **benefits** that your service or product provides. While features are inherent to the product or service, the benefits are only created *in connection* to the client. A message that communicates the benefits is more compelling, because it highlights what's most important to the buyer. Examples for benefits include:

- Butterfly, symbolizing *transformation* for a life coach.
- Scales, symbolizing *fairness* for a lawyer.
- Swan, symbolizing *elegance* for a fashion brand.
- Silhouette of a person jumping, symbolizing *vitality* for a nutrition specialist.
- Heart-shaped hands, symbolizing *care* for a hospital.

Benefits are often more abstract than features, and challenging to depict visually. The choice of typography and color plays a large role too. Your unique value proposition can serve as inspiration for this type of logo.

The third level of brand message are the **brand qualities**. If benefits are what the business *achieves* for the client, qualities are how the business *feels* to the client. In services which are highly aesthetic (arts, crafts, fashion), benefits and qualities may, in fact, be the same. For other services and products, the brand qualities are based on *how* the business does what it does and what kind of impression it leaves on the clients. Examples of these include:

- Script monogram, representing *refinement* of an opera house (Dallas Opera).

- Cartoon chipmunk, representing *friendliness* of a travel agency (Hipmunk).

- Letters made out of tree branches, representing a music band inspired by *nature* (Komfor).

- Stylized olive tree and boat icon, representing the *tradition* of a French family (RPSA).

- Unicorn icon, representing the *playful* nature of a digital agency (Rimake).

The fourth and deepest level of message your business can communicate are your **core values**. We've discussed them in the third chapter, and I hope that by now you have identified yours. Broadcasting your core values through your visual identity is a powerful way to capture the attention of people who are a great match for your business. Examples of values expressed through visuals include:

- Torch icon, representing the *liberty* of a radio station (Radio Free Europe).

- Abstract art human silhouette, representing the *humanity* of a plastic surgeon (Doctor Barret).

- Devil's tail shape, representing the *fun* of a copywriting & PR agency (Savarakatini).

- Green and brown flowing lines, representing *nature* and *health* for an architect (Pere León).

Since values are mostly abstract they present a design challenge, but are in my opinion the most powerful and most rewarding type of logos.

Now that you're aware of these conceptual differences in logos, you can play a little game as you're walking down the streets of your town: pay attention to the shop signs and try to guess which logo would fit in which category? (Yes, it's a very nerdy game. I happen to like those best.)

Which one of these approaches should you choose for your own business? I recommend the deepest message that you're able to identify. The more you dig into the essence of your brand, the more permanent your brand message will be, and the longer your logo will last. Features may change as your offers and business model evolve. You might uncover new benefits that your services provide. Brand qualities are more permanent, since they depend more on the personality of the business owner than on the services they offer. Core values are the most permanent of all—brands that are based on them will last the longest, despite other changes that may happen in the business. This is especially true if you have an expansive vision for your business that is far beyond what you're able to do right now. If you want to avoid rebranding every time your business pivots, focus on your core values, not on the more superficial aspects.

## TYPES OF LOGOS

When we say the word 'logo', most people imagine a symbol: the Nike swash, Target's concentric circles, Starbucks mermaid, Mercedes three pointed star in a circle, etc.—but not all logos feature symbols. Here is a rough classification of the different varieties of logos in use today:

**Typographic wordmark** logos feature only the company or a product name set in a font, without any kind of symbol. Some typographic logos may have tiny decorative elements (like the yellow underline under the Olympus logo), or the shapes of letters may be slightly changed so that the logo looks more unique. A typographic logo may be surrounded by a geometric shape (like the Samsung logo placed on a dark blue ellipse).

**Hand-lettered wordmark** logos are uniquely drawn company or product names by hand-lettering artists. These logos often feature a more organic, hand-made, or retro look, but this isn't always the case. Letter shapes may be illustrative, entwined with lots of ligatures and swashes, or tightly fitted inside a silhouette.

**Monogram** or lettermark logos consist of the company name and an icon featuring the first letter of the company. The monogram can be abstractified to a basic geometric shape, ornamental, or illustrative. It may be placed inside a circle or a square to make it more robust.

**Pictorial symbol** logos feature a graphic that represents a recognizable object: animal, plant, person, the elements, or a man-made item. The company or product name is written in full next to the symbol. Simple pictures surpass language barriers, improve the speed of recognition, and make differentiation among competitors easier.

**Abstract symbol** logos feature a graphic that may not be easily recognizable at first, but are often inspired by a physical object or an abstract concept. (For example the Nike swoosh is based on the wings silhouette on the statue of the Greek goddess of victory, Nike of Samothrace.) Abstract symbols often feature geometric shapes such as circles, lines, triangles, rectangles, hexagons, stars, spirals, etc.

**Emblems** are graphics that combine letters, pictures, and geometric shapes into compact forms shaped like badges and seals. They are most often used in governmental and educational institutions and sports clubs. Because of their high visual complexity, they're rarely used by businesses.

**Mascots** use the likeness of a human (e.g. Mr. Clean), animal (e.g. MailChimp), or a personified object (e.g. Reddit) to represent a company or a product. The illustrations are often more detailed than in a pictorial symbol, and the mascot may be depicted in a variety of situations, or even animated.

With so many options, choosing the right type of logo for your business may seem difficult, but as a service based business you can safely eliminate some of them. Mascots and emblems are rarely appropriate for service professionals (though there are always exceptions). Pictorial symbols can become a cliché in certain industries, as we've already seen when discussing symbolic messages, so this approach should be considered carefully. If your business name relates to a subject that may be depicted, but that isn't very common among your competitors, then a pictorial logo may be the best choice since it has many advantages. (For example, the wedding planning business Lemon & Lime.)

Professionals who use their own name as a business name typically turn to monograms which are very versatile, as well as hand-lettered logos that resemble signatures. Of course, just because something is typical for an industry, it doesn't mean that you should do it.

The pitfall of abstract symbols is that they often lack distinctiveness, especially if they're based on geometric objects. In my experience, whenever you base a logo on an abstract symbol, you're bound to find some existing logos that look similar. Still, if you or your designer take great care in devising a unique shape, it can work.

A typographic logo is the safest choice. Many prominent businesses have pure typographic logos, and it didn't hurt their success. If you're creating a logo for yourself and don't have a lot of design experience, this is the approach I'd recommend.

If you decide to work with a professional logo designer, they'll probably create multiple ideas involving different types of logos, and then narrow down the choice to the type that suits your business best. Some designers on the other hand specialize in certain types of logos, so if you already know what type of logo you want, look up people whose portfolios show similar examples.

## LOGO DESIGN BEST PRACTICES

If you decide to create a logo for your own business yourself, here are some tips to make sure that the design you come up with looks as professional as possible.

**Use only one font family.** You can combine two typefaces like regular and bold, but using more than one font family is risky if you're not an experienced designer.

**Don't use overly decorative fonts.** We've already covered this in the Typography section, but it bears repeating. Fonts that are too curly, too futuristic, or too funky may be difficult to read, especially at small sizes. If you want to use a cursive or hand-written font, select the cleanest and the simplest one available. Print it at around 2–3 centimeters wide (1–1.5 inches) and see if you can still read it. Ask someone who doesn't know what it says to read it for you. (I always do this when I'm using cursive fonts or hand-lettering.)

**Use one strong color.** Too many strong colors in a logo can make your brand appear juvenile and unprofessional. Stick with one bright, saturated color that will draw attention, and complement it with a neutral color like gray, black, dark blue, or brown. If your brand is more classical and serious, you can avoid bright colors altogether and stick with a classy, neutral palette.

**Avoid using symbols if you can.** I often see business owners mess this one up, so I would advise not to use them at all and stick to pure text. The common mistake people make is to use a complex symbol that has too many details. When complex logos are scaled down, the detail is lost and the graphic looks unclear. A logo is not an illustration. It needs to be extremely simple so that it comes out clearly on a stamp or a miniature social media icon. If you want to use a symbol, make sure you're not violating anyone's copyright—don't use an image you've found online. There are royalty free graphics you can purchase to use as a logo, but in that case you may be using the same image as another existing business.

**Ask your friends to double-check your logo** before you send it off to print. Ask them what the logo reminds them of. If anyone mentions any unflattering imagery or unwanted symbolism, you'd be better off by changing it. If one of your friends has noticed that your graphic reminds them of a penis, other people may think that way too (you'd be surprised how often this happens).

If your goal is to become a professional logo designer, I recommend the following books that go into far more detail than I covered here:

- *Designing Logos: The Process of Creating Symbols That Endure* by Jack Gernsheimer.
- *Decoding Design: Understanding and Using Symbols in Visual Communication* by Maggie Macnab.
- *Smashing Logo Design: The Art of Creating Visual Identities* by Gareth Hardy.

For an aspiring brand designer, the book *Designing Brand Identity* by Alina Wheeler is an indispensable reference book that covers a wide range of topics.

## VECTOR VERSUS RASTER GRAPHICS

There are two types of computer graphics: vector and raster. Each of them has certain advantages and disadvantages, so it's good to know which one is the most appropriate for your needs.

**Vector** graphics are made up of geometric curves, called the Bézier curves. For example, the letter O is outlined by two ellipses: the larger outer one and the smaller inner one. The space between these two ellipses is filled with color. Vectors may also be quite complex, and made up of thousands of curves in different colors.

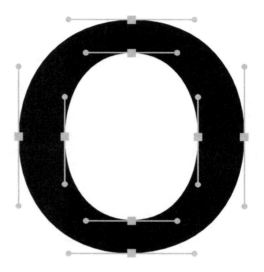

The advantage of vectors is that they can be scaled up to very large sizes without the loss of quality—the edges of the graphic remain crisp and clean. **Logos are always created as vectors** so we can apply them to business cards, websites, billboards, and trucks and they will look great at any size.

Popular programs used for creating vector graphics are Adobe Illustrator, CorelDRAW, and the open source program Inkscape. File formats for vector graphics include the standard format EPS, open source format SVG, and proprietary formats AI (by Adobe) and CDR (by Corel). If you're working with a professional designer, make sure they send you the files in the EPS or SVG formats, so you can use them in different programs from those they used to create the logo.

**Raster** graphics are made up of a grid of tiny squares called pixels. A photograph of a red rose flower will have thousands of pixels in different shades of red and green, and when you enlarge it with a 'zoom' tool in a graphic program, it will resemble a mosaic. The raster letter O is also made up from tiny individual colored squares. The advantage of raster graphics is that they can store very complex images with millions of colors, such as photographs. The downside is that when the raster graphic is enlarged, the details are lost and the image becomes blurry. This is why we never, *ever* make raster images bigger than their original size—we can only make them smaller.

Raster graphics are used for photography and illustration. There are many different programs that can be used to edit photos and create digital illustrations like Adobe Photoshop, GIMP, Corel Photo-Paint, Corel Painter, Pixelmator, Krita, and ArtRage. Each of these programs has their proprietary file format. Standard raster file formats that can be opened in pretty much any program are JPEG, PNG, and GIF.

Vector logos can easily be saved in a raster file format so you can use them in presentations, Word documents, on social media etc. Since raster images are more difficult to turn into vectors, we don't use raster graphics programs like Photoshop or GIMP to create logos.

## 5. Photography

Photos are becoming more and more important in online promotion. Social networks feature photos prominently, and written content looks much better when you break it apart with a couple of relevant photos. Conference presentations are starting to feature more visual content and less text, which increases audience engagement. Long story short: **you need good photos**.

Custom photos taken by professional photographers specifically for your business is by far the best way to use photography. Unfortunately, this may be out of budget for many new business owners. As soon as your budget can allow it, I recommend booking a professional photo-shoot, because these photos will enable you to create more appealing marketing materials for years to come.

The second best way to use photography is to **take your own original photos** as frequently as you can, especially if your work process is visually interesting. If you can, purchase a decent quality camera and take a beginner photography class to make the best photos possible. This is the closest to reality that your clients can get online, and it's worth getting it right. Here are some ideas for photos you can take that will increase the appeal of your website, social media, and other marketing channels:

- Your portrait (face and full body).
- Your office/studio/shop.
- You working in your office/studio.
- You giving a talk or teaching a workshop.
- Behind-the-scenes of project or event preparations.
- Finished creations.
- Lifestyle photos featuring your creations.
- Close-ups of your workspace or tools.
- Close-ups of your work in progress.

For professionals whose work involves other people, for example hairdressers, massage therapists, makeup artists, tutors, tattoo artists, etc. taking photos may be tricky. You can either pay a professional model for your photos (which is what big brands do), or take the more affordable route of bartering: offer a free session to the person who agrees to have their pictures taken and used for promotional purposes. Have the client sign a model release form,* so you can prove you have permission to use the photos in for marketing purposes.

Some industries have strict confidentiality regulations, like lawyers, medical professionals, and therapists. If that's the case, you can't use any actual client photos, or any identifying information in your marketing. You could stage a pretend client session with professional models or ask your friends to model for you.

Apart from the typical photos of people and office spaces, you can get so much more creative and expressive with your photo shoots. Amy Walsh, artist and the founder of The Bureau of Tactical Imagination, collaborates with clients and photographers in order to create scenes that tell a story about the business owner and their work. The photo shoots she art-directs use unique and interesting backdrops, props, and outfits that elevate her client's visuals from the run-of-the-mill corporate photography. In one of her articles, she shares how costumes and performance can help people overcome the discomfort they feel when having their pictures taken:

> *"Rather than see performance and dressing-up (in all its forms) as some kind of contradiction to the idea of authenticity in our business communications, why not recognize that we are more vast, more complex, more genius and beautiful than one photo of us with our laptop on the beach can ever show?*
>
> *Performance, drag, dressups, composing, posing, and constructing—these are all the tools of the artist and visionary, using multiple languages to express the complexity and emotional range of their visions."* †

I love Amy's playful approach to professional portrait photography, and have personally used costumes, theatrical make-up, and digital image

---

\*   A model release is a legal release typically signed by the subject of a photograph granting permission to publish the photograph. Source: *wikipedia.org*

†   *"On getting comfortable with pictures of ourselves: we contain multitudes!"* by Amy Walsh (July 7, 2017).

manipulation in my own work in an effort to create visions that can't be photographed in real life. A single still photograph can't capture the richness of our personality, and we shouldn't limit ourselves to it.

## TIPS FOR USING OTHER PEOPLE'S PHOTOS

If you're not able to take any photos of your own at the moment, but you need to create a website, social media graphics, or a presentation, you're allowed to use other people's photos—but there are rules to what you're allowed to do.

First of all: **always respect other people's copyright**. Don't just lift images off of Google, Pinterest, or other people's social media channels or blogs. Assume that every image you've found online is protected by copyright, unless the website specifically states it's not.

There are different licenses that enable you to use other people's photos: Public Domain (also called CC0) and Creative Commons (which comes in many variants). Public Domain images are free to use without restrictions. Creative Commons licenses come with different restrictions that require you to:

- Credit the original photographer in your publication.
- Use the photo without editing it in any way.
- Only use the photo for non-commercial purposes.

Many free stock photo websites, such as Pixabay, Pexels, Unsplash, and many others feature photos that are either free for use or in the Public Domain, but read the terms of use carefully for every photo. You'll usually find this information right under the photo, or in a column next to the photo under the photographer's name.

Apart from the free stock websites, there are also paid stock photo archives where you can get professional quality photos. Many such websites today have a subscription model, which means you pay a monthly fee to download a certain amount of photos. Some websites also allow for buying individual photos at a fixed price, though this is usually more expensive. Examples of paid stock websites include: Shutterstock, Adobe Stock, Alamy, and PhotoDune.

There are some restrictions on paid stock photos: some may be used in any way, while others are marked 'editorial use only', which means you may not use them in marketing materials—only in news articles. There's also a limit to how many times you may reproduce the photo you've bought. Typically, you may only use a photo on your website once, and if you want to use it in multiple marketing materials (poster, brochure, presentation) you'd have to buy the photo again for each use. If you're publishing a book or a brochure, you may only print a certain number of copies (which goes in the thousands, but you should still keep in mind).

When selecting photos, try to find those that have a similar color palette and light-to-shadow ratio, or edit them in a photo editor so they look more similar when viewed side by side. For example, you can turn all your photos into black and white or sepia, if those colors are dominant in your color palette. You can also make sure that your photos always include a colored detail that corresponds to your main brand color. Your brand mood board is a great source of inspiration for the style of photography that best suits your brand.

## 6. Illustration

Not every business needs illustration. Since stock photography and digital cameras have become so readily available, the majority of advertising today is based on photographic visuals. Still, illustration is a powerful medium that helps differentiate your brand from others, especially for creatives whose primary skill is in the visual arts.

**Descriptive** illustration assists the audience in understanding new concepts and how different parts connect together. Research has found that people learn better with descriptive visuals and narration, than from verbal instruction alone.* If your services or processes are challenging to grasp for an average Joe or Jane, using visuals such as charts and diagrams can help make them more accessible to your audience. If these illustrations are also skillfully drawn and aesthetically appealing, all the better. This type of

---

\*    *"Multimedia Learning"*, Richard E. Mayer (2001).

illustration is usually seen in instructional booklets, presentations, worksheets, book content, articles, videos, brochure pages, and infographics.

**Symbolic and decorative** illustration communicates the deeper meaning or the atmosphere of the piece by focusing on a certain detail, and interpreting it in a visual manner. This type of illustration doesn't usually help with understanding and remembering the information itself, but it helps with creating an emotional connection to the audience. It's often present on book and music record covers, product packaging, website headers, brochure covers, posters, ads etc.

In the age when stock photography has become ubiquitous and a tad overused, illustration can give your brand that much needed originality boost. This is one reason why we've seen a resurgence in hand-drawn and hand-painted sketches and lettering pieces in the past years. For some companies, people and publications, illustrations make a recognizable part of their brands. Notable examples include: Google (especially with their anniversary 'Doodles'), MailChimp, Shopify, and A List Apart. Technique-wise, illustration covers a variety of visual media:

- Traditional drawing and painting
- Traditional collage
- Sculpture
- Assemblage
- Paper-crafts
- Digital vector drawing
- Digital painting
- Digital collage (photo-manipulation)

These techniques may be mixed in any combination to produce an original and fresh approach, unique to the illustrator or the brand.

Typically, small business owners who use illustration in their content and marketing are artists themselves. If that's you, this is a great way to use your skills to your advantage. Even if you're not an artist yourself, you can still benefit from illustrated visuals by collaborating with a talented artist whose visual style matches the qualities of your brand.

Illustration may be used in many different mediums instead of photography—like websites, brochures, presentations, and videos—but also in places where photography wouldn't work because of color limitations or small areas. Here are some items you could decorate with simple, single-color illustrations, patterns or icons:

- T-shirts and other apparel
- Business cards and gift cards
- Stationery (letterheads, envelopes, folders, notebooks)
- Shop windows or glass doors
- Wall decals
- Wrapping paper
- Paper bags
- Table mats
- Badges

The list can go on, and not all of these items may be appropriate for your business, but I hope this gives you an idea of how you can lift the appeal of your brand by using custom-designed visuals which communicate the spirit of your business, whether it's fun or luxurious, elegant or expressive, simple, or elaborate.

All of the elements of visual brand identity work together to communicate a specific message. This is why we need to choose elements that are harmonious, and focus on one clear message instead of multiple conflicting messages. When it comes to design, 'more' is not necessarily better. When in doubt, remove the extra elements that may add to the visual noise.

In the next chapter, we'll examine how visual brand identity is documented for future use in a brand style guide.

*chapter VIII*

# Brand Style Guides

If you're learning how to design logos on your own, you may have encountered the term brand style guide—also called the brand identity guidelines, branding manuals, or branding guidelines. (Don't ask me how we've ended up with so many synonyms for this thing.)

**Brand style guide is a document containing rules for how a brand is to be visually represented throughout the various media.** It's supplied by the brand designer, usually as a PDF booklet. Some designers may also give their clients printed copies, which is more common for high-end branding projects. A brand style guide may also include non-visual brand elements.

If you're designing your own brand, this chapter will provide pointers on what to include in your own style guide. If you're collaborating with a designer, it will explain all the design lingo that will help you communicate your needs.

## Why Brands Need Guidelines

A brand style guide enables people to create designs that are aligned with the brand, and that look consistent and professional. Brands are ever evolving, and may be used by many people throughout their lifetime. Not all of these people are designers who understand how brand design works. Giving people the logo and sending them on their merry way without any instructions can end up in a disaster.

The designer creates a logo with a set of constraints which are defined by the client before the project starts—for example where the logo will be displayed, and what technology will be used to apply the logo to different surfaces. During the logo design process, the designer ensures that the logo they're making fits those constraints. If the client intends to use silk-screen printing on T-shirts, the logo must look good in a single color (like white on dark). If the client intends to apply the logo to the uniforms using embroidery, then the logo must look recognizable even when slightly 'pixelated'—it can't contain delicate details, or too many shades of color. At the end of the project, it's the designer's job to reiterate those constraints back to the client and everyone on their team, so that the correct logo is used for each application.

Another important consideration is how the brand will be represented when surrounded by other brands. A common example for this is the list of sponsors. In order to avoid being confused with other brands, there are limitations to where the logo may be safely placed, what's the minimum distance between your logo and the other logos, the minimum size of the logo, and which colors the logo may be reproduced in. If your business anticipates this kind of use, then you definitely need clear guidelines to supply to your partners and the press.

Apart from the logo itself, branding guidelines also define the colors and fonts that a brand may use. You need a consistent color palette and typography if you want your brand to look professional. (Do these two well, and you can even get away with not having a logo.)

## BRANDING GUIDELINES EMPOWER BUSINESS OWNERS

Imagine you've just bought a new car. It's perfect: it's painted your favorite color, has all the gadgets you need, the seats are comfortable, and it's environmentally friendly... But there's one problem—you can't drive it, because you don't have the keys. Every time you need to go somewhere, you need to call the professional driver who has them. This driver serves several clients every month, so you need to call them in advance and book your appointment to make sure you get where you need to go on time.

Sounds ridiculous? It should, but that's something that business owners routinely agree to when working with designers. When a designer gives the client their branding guidelines, it's like giving them the keys to their new car—they can now take full ownership of it. If the designer gives the client just a logo without any other guidelines to rely on, they're essentially keeping the 'keys' to themselves. If the client wants to get even the simplest thing done, they must come back to the original designer if they don't want to risk messing it up. What if the designer is unavailable? What if they're on vacation, parental leave, sick leave, or are booked 6 months in advance? What if they went out of business? The client is stranded. They need to find someone else, and pray that the new person will be able to recreate what the previous designer did. Branding guidelines help business owners by answering questions and dilemmas like:

- What's the name of the font used in the logo?
- Which colors may I use in this Facebook ad?
- Can I put the logo on this photo? What about that photo?
- How will I keep my brand integrity if I don't have the last say in where my logo shows up?

You may not be thinking about these questions now, but they do pop up frequently as you start building your website, and your brand gets more exposure. Having clearly spelt guidelines makes all the design decisions much easier.

## WHO REPRESENTS YOUR BRAND?

Anyone who does *any* communication for your brand, whether it's in person or online, needs to adhere to the branding guidelines. These people may include:

- Virtual assistants
- Customer support
- Developers
- Designers
- Photographers
- Social media marketers
- Copywriters
- Trainees and interns
- Helpful family members
- Reporters

Every piece of information that comes out of your office needs to be carefully examined for potential inconsistencies that may arise when several people work on the same project. Each person will do things their own way, unless instructed to do them a certain way. If it's obvious that your website, business cards, posters, brochures, and social media updates are all done by different people, this means that either you don't have any branding guidelines in place, or you do have them, but people don't respect them. Both of these spell trouble for your brand.

Branding guidelines are not open to 'artistic interpretation'. Once in place, they are a pillar that supports all of your visual marketing activities.

## What Goes into a Brand Style Guide

Branding guidelines can be just one page long, and the largest I've seen had over a hundred pages. The ones I create for my clients can be anywhere from 10 to 30 pages long. I'll share some typical contents of style guides that may be appropriate for your business. (If you'd like to see visual examples of this, I've included them in my article *Branding guidelines (style guides) demystified*.)

### 1. BRAND ESSENCE

The first thing to define are the general, intangible elements of your brand that will be reinforced with the graphics later on. If you've answered the questions in the bonus workbook, you already have all the information you need for this part, it's just a matter of presenting it in a clear and organized manner. In the introduction, we get the reader acquainted with the foundations of our brand:

- Core values
- Unique value proposition
- Target audience
- Tagline

While this part is not obligatory and is left out of many brand style guides, it helps to set the stage for the following pages of the document. It explains in clear words something that all company employees and contractors have to be on board with in order to accurately represent the brand.

## 2. BRAND VOICE

As we've established in the fifth chapter, every company employee takes on the qualities of your brand's voice when communicating with your clients. It does help if they have a natural tendency to communicate in this way, since it will sound more natural. This section covers:

- Brand voice qualities.
- What you want your business to be known for.
- Your business's role in your client's lives.

## 3. THE LOGO

After introducing the general brand, it's time to introduce the logo (if you have one). If you don't have a logo, simply type your business name in the font you've chosen in the exercises in the last chapter. In my style guides, I allow a full page to show the logo with plenty of white space around it, and include a little background about its development:

- Inspiration from the company's core values and brand qualities.
- The meaning of the logo.
- Construction of the icon.
- Typefaces used in the logo.
- Colors used in the logo.

This part serves to tell a story of the logo graphic, and it can be as short, or as elaborate as you want. If you want to keep it simple, one paragraph of text explaining the idea behind the logo is enough. Here's a fill-in-the-blanks example you can use:

> *"The [company name] logo consists of the [description] symbol, and the company name set in the [full typeface name] typeface. The colors used in the logo are [color names]. The symbol and the colors represent the [core values and voice qualities of the brand]. The typeface used gives off a [quality] impression."*

## 4. LOGO VARIATIONS

Once completed, the logo *may not be changed in any way* from the original files because this could ruin the professional perception of the brand. It's the designer's job to anticipate all the use cases for the client, and provide the logo versions for each use. Here are some logo variations that I create for my logo design projects:

- Full color logo
- Inverse logo (typically white)
- Black logo
- Vertical logo composition
- Horizontal logo composition
- Icon only
- Logo with a tagline

The **full color logo** may be designed for print and web in mind, so files are created in two different color modes: RGB and CMYK. Additionally, a Pantone version may be provided.

The **inverse logo**, also called the knockout logo, is used on dark backgrounds. It's often white, but it may also be set in other light colors.

The **black logo** is used for rubber stamps, engraving, foil stamping, and other less common print uses. A black logo may also be used on printer-friendly documents, such as invoices and contracts. (Back in the day, we've also used black logos on documents sent via fax machines.)

Different compositions may be used when a logo includes both the wordmark (pure text) and the symbol. In the **vertical composition**, the symbol is placed either above or below the text. This composition is of roughly square proportions. It's typically used on business cards, as well as promotional materials where there's plenty of space to fill with graphics.

In the **horizontal composition** the symbol is placed to the left of the text (rarely on the right, at least in the countries where text is read left-to-right). This composition is typically used in website headers, email signatures, invoices, and other situations when there's a need to fit as much information as possible in the least amount of vertical space.

The **symbol** itself can be used on its own as an app icon, a social media profile photo, or on promo goodies such as badges, apparel etc. Some logos don't have symbols. In this case, brands often use the first letter of the wordmark as an icon.

**Logo with a tagline** is used when frequent use of this type is expected on marketing materials. Many businesses don't need a tagline in their logo, so feel free to skip that. The tagline often uses the same font family as the wordmark (only a lighter, or an italic variant), or a contrasting yet compatible font.

## 5. LOGO REPRODUCTION

Once the logo is complete, the designer needs to explain how the logo is allowed to be used, so that no one tries to do something that the logo was not designed to do. Typically these constraints include:

- Minimum clear space.
- Minimum reproduction size.
- Colors the logo may be reproduced in.
- Allowed logo backgrounds.
- Examples of incorrect logo usage.

**Minimum clear space** is the area around the logo that must remain empty to preserve the integrity of the logo. If you put other graphics or text too close to the logo, it will blend with it and the resulting look will be unflattering for your brand. This part is especially important if your logo is displayed in media you have no control over (like a partner's website or a poster for an event you're sponsoring), where your logo is displayed along with many others. Whenever there are other people involved in representing your brand in the media, insist on them respecting the logo clear space.

**Minimum reproduction size** specifies the smallest allowed dimensions of the logo in the print and digital media. The dimensions are defined in pixels for digital use, and in millimeters or inches for print. Typically, only one logo dimension is defined (width or height) for each variation, since the logo proportions are not supposed to be changed.

Logos are designed with specific **background colors** in mind. Certain variations are designed to be placed on light backgrounds, others on dark backgrounds. Mixing them up may result in poor visibility of the logo. Some logo designs may be placed on photographs, others may not. Usually putting a logo on a uniform photographic background is OK, but you need to be careful and make sure the logo reads well. When in doubt, solid colors are better.

The main rule of proper logo use is: *don't change the logo in any way.* Don't change the logo color. Don't change the font. Don't change the orientation. Don't change the proportions. Don't add drop shadows, outlines or any effects to the logo. An **incorrect logo usage** sheet reinforces this message with visual examples of what people are not supposed to do.

The length of the logo reproduction guidelines can range from one page, to five or more pages—depending on how many logo variations there are, and how detailed the instructions are.

### 4. COLOR PALETTE

Choosing a color palette that you'll be using consistently across all media is the easiest way to strengthen your visual brand identity, even if you don't have a logo. We talked about how to choose a color palette in the previous chapter, so here I'll just recap some of the most important points.

I typically divide the colors into the primary palette and the secondary palette. The **primary palette** includes all the colors that are present in the logo, and may also contain shades (or tints) of these colors. The **secondary palette** includes compatible colors that may be used as neutrals, or as accents, and will enable designers and illustrators to create interfaces and visual art that's visually appealing and easy to understand. Websites typically need a range of colors so we can distinguish elements like:

- Regular text
- Highlighted elements
- Fine print
- Links and buttons
- Errors
- Warnings
- Success messages

Ideally, all of these should have their own corresponding color that is used *consistently* across the entire website or app. It's a little easier with printed materials, because there's no interactive elements, so just a few colors to highlight important elements will do.

In the branding guidelines, each color swatch is described using several formulas, which we've examined in the previous chapter:

- HEX code: #123456
- RGB formula: 100/100/100 or R=100 G=100 B=100
- CMYK formula: 10/10/10/10 or C=10 M=10 Y=10 K=10
- Pantone color name

As I explained previously, the HEX code and the RGB formula both respond to the RGB color system, which is used in all the digital devices (computers, tablets, mobile phones, projector screens, TV, etc.). The CMYK formula corresponds to the four-color printing process, and is used in print. Spot colors such as Pantone may also be used in print if higher color accuracy is needed.

Color guidelines may also explain in which cases certain colors are allowed to be used, and how large the areas of color are allowed to be. Some colors (for example, accents) may only be used in small quantities.

## 5. TYPOGRAPHY

Typography guidelines are used to define which fonts are used in which media, and there also may be additional guidelines on how body text and headlines are formatted, with their minimum text size, weight, style etc.

I typically define the primary fonts and secondary fonts in typography guidelines. The **primary font family** often includes a font that's used in the logo, but that doesn't always have to be the case (especially if the logo is completely hand-drawn). In any case, it's the font family that's used most often across the media. The **secondary font family** is used for emphasis or to create variety in the design. The font specimens are typically displayed as a set of alphanumeric characters, or as a pangram.[*]

---

[*] A pangram is a sentence that contains all the letters of an alphabet. A well-known English pangram is: *"The quick brown fox jumps over the lazy dog."*

Apart from the preferred fonts, we need to take into account that sometimes they may not be available. Examples include invoicing or newsletter software that have a limited range of available fonts. In that case, we need to also define **alternative fonts**. Typically these are so called 'system fonts' or 'web safe fonts', and they may include Helvetica, Arial, Times New Roman, Georgia, Palatino Linotype, etc. Here's an example of what the font definition in a style guide may look like:

*"The primary font family for print and digital media is Alegreya, which may be used in headings, paragraphs and quotes. If the primary typeface is not available, the alternatives are Palatino Linotype and Georgia."*

## 6. GRAPHICS

Apart from logos and solid colors, you may use additional images across your marketing communication to signal your brand in a subtle, or an eye-catching way. Some examples include:

- Decorative details
- Icons
- Patterns
- Textures
- Illustrations

Designing marketing communication is so much easier when there is a predefined set of assets you're able to use. When you have your own custom-made graphics, you don't need to rely on stock libraries and end up using the same graphics as your competitors. The brand style guide displays examples of these resources, and may provide guidelines on how to create new icons or illustrations if needed.

## 7. APPLICATION FOR SPECIFIC MEDIA

Often the designer will create solutions for different brand applications, such as:

- Business cards
- Letterheads & envelopes
- Website design
- Application interfaces

- Social media graphics
- Email signatures
- Indoor & outdoor signage
- Documentation
- Staff uniforms

These designs may then be documented in the branding guidelines, so that any graphic designer, textile designer, print technician, or web developer can step in and follow the instructions. This part of the guidelines may be expanded as time goes on, if the business needs new applications that weren't a part of the original branding package.

## 8. PHOTOGRAPHY

Photography is one of the most impactful elements of a brand, because it's so effective in conveying the atmosphere you want your customers to experience. If you don't have a set photography direction, what might happen is that your blog and social media is filled with a bunch of inconsistent and off-brand visuals:

- Photos featuring colors that clash with your brand colors.
- A mix of photos that give off contradicting atmosphere: corporate and serious, fun and leisurely, natural, luxury, etc.
- Photos that are overused on other blogs and social media, so you look like a copycat.

I like to include photography style direction into a brand style guide if we expect a lot of stock photo use, so that my clients know what type of photos to look for when creating their own presentations and social media graphics. If you're an artist, or rely on commissioned illustration for your marketing materials, you can also include an illustration style direction.

## 9. CONTACT INFORMATION

Typically, the last page of the style guide contains contact information of the brand designer, so that anyone can reach them with questions and concerns. If you're a business owner creating your own style guide, you'll include your own contact information.

## Where to Keep Your Brand Style Guide

Some companies and nonprofits publish their vector logo files and branding guidelines on their website, so they're accessible to all the employees, partners, and press. If you expect to deal with press and advertising agencies a lot, I recommend creating a 'media kit' page where anyone can access them.

If you don't deal with press, and don't want your branding assets to be visible to everyone, upload them to a cloud service like Google Drive or Dropbox so they're always accessible to you, and you can easily share a private link with your team members and contractors.

**Keep multiple backups of your logo, brand style guide, and other assets.** Don't expect your designer to keep your files forever. (We deal with many client projects and sometimes need to purge our disks to make room for more.) Create as many copies as you're able to—with the technologies available today, you have no excuse not to keep backups of your important business assets.

Your brand style guide is a tool to be used almost daily. I keep referring to the brand style guides I've created for my clients when designing marketing graphics for them, just to make sure I'm adhering to the same rules. While creating a style guide takes time, it saves so much more time in the long run. You never have to wonder if a contractor you hire will interpret your brand correctly, because it's literally spelled out for them.

## The Brand Style Guide Bundle

If you've decided to take on the challenge of creating your own brand style guide by yourself, I've created a resource that makes it super easy for designers and non-designers alike. The Book & Brand Style Guide Bundle contains:

- Fill-in-the-blank templates for Adobe InDesign, Microsoft PowerPoint, and Google Slides.
- Step-by step video instructions.
- Written transcripts of the instructions.

Visit **humancenteredbrand.com** to learn more, and use the discount code **bookdeal** to upgrade to the bundle and save the price you've already paid for this book.

*chapter IX*

# Creating an Impeccable Client Experience

Up until now, we've been creating the building blocks of your brand strategy and visual brand identity. In the previous chapter we've talked about how to document them in your brand style guide to make future use easier. Now it's time to use those building blocks in creating all of your pieces of client communication and marketing materials, so that other people can see and interact with your brand. Your brand strategy is useless if you don't implement it in your daily business tasks. If you've come this far, I ask you to push forward just a bit more, so you can start seeing the results. **Give people the opportunity to see your brand—*to see you.***

Implementation of your brand has different components:

- Making business decisions that align with your core values.
- Adding features and services that leverage your unique value proposition, and discontinuing those that don't.
- Writing every piece of text in your natural brand voice.
- Allowing your natural voice and personality to come through your speaking.
- Choosing marketing channels that allow you to use your greatest strengths, and where your ideal clients spend time.
- Designing every piece of marketing communication and documentation with care and consistency.

By taking care of all these steps, you're creating a superb **client experience** which affects your brand perception. A refined work process and an impeccable client experience positions you as a trustworthy expert, because your clients feel safe in your hands. It also demonstrates that you care about the wellbeing of your clients, not only about their money. Clients who have a pleasant experience with you are more likely to recommend you to their friends and colleagues, so you'll receive more word of mouth referrals.

I wrote an article about this so method so you can read it for more details and visuals,* but here's the short version of how to approach crafting your impeccable client experience:

1. Take a piece of paper, post-its, or a sketching app, and map out a flowchart with all the steps you and your clients take from the first time they hear about you, to the completion of your project.

2. Ask yourself: could you eliminate or combine certain steps in order to optimize your process?

3. Examine each individual step and ask yourself: how could you make it more pleasant and easier for your clients by using applications, educational materials, online interaction, etc.?

4. Examine each step and think of how could you make it easier and more efficient for yourself by using automation, templates, documentation, etc.?

5. Make notes of all the applications, educational materials, templates, and documentation you need to create in order to improve your client experience.

6. Commit to implementing this new process for your very next client.

The last point is critical, because if you don't give yourself a deadline, this project will remain on your 'someday maybe' list forever, and you'll miss out on the benefits that it provides. I've taught this process in live workshops, and when people see how their business could be transformed using a better

---

* *"Improve your business & brand with a client journey map"* by Nela Dunato (July 15, 2018).

system, it blows their mind. If you can't visit my next live workshop, web designer Leah Kalamakis has a course *Stress Less & Impress* which teaches how to systematize and improve your process tailored specifically for free-lancers. (I haven't taken the course, but I've used and taught some of the same methods.)

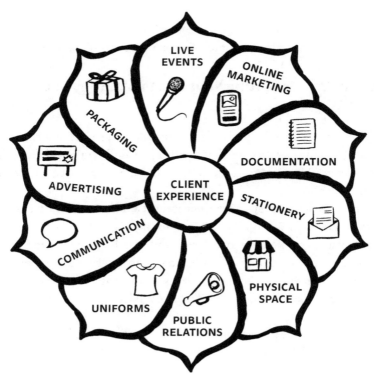

In this chapter, I'll address different examples of business communication, marketing, advertising, and other client experience elements, and give tips on how to weave your brand through them. Which of these you end up using depends largely on your business—some conduct their business exclusively online, while others do their work in person, or have a dedicated physical space to meet their clients. The graphic above gives an overview of the applications we'll examine.

If you encounter an example that seems like it doesn't fit your business, you can either ignore it entirely, or think about how you *could* potentially apply this to go the extra mile and differentiate from your peers.

I don't cover technical or design instructions in this book, so I assume that you either know how to do this already, or that you'll be able to find a relevant and up-to-date tutorial for any given task. Consider hiring a professional copywriter, designer, photographer, videographer, marketing specialist, or a virtual assistant to help you with some of these tasks.

## Tips on Implementing Your Brand Strategy and Identity

Implementing a new brand is a long, difficult, and sometimes expensive process. You may feel overwhelmed with all the different possibilities that I've listed in this chapter. If that's the case, here are my tips on keeping overwhelm down.

**Take this project step by step, one item at a time.** Rome wasn't built in a day and all that. When I do this work for my clients, it takes us about a month just to complete the logo design and brand style guide, and then it can take us anywhere from a month to a year to redesign all their existing documentation and marketing materials, or to create new ones. By that I don't mean a year of non-stop work, but completing work in phases with breaks in between. Even when I do this for myself, it always takes me longer than I expect. To be honest, this work never really ends. Don't think about what there's still left to do—focus on the next immediate task.

**Tackle the items in the order you need them.** Take a look at your schedule in the next few weeks: are there any events or opportunities to meet people in person? If so, prepare some business cards. Are you launching a new service offer? Then you'll need to design a nice sales page that will get people interested in it, and maybe some Facebook graphics as well. Giving a workshop or a talk? Then you need to create a presentation. Look for highest leverage opportunities, and handle those first. Everything else can wait for the time being. Next time you need to send a proposal to your client, redesign your document template and edit the text to include more of your brand voice in it—but do not stress about the proposal document before you need it. **Stick to the design tips** I've outlined in the seventh chapter:

- Use two different font families *at most* (preferably one) that are easy to read.
- Don't use too many colors.
- The larger the white space around the elements, the classier the design looks.
- Don't place text or your logo on busy backgrounds.
- Make sure the color contrast between the text and background is sufficient.
- Print the design at home to check if the font size is large enough.
- Ask your family members or friends to double check the design and spelling before publishing your pieces.

Consult the seventh chapter as often as you need to if you're going to design things on your own. (In addition to this, you may want to read the article *Top 11 Easy-to-fix Beginner Design Mistakes* on my blog, and download the visual checklist to keep on hand.)

**Use templates provided by the print shop to design your marketing materials.** There are many affordable online printing services, and they typically provide templates you can use in design software to create items such as business cards, postcards, flyers, etc. Pay special attention to the color space (CMYK for print), resolution (300 dots per inch for raster graphics), and bleed. **Bleed** is a safety margin that makes your artwork slightly larger than its final trim size to accommodate for any errors in cutting. The template your printer provides will include this area. When in doubt, ask them to check your files and let you know if there are any problems.

**Outsource technically complex tasks.** As small business owners, we're used to wearing many hats and doing everything ourselves. While this resourcefulness is helpful and saves us lots of money, sometimes it's more trouble than it's worth. You can hire a virtual assistant to handle any website updates. Perhaps you can call in a favor that one of your friends owes you. If you have older tech-savvy children, enlist their help. (And make sure to tell them how in ye olden days kids had to help out their parents in the field and tend to livestock, so they're lucky to only have to tweak a few lines of code.)

**Let this process take the time it takes.** If you have a slow work week, you can take this opportunity to work on your branding. During the times when you're busy with clients, you'll probably have to put this project to the side. It's all good. You're doing your best, and that's what counts. Don't compare yourself to anyone else. Your brand is *your* responsibility, and how good or bad other businesses are doing this should not concern you.

In the remainder of this chapter, I offer tips specific to certain communication channels. Pay special attention to those you're already using in your business, and write down any ideas for improvement as you're reading.

## Everyday Communication

We'll begin with some brand applications that most service businesses use on a daily basis. While some of these aren't usually considered a part of a brand identity, they all rely heavily on communication, which means that your brand voice plays the biggest role in them.

### EMAIL

Email is the most frequently used method of business communication today. We've already hinted at the ways your brand voice affects your email correspondence in chapter five, and now we'll take a more big-picture look at how you can weave in the rest of your brand as well.

Email is first and foremost a vehicle for your brand voice to radiate through the personalized messages you send to your clients, prospects, and partners. Sometimes our emails are happy and excited, but sometimes we need to say "No" to the inquiry with compassion and grace. If you're worried about how something you've written comes off, consult your brand voice qualities and ask yourself *"Is this quality coming through my writing?"* If the answer is no, adjust your message.

People used to frown upon smilies, emojis, and exclamation marks in business correspondence, but nowadays many businesses have embraced them as they help to clarify the tone of the message.

The problem that often comes up for small business owners is how to address your prospects and clients: do you use a formal way with their last name, or a more informal way and their first name? This comes down to personal choice. I prefer to get on a first name basis as soon as possible. So far none of my clients have complained. In some countries like Japan, addressing a business contact by their first name is unusual. Do what is sensible in your and your client's cultures. If you're not sure, ask.

In languages that have a formal 'you' used as a sign of respect, that first contact can be a bit awkward. I follow my client's lead—if they address me with a formal you in their inquiry, I address them the same way. I bring up the subject in our first meeting and ask if we could switch to informal you, and they invariably say yes. Even when I teach, I ask my students to call me by my first name and address me with informal you. If your native language doesn't differ between formal and informal you, this paragraph made no sense whatsoever, but many languages do have such tricky bits that we need to navigate.

When it comes to visual brand identity, emails are not the best place to go crazy with fonts and colors. Choose one of the default system fonts offered by your email client. Keep rich formatting to a minimum, but feel free to highlight the most important information in bold letters.

One area where you may feature your visual identity is the **signature**. If you have a logo, place it in your signature, but don't make it too big. If you have a tagline, add it under your company name.

Another way to use this often neglected space is to offer a **call to action**. The call to action should be as short as possible, and point to a resource or a service on your website, like a free 'discovery' session, free trial, your newsletter, latest article or video, or an inexpensive product. The point of a call to action in your signature is to get as many eyes as you can on something that you consider highly valuable to anyone who reads this email (whether they're an existing client, a prospect, or someone you'll never work with). Make it related to the most important topic you want to be known for (as we established in the fifth chapter). At the moment of editing this text, my signature call to action promotes this very book: *"P.S. My book 'The Human Centered Brand" is coming out on July 30! Learn more & download the sample* *chapter."* I change this call to action regularly based on what's going on in my business.

If you send certain types of emails often, you can write **canned responses** and start your replies from a template, instead of having to scramble for words every single time.* The great thing about canned responses is that once you find a graceful and clear way to respond to a question or an issue, you can simply keep using it whenever that question or issue pops up again. It speeds up email processing, keeps your brand voice consistent, and saves you from the stress of mulling over a difficult email.

## IN-PERSON MEETINGS

How do you apply your brand to in-person meetings? If your brand is based on your authentic personality, you don't have to put in any extra effort. Getting your personality to show through less personal methods of communication is the hard part!

The most challenging part about in-person meetings is staying calm when the stakes seem high. The first meeting with a prospective client, and the first presentation of the result of your work may invoke a lot of anxiety. Use whatever method of calming yourself down you have before a meeting to make sure that nothing can impede your ability to connect with your client. (You can try 'power posing' which supposedly lowers your stress levels.)†

One 'trick' I have for my first meeting with a client is to wear something in my main brand color, which is red. I also do this for most of my speaking engagements and conferences, though it's becoming hard to find a fresh outfit for every event! You could purchase an accessory in the color most closely resembling your main brand color like a bag, a phone case, glasses, a water bottle, etc. That way, you'll always have something 'on brand' when meeting people. Custom branded products are also an option, though they might cost more.

---

* A good selection of examples is featured in the article: *"Canned Responses: 10+ Helpful Email Templates That Save Time"* by Laura Spencer on TutsPlus.

† *"Your body language may shape who you are"* by Amy Cuddy, TED (June 2012).

## ONLINE VIDEO MEETINGS

Video meetings are the closest we can currently get to in-person meeting in the digital world. (I expect that in a few years we'll be conducting meetings in virtual reality.) Since the screen shows only a limited portion of your body and environment, you don't have to pay as much attention to your attire as with in-person meetings. Still, body language and how you appear on camera is important.

Try to keep your surroundings clutter-free. If you have a dedicated office space, make sure that the wall opposite your computer screen looks as neat as possible, and maybe add a few elements to make it look nicer, like a vase, a candle holder, or a potted plant. Bonus points if you can find items in your brand color to place there. The rest of your house may be a complete mess, but that single square meter that shows up on camera better look nice.

Here's a trick I've learned from the human behavior researcher Vanessa Van Edwards: when you're on video, keep both hands in view.* When our hands are hidden, it sends a subconscious signal to the other person that they may not entirely trust us, because we may be hiding something in our hands. Hands in view mean *"I've got nothing to hide,"* and this increases the other person's trust.

## PROJECT MANAGEMENT SOFTWARE

For those of us whose work is project based (like designers, developers, writers, engineers, etc.) a lot of the communication happens in a dedicated project management app. I've switched from managing my projects through email to a free tool called Trello, and I've never looked back. I won't be getting into all the benefits of project management software now, but if you need any convincing, I suggest checking out the website Systems Rock by a small business systems expert Natasha Vorompiova—she was the one who persuaded me to take the plunge.

There are many different project management systems, and some of them are great for small teams, like Trello, Asana, Teamwork, and Basecamp.

---

\*    *"Body Language for Trainers and Teachers"* interview with Vanessa Van Edwards, MNIB Consulting (May 20, 2014).

Their features and pricing differ, so check out the demos of each one and decide which one you prefer. Some of these apps allow you to use custom colors and graphics, which you can use to design them to look sort of like an extension of your website. Trello has that ability, that's why I love it so much. Be sure to customize the language you use in your task names and descriptions, and avoid overly technical jargon when possible.

One of the greatest benefits of using a project management system is being able to duplicate task lists and entire projects, so that each of your clients gets a consistent experience, plus it saves you time. A great project management solution can enhance your process, and your clients will be impressed by how well organized you are.*

### APPOINTMENT BOOKING

People whose work is session based (like coaches, psychotherapists, consultants, hair stylists, medical doctors, massage therapists, etc.) can benefit from automated appointment scheduling. There are more apps dedicated to online booking than I can count as new ones seem to pop up every day, but a few that come to mind are Calendly, Acuity Scheduling, TimeTrade, and YouCanBookMe. Most of these apps have the ability to synchronize with your calendar, and some are even able to process payments. Some have a free option, while others require a monthly subscription.

Some appointment booking apps allow limited styling, like choosing the colors of the booking interface and uploading your own logo. Use these options if they're available. Customize the language of the email reminders that are sent to clients, because the default messages typically sound very dry and boring. Add a dash of personality and prepare them for what they might expect when they meet you.

## Stationery

Stationery is the staple of every visual brand identity. Even though many businesses have switched from paper to electronic communication, there

---

* *"Why I love using Trello with clients"* by Nela Dunato, Systems Rock (August 2, 2016).

are occasions when you need to send someone a nicely formatted document.

Printed stationery is another touch point that your brand communicates through. Your choice of papers and inks emphasizes your core values and brand qualities. For example, a business whose core values are 'nature' and 'sustainability' might use recycled paper and eco-friendly inks. Brands that wants to communicate the qualities of 'luxury' and 'exclusivity' often use gold foil and dark, velvety papers.

Your stationary doesn't have to be too fancy, if that's not what your brand is about. What we're aiming for is making your job of keeping a consistent and authentic brand easier.

## BUSINESS CARDS

I've heard some marketers say that business cards are dead. As a person who meets lots of new people at conferences and industry events, I vehemently disagree. If you meet potential clients or business partners in person, you need business cards. If you never get out of your house for work, then I agree that you probably don't need them.

Typically business card feature the company logo, contact information, and tagline. Business cards may look plain and simple with black text on white paper, or fancy and elaborate with double-sided full-color print. You can even add your own photo or artwork on the back side of the card.

Apart from the standard sizes (90 x 50 millimeters, 85 x 55 millimeters, or 3.5 x 2 inches), they can be also cut to custom size, or any custom shape.

Business cards are not just about the artwork—the **paper** can affect the look and feel of the card tremendously. Apart from plain smooth white paper, there are other specialty papers you can choose from like off-white, brown, textured, recycled, colored, or pearlescent paper. These papers can make even the simplest business card design look more appealing.

The finish of the card can be plain, gloss laminated, or matte laminated. If your business card features artwork or a photo, glossy lamination will increase the vibrancy and protect it from fingerprints and scratching. Matte lamination looks sophisticated, and the cards feel soft to the touch. There are other special printing features that can make a business card look even more striking, like metallic or neon inks, foil stamping, embossing, spot UV gloss, etc. These effects increase the printing costs, but if you want to make an exceptional impression, it's a good investment.

Some businesses go even further in their quest to make a unique card. Canadian bike repair shop Broke Bike Alley had a business card made from metal, shaped like a tool you can use to unscrew and tighten the lug nuts on your bike. Their other business card was made from rubber which you could use to patch a tire. It's clever, relevant, and their brand awareness exploded because blogs and magazines all over the world shared photos of their business cards.

Artist Ivan Turčin created a foldable business card which turns into a tiny finger puppet for his former character design brand Mogibo. Fun solutions like this are most often used by creative professionals, but there's no reason why a business consultant or a dentist can't have them, as long as it's aligned with your core values and brand qualities.

When your cards finally arrive from the printer, here are some ways you can use them:

- Always carry at least five business cards in your wallet.

- Take 20–30 cards with you to conferences, and take all of your cards to fairs and networking events.

- Give a few cards to your clients and friends, so they can forward them to other people.

- Leave a small bunch in places where your ideal clients regularly hang out (see section on flyers).

- Include a business card to any letter or package you send to clients.

Some of my clients feel awkward about handing their business card to people, because they don't understand that offering a business card is *normal* and even desired. If someone has expressed interest in your services, the next logical step is to give them your contact information so they can reach you at their convenience. Don't overthink it, just give them the darn card. If they don't want it, they'll throw it away and you'll lose 20 cents worth of paper. It's fine.

## LETTERHEADS

A letterhead may be used for any official internal and external business correspondence. It features the company logo and contact information in the header or the footer of the document, so you don't need to add them manually when composing the letter. In some countries, companies are required by law to include additional information, like a business registration number or a VAT number.

For printed letterheads, you can use either plain white printer paper, or other types of paper like textured, off-white, gray, colored, or recycled. Consultants and B2B\* service providers usually stick with plain white paper, while businesses in the wellness, beauty, leisure, fashion, and food industries can get more intentional about their choice of paper to better portray their brand qualities.

Some companies have stacks of their blank letterhead printed professionally, which ensures color consistency, and enables you to use special inks or metallic foil. If you intend to print all of your letterheads at home or send your documents electronically, create a Word or Pages document template with your logo and contact information. Make sure to leave plenty of space for the content.

When creating a new document, add content to your template and then either print it, or save it as a PDF file. If you send your original text documents to other people, they may not see the proper text formatting, especially if you're using custom fonts. **Always send your documents as PDF files, and they'll appear accurate when viewed on all other devices.**

## ENVELOPES

If you send a lot of printed correspondence, custom envelopes appear more professional. You can also print envelopes at home by creating a text document in the exact envelope size, and adding your logo and contact information in the upper left corner of the page. The recipient's address is placed on the bottom right side. If you're using special letterhead paper, get matching envelopes. Even if you use plain white paper for your letterhead, you can

---

\*    Business to business

send it in a colored envelope to make it immediately stand out from bank statements and junk mail. I always send holiday greeting cards to my clients and associates in beautiful, metallic burgundy or silver envelopes. While they cost more than the plain ones, I want my clients' experience of receiving the greeting card to be as exquisite as possible. We all like getting nice things!

This may seem like a ridiculously small detail to fuss about, but the more high-end your services are, the more it matters that every touch point with your clients looks and feels well thought out.

## FOLDERS

If you're a consultant that delivers printed project documentation to your clients, custom paper folders are a great way to package it. From that first meeting where you can bring samples of your previous work or question-naires for them to fill out, your folder sitting on the table with the logo emblazoned over the cover is saying *"This consultant has their act together."* It also serves as a reminder of who they need to call when they need more help.

If you teach in-person classes, workshops, or retreats, investing in beautiful packaging of your handouts adds to the perceived value of your teaching. For some reason, people are willing to pay more for physical items than they are for experiences or digital products. If you leave them with something solid they can take home, it will make a better impression.

## STAMPS

In some countries, registered business are required to have a stamp to mark official documents and transactions. The contents of the stamp is regulated, and typically it includes the full business name and the address of the headquarters. Include your logo on the stamp if possible, and make sure it's simple enough so it looks good scaled down.

Stamps offer an inexpensive way to personalize any paper correspon-dence, so it's a good idea to get one even if you're not legally required to have it. Stamp pads come in a variety of colors (even metallic!), so you may be able to find one that's close to your brand color at a local craft store. Some busi-nesses decorate their stationery, gift cards, and envelopes with embossing stamps or wax seals to add a tactile dimension to them.

## Documentation

Providers of intellectual services, especially those whose work engagements last for weeks or months, often need documents that educate prospective clients about their services, and cover their backs in case of any misunderstandings or unexpected events. The extent of this documentation depends on the type of work you perform, how you handle your client communication, and how you market your business.

Some of the documentation will be the same for all of your clients, and other will be customized for each client. If you're sending the same files to everyone, it might be easier to store them online and send people the direct download link, instead of having to look them up and attach them via email. If your documents change for each client, creating templates with the typical content saves you time and gives all of your clients a consistent experience.

The content should be formatted in a way that enhances the clarity and readability of the text. Break it into sections with headings, and use bold text or color to emphasize the most important information. People may need to read over your document more than once, so make it easy for them to find what they're looking for.

When inserting your logo graphic into writing or invoicing software, make sure it's large enough so that it looks nice on the screen and when you print it. Most applications will require a raster image file, like JPEG or PNG.

### CONTRACTS

Contracts or agreements are documents that outline the rights and responsibilities of each party signing the document (usually the client and the service provider). The agreements used by small businesses include service agreements, licensing agreements, and non-disclosure agreements.

The service agreement covers the nature and scope of work, project timeline, milestones, pricing and payment, intellectual property rights, cancellation policies, indemnity clauses, disclaimers, and jurisdiction. **Signing a contract is a mark of professionalism and mutual goodwill.** If your prospective client doesn't want to sign a contract, this is a red flag, and they're not your ideal client.

Licensing agreements determine how your work can be used commercially by another party in exchange for a fixed sum and royalties, whether that's your artwork, software, or a proprietary coaching framework.

Non-disclosure agreements prevent parties from sharing information about the project with anyone who is not a part of it. If your clients are in an industry that's highly protective of their intellectual property (like the electronics, automotive, pharmaceutical, and military industries), you'll most definitely be required to sign it, but at least make sure they're paying you well.

The agreement contents may be negotiated, and you're allowed to ask for certain clauses to be removed or amended. Ideally, you'd have your contracts written up by a lawyer who understands your industry and is keeping your needs and interests in mind. If you're not able to find one at the moment, an affordable alternative is to purchase agreement templates from a service such as Small Business Bodyguard, and customize them to your liking.

Agreements often use legal jargon, especially disclaimers and indemnity clauses. On the other hand, clauses that deal with straightforward issues such as the scope of work and how much it costs may be written in plain language. I'm in favor of plain language, and this is another instance of communication that depends on your brand voice. The purpose of your contracts is for you and your clients to know what you're agreeing to—the two of you need to be able to understand what they mean without the help of lawyers.

Contracts may be signed with the old pen and paper method, or electronically. Electronic signatures are binding in the EU, United States, and most developed countries. This is another way to improve your client experience by making things easy for them. Popular electronic signature services include HelloSign, DocuSign, and Adobe Sign. There are also services that combine electronic signature features with project management and customer relationship management, like Dubsado.

## PROPOSALS

Proposals are documents created individually for each client, outlining the key aspects of your project:

- The problem you're solving
- Project goals
- Scope of work
- Phases and milestones
- Cost
- Timelines

They're used in consulting and creative services as a part of the sales process. Proposal writing can be time-consuming, so vet your prospects before you move onto that stage. You don't want to waste time on people who would only balk at your prices (putting your prices on your website helps prevent that). If you offer a few types of services which may be packaged, you can create templates for your proposals and customize them for each client.

Anticipate that your proposals might get circulated if your client wants to get a second opinion, so don't disclose any proprietary information. Keep your project description focused on outcomes, and less on your method. You can use your authentic brand voice as you would in an email or a blog post. The format of the proposal can vary. Some business owners write them as simple emails, and a more professional approach is a written document delivered on the company letterhead.

**The trick to a super effective proposal is to echo the words that the client has used** in their previous communication with you. Use the problems and goals they have expressed, verbatim. This is not lazy writing, it's a sign that you're truly listening to them. The proposal is your chance to tell them what you envision the results of your collaboration to be, and how you intend to achieve them. It's a balance of aspirational language, next steps, and hard numbers. If you do this right, your proposal will:

- Demonstrate that you listen to your client's needs.
- Explain your unique value proposition.
- Reinforce that you're the right person to solve their problem.
- Clear out any ambiguity over what is delivered and how much it costs.

- Demonstrate that you're a well-organized professional who takes their work seriously.
- Give a glimpse into what working with you will be like.
- Create familiarity with your brand.

For all these benefits, they're well worth spending a bit of time on.

## INVOICES

Invoice content is determined by the local tax authorities of the issuer *and* the recipient. (If you work with international clients, this can get frustrating.) Unfortunately, most global invoicing apps are US-centric and typically don't accommodate for these diverse regulations so it's best to use a localized invoicing application. If you don't want to use invoicing applications, you can also write your invoices as a text document on the company letterhead (remember to save them as a PDF).

The invoice text is usually short and straightforward, but you can add a personal note, a funny remark, or an 'Easter egg' at the bottom of the invoice if that works for your brand. If you're using an invoicing app, you'll have less options for customization. Most likely you'll be able to add your own logo graphic to feature at the top of the invoice.

## WHITE PAPERS & EBOOKS

White paper is an old-school marketing term for a free publication that you give to prospects to get them interested in your work. People used to print them and share them at fairs, or leave them in public places, but nowadays they're mostly digital because it's cheaper and more accessible to a wider audience.

We often refer to white papers as 'ebooks', but remember that your white paper doesn't have to remain digital. In fact, it can be a valuable sales tool when you get face to face with your ideal prospects. You can hand them out to interested people at fairs, conferences, and networking events, or give them to your prospects after an initial meeting. My friend and colleague Višnja Željeznjak of Logit created a 40-page full color booklet printed on quality paper featuring the results of their original research.* This paper is available for free download on their website, but it looks so much more substantial and valuable when you hold it in your hands. Print is here to stay, folks.

Ideally, a white paper will help your prospects score a quick win with a problem they're facing, either by offering them the information they need to make a decision, or a step by step solution. Some examples of such content are:

- In-depth explanation of a topic (e.g. *Everything You Need to Know about Cryptocurrency*).
- Step by step tutorial (e.g. *How to Create a Landing Page with Divi*).
- Buying guide (e.g. *10 Things to Look For in a Therapist*).
- Curated collection of tools or resources (e.g. *40 Digital Marketing Tools for Your Wellness Business*).
- Demo version of a book or a class you sell (e.g. *5 Quick & Easy Recipes for High Energy Mornings*).

You've probably seen hundreds of white papers by now, offered in exchange for your email address. Maybe you already have one of your own. White papers may be freely distributed with no strings attached, and they may also serve as a newsletter opt-in incentive.†

I've heard a great piece of advice from Naomi Dunford, marketing consultant and founder of IttyBiz: *"Make a freebie that hurts to give away for free."* In order for the white paper to be worth downloading, it has to be something people may otherwise be willing to pay for. With so many ebooks floating around, it's hard to create one that's irresistible.

When it comes to creating a white paper, you have a lot more freedom both with language and design. This may be the first contact the reader has with you, so lay your cards on the table. A person should be able to decide if you're the right professional to work with, or at least stay in contact with, after reading that one document. Add an *"About the Author"* section at

---

\*  *"Results of Our New Research: 46% of B2B Companies Lack the Foundations of Digital Marketing"* by Logit (October 26, 2015).

†  This practice is changing in post-GDPR Europe.

the end, and provide a call to action for people who may be interested in working with you.

Design-wise, white papers can vary between looking like a book, a magazine, or a presentation. If it's a bit longer, you can add a table of contents in the beginning, especially if it's a resource that your readers will return to again. In addition to text, white papers may contain graphics and photos to make them more engaging and visually pleasing.

Consider the **cover** of the white paper like a proper book cover. It should look nice and attract attention when featured on your website.* If you offer more than one white paper, give them all a harmonious look. Use the same cover design, just switch the title and the photo. The inside formatting should look the same. You can literally start with the same file, save it under a different name, and replace the content. It's not lazy—it's smart.

### WORKBOOKS & QUESTIONNAIRES

Workbooks are interactive documents designed to help your prospects or clients identify their own answers to the problem they want to solve. They're often created by consultants, coaches, and therapists. These workbooks can have different purposes, such as:

- Project questionnaire
- Free gift
- Workshop handout
- Supplementary book material

The advantage of a workbook over a white paper is that it's more engaging and gets people to commit to your process, since it requires people to invest more effort into it. That is my motivation with the workbook that accompanies this book: I want you to start engaging deeper with this content, so you'll be more likely to understand it and implement it in your business.

Workbooks don't have to be wordy, but you need to know which questions

---

\* For tips on designing a cover, check out the article: *"5 Tips for Designing the Perfect eBook Cover"* at *designshack.net* will invite the most useful answers. The questions may be **open-ended** and allow for several lines of text, or they may be **multiple choice** from a list of options. Some multiple-choice is fine, but open-ended questions push the person to think deeper, and are more likely to give them valuable insights. Use the language you'd normally use in a dialogue with your clients. Make this experience as close as you can to working with you. If the workbook is offered as a gift, it can prepare prospective clients for becoming ready to work with you, or filter out those who are a poor fit.

The design of a workbook is optimized for print and ease of interaction on digital devices. This means that you should keep images to a minimum, although I've seen some workbooks that are heavier on imagery. Jennifer Lee, the author of *The Right-Brained Business Plan*, April Bowles Olin of Blacksburg Belle, and Leonie Dawson make a point of having every single page of their workbooks and planners illustrated. This makes sense for their brands as artistic women providing business training for other creative people. Reading comfort is paramount. While I do like hand-drawn elements, the questions themselves need to be set in a typeface that's easy to read.

What makes workbooks different from other documentation is the addition of **interactive input fields**. Advanced text editors like Microsoft Word and OpenOffice have this feature. Professional designers use Adobe Acrobat and Adobe InDesign to make interactive PDF documents.

When you're done formatting your workbook, save it in PDF format and test how it works in different PDF viewers, and on different devices such as tablets and phones. Send them to a group of friends and family members with varying levels of computer skills, to see if they're able to fill them out.

Lastly, print your workbook with different settings: double-sided, color, grayscale, normal quality, and draft quality. This shows you the wide range of experiences your clients will have with the workbook, and identify glitches that only appear in print. There's no point in your workbook looking gorgeous on your own computer if your clients and students can't *use* it!

## CLIENT GUIDES

The term 'client guide' encompasses any document that is designed for your warm prospects (those who have inquired about working with you), and existing clients. It's similar to a white paper in a way, but its purpose is entirely different. White papers can be useful to people whether they decide to work with you or not, but client guides are just for clients.

Here are a few examples from my own business. My Welcome Guides offer information that helps prospects make a decision on whether they want to work with me, or find a different designer that may better suit their needs and personality. They outline my design philosophy, my core values, what happens in each phase of the design process, how to give appropriate feedback on my proposals, and my business policies. The Website Design Welcome Guide also lists all the steps the client needs to complete in order for me to start working on their website. Another example is my Website User Manual, which I give to clients at the end of a website design project that provides customized instructions on how to use their WordPress website.

**Client guides can help you cut down on communication and support time by providing the most important information upfront.** If used in the client onboarding process, they also help you filter out any people who may not be the right fit. The language you use in your client guides is like that of a proposal: serious enough to reiterate that yes, this is a business transaction and we're making things happen, and relaxed enough to show that you are indeed a real person they can rely on and talk to. Let your warm personality glow through your writing, and refer to your brand voice qualities to help you evaluate your writing.

The design of your client guides may look resemble a brochure. They may include illustration and photography, since it's not likely that people will print them. You can feature your best portfolio pieces, or photos from your events or speaking engagements. Done well, client guides can save you time, communicate the essence of your brand, and improve your client experience tremendously.

## Online Marketing

The main benefit of having an online presence is that it enables people from all over the world to access information about your business at any time, regardless of whether you're working or sleeping. Online marketing can help you reach a larger audience, and the resources you create and share once can be used multiple times at no additional cost to you.

While most of us imagine that random people will type our service into Google, like *"massage therapy Toronto"* and call us immediately, the truth is that most of your inquiries will come from people who have been directly referred to you, or who have been following you online for a while. When your friends, former clients, or colleagues recommend your work, people might look you up online. What will they see when they enter your name? If your first result is your personal Facebook profile, you might need to work a bit harder on your online presence.

Word of mouth referrals, combined with an informative website, and active social media channels can produce a more powerful effect than either of them separately.

## WEBSITE

Everybody knows what a website is, but few people know how to create an effective one. Websites serve multiple purposes and goals, and balancing all of those goals is challenging. If you focus on optimizing your website for sales, you might be losing out on building goodwill and authentic connections. If you optimize for connections, you may be taking a hit on the sales. Creating a website that serves your needs and the needs of your clients requires strategic thinking.

A website is the first marketing tool I recommend business owners to create—even if it's a simple one with basic design and minimum content. The better your website, the better your results, but a modest website is better than having no web presence at all. A great website can reduce the need for printed marketing materials. Websites can be easily shared with friends, so your clients, colleagues, and fans can do word-of-mouth marketing more effectively. You can use a website to inform your audience about your services and the benefits they offer, and to collect leads (which we'll talk about in the section on newsletters).

I've been building websites professionally since 2005, and a lot has changed since then. We used to make websites by coding individual HTML,

PHP, or ASP pages. Later, **content management systems** (CMS) became the norm—most of the websites you visit have been created using one of the open-source, commercial, or custom built CMSs. Content management systems are simple to install, so even the average internet user can make their own website. Some CMSs have a rich support community, so if you need professional help, you'll be able to find someone who knows that system inside out.

For a typical service based business website (also called a presentation website, or a brochure website), popular CMS choices are WordPress, Joomla, Wix, Squarespace, and Weebly. WordPress and Joomla are open-source and free, but they require purchasing your own hosting. Wix, Squarespace, and Weebly are commercial platforms that include hosting. Ecommerce websites are built on CMSs like Shopify, WooCommerce, or Magento. Other industries have ready-made solutions as well, like accommodation booking, conference management, etc.

If you can't find a CMS that can be adapted to your needs and want a tailored solution, web development agencies can build a website from scratch for you, which integrates all the functionality you need. This is the most expensive option and will take the most time. Be clear about your needs, and ask around before you commit to working with a web agency. Every website will require a bit of customization, but not every website needs to be custom-built from scratch.

In addition to website hosting, you're going to need a custom website **domain**—a short and meaningful name that ends with .com, .org, .eu, .co.uk, .me, .info, .tv, .photo, or other type of top-level domain (TLD). Domains can cost anywhere from $10 per year, up to hundreds of dollars, depending on the TLD. Usually your domain name is going to be the same as your business name. Shorter domain names are better than longer ones because they're easier to remember, but uniqueness is an even more important factor. If your business name is generic and the .com domain has already been taken, it's better to consider a different domain if possible because people will likely go to the .com domain in error. For example, if your name *janedoe.com* is taken, consider an alternative like *janedoewriter.com*, *janedoeart.com*, *janedoelaw.com*, etc.

Technology is important, but the most important marker of a quality website is its **content**. Whether you're hiring a designer and a developer, or are making your own website, best practice is to create *all* the content beforehand. That way, you'll know exactly what the scope of your project is, and your website will be completed faster. The basics website content a service oriented website needs is:

- Homepage introduction
- About us
- Contact us
- Case studies
- Services
- Service sales pages
- Newsletter call to action
- Blog or news
- Legal pages
- Microcopy

Provide **clear information** for your clients in your content. The easiest way to go about writing content is to list all the questions your clients might have about you or your services, and start answering them one by one. If you don't know what questions your prospects have, ask your existing clients. If you regularly get questions from your friends or random internet people, use those to guide your content.

Often, the **homepage** is the first page your visitors see. Its main purpose is to help them identify whether your website is relevant for them. If your site visitors already know you from elsewhere, your website should be consistent with what they've already seen, so it appears familiar. We do this largely through design, and by highlighting the most important information. For example, if you're actively promoting a new offer through advertising, social media, or speaking, your offer should be prominently featured on the homepage. The top of your homepage is a place where you'd typically include your logo, tagline, and navigation. Many modern websites use this space to feature a large photo and a call to action.

**About Us** is one of the most viewed pages of your website. Your potential clients are interested in seeing who's behind the website, in order to judge how trustworthy you are. If you're a sole business owner or an independent artist, include your own biography. If your business, organization, or music band is made up of a team of people, write a group biography—when the organization was founded and why, important activities throughout the years, how it evolved, and where it's headed. This is also a good place to mention your unique value proposition, and what makes you uniquely qualified to provide it.

Include a photo of yourself and your team members on your about page. People need to be reassured they're working with real, living, breathing human beings. **Photos increase the trustworthiness of your business.** You can even create a short video featuring you and your team. Don't hide your team behind a *"we"*—present them all and highlight what they're like *as people*. Use your friends' and your clients' words to describe who you are. You can start the sentences with: *"Our clients call him...,"* or *"Our clients say she's...,"* or *"Our clients always admire their..."* Another person's endorsement is more powerful than tooting your own horn.

Copywriters often emphasize that when users read your About page, they don't really want to learn about you—they want to learn how you're relevant to them. For this reason, you'll notice that many About pages use the 'you language', or customer centered language. This is smart, but it's not an excuse not to write about yourself at all. This is the place where you can share your unique point of view, your core values, your big vision, and even personal details that you may have in common with your clients. If there's any place where it's totally legitimate to let your freak flag fly, it's the About page.

**Case studies**, **portfolio galleries** and **references** are proof of your past successful work. The format of your case studies will differ based on your industry. Visual creators such as illustrators, designers, animators, 3D modelers, architects, fashion designers, tattoo artists, hair stylists, makeup artists, etc. benefit the most from a gallery featuring reproductions of their work, in image and video format. Writers may provide writing samples (either hosted on your own website, or linked to publications). Musicians may provide audio clips, and filmmakers may provide video clips. Even if your work is easily reproduced through visual media, detailed written project descriptions help your prospects understand the context and the work it took to create it. Case studies (as opposed to finished portfolio pieces) will often feature 'work in progress' images as well.

What do you show to people when your creations—such as reports and strategy documents—are confidential? You write case studies. Case studies describe the *before* state your client was in, the process you've used to solve their problem, and the *after* state (results). Include the client's own words, and provide numeric data if applicable (exact numbers or percentages, depending on what the client is willing to reveal publicly).

MNIB Consulting is a company that helps small businesses scale. Their story driven case studies offer a 'behind the scenes' look at the process, and their client's thoughts and experiences highlight the most important turning points. Case studies provided by the digital marketing company Logit are visually well-organized and highlight the benefits their clients received with large headlines and bullet points.

People who do sensitive and confidential work in the medical, counseling, and legal professions are not allowed to reveal any identifying information about their clients. In that case, you could write an anonymous case study with your client's permission. If all else fails, create a reference list of your typical clients, with the typical problems you help them with, and typical results (avoid exaggerating or generalizing from rare and exceptional client results). This type of page is often called *"Is this You?"* or *"Who We Work With."*

**Contact page** is another must have page for every business website. People who want to get in touch with you need to know what the best way to reach you is, and how long it may take for you to respond. If you have a physical office space where clients visit you, include your working hours, business address, and an interactive map. Many websites use a contact form, which are easy to integrate on most modern content management systems.

Dedicated **inquiry forms** are useful if you need to know more details before you can proceed with the sales conversation. Most clients don't offer this information on their own, so it's your job to ask them everything you need to know.

Your **Services page** is the most important one for your potential clients to visit. Some people list all their services details on one page, but I prefer having separate pages for each service. A general Services page may include the individual services names, short description (the benefits and who it's intended for), and a link to learn more. A great way to make this page look more interesting is to illustrate each service with a photo, an icon, or an illustration.

Your potential clients need a little more information and reassurance before they commit to buying your services. This means you need to create a **Sales page** for each service you sell. Individual pages allow you to share the link to people that you believe are a good fit for it, or to highlight this service on your blog, newsletter, or social media. Effective sales pages are a mix of art and science. At the very minimum, a service page should include:

- Attractive and needs-oriented title.
- The unique value proposition.
- Who this service is intended for.
- Details on what's included.
- The delivery time and date.
- Price (exact, typical range, or "starting from").
- Call to action (*"Send an inquiry"*, *"Contact us"*, *"Book a session"*, etc.)

Additional elements such as client testimonials and guarantees can help the prospective client to evaluate the risks and benefits of this service. Sales pages can get rather long, so text formatting and graphics play a key role in content organization and ease of use.

**Blogging** is an effective way of driving visitors to your website. It helps you expand your reach, because people are more likely to share your free content then they are to share your paid offers. It also helps with improving your search engine rankings. Blog can be less formal than other written marketing content, so this is another opportunity to show your personality. The format of your blog will depend on your industry and your target audience. Here are some ideas of the types of posts you can publish:

- Interesting and little known information related to your industry.
- Debunking a common myth about your industry.
- Documenting your creative process with photos or video.
- Teaching a technique through a short tutorial.

- Giving people a tour of your office or studio.
- Announcing and reporting on events you'll be attending or hosting.
- Writing stories about how you got started, the challenges you've overcome, etc.
- Reviewing resources, such as books, tools, and courses.
- Educating potential buyers on topics relevant to your work.
- Writing about the 'big why' behind your work.
- Interviewing your past clients or people you admire.

Take inspiration from your Human Centered Brand Workbook. Find bits that you'd be willing to share publicly, and craft stories around them. This is how you offer people the pieces of the puzzle, so they can form a complete image of who you are as a person as they get to know you more through your writing.

A **Newsletter page** is similar to a sales page in many ways, and its purpose is to sell the value of hearing from you regularly. People are not as eager to get on your email list as they used to be, so you'll need to create a compelling pitch as to why they would enjoy your newsletter. (We'll get into the newsletter details later in this chapter.) The page doesn't have to be long, but it should at the very least contain the benefits of receiving your newsletter, and how often subscribers can expect to hear from you. Words of reassurance that unsubscribing is easy, and that you won't give away or sell their contact information are also helpful. Close the pitch with a call to action and the sign-up form. You can also include the sign-up form and a shorter version of the call to action on every page of your website.

**Legal pages** include terms of service, privacy policy, cookies policy, and other pages that may be required in your country. Barely anyone reads these pages, but you can go the extra mile and write the content in a way that those few visitors will appreciate.

**Microcopy** are short snippets of text that appear all over your website. It's often an overlooked element, but it can make the website more clear and engaging. Examples of microcopy a small business website might need are:

- Button text.
- Newsletter form text.
- Contact form success and error messages.
- Footer copyright information.
- Legal disclaimers.
- *"More information"* links.
- Registration process messages.

If creating content for your website is next on your to-do list, here are some suggestions on what to read:

- *Content Rules* by Ann Handley
- *The One Hour Content Plan* by Meera Kothand
- *Managing Content Marketing* by Robert Rose and Joe Pulizzi
- *The Art of SEO* by Eric Enge, Stephan Spencer, and Jessie Stricchiola

(Please read the reviews on Amazon and Goodreads to make sure you're getting a book that's appropriate for your current level of understanding. Some books may be too basic if you actively follow online marketing blogs.)

If you run a business to business company and need more hands-on guidance, digital marketer and content writer Višnja Željeznjak has created a resource called the *B2B Website Content Writing Guide.*\* (When I told her I've mentioned it in this book, Višnja generously offered to give 20% discount for the readers with the code **hcbbook** that you can enter on the checkout page.)

What you say is not the only thing that matters—it's how you say it. Refer to your brand voice qualities to check that all of your website content sounds like it was written by the same person. If you're using templates or plugins that contain text written by other people, customize it all so that it aligns with your brand. It's not uncommon for business owners to rewrite

---

\*   *b2bwebsitecontentguide.com*
Disclaimer: I'm not receiving any compensation for mentioning this resource.

their most important web pages over and over until they sound *just right.*

If you're writing a high stakes web page, like a sales page or an about page, ask other people to review it—your friends, colleagues, mastermind buddies, former clients, etc. It's difficult to put ourselves into the shoes of a person who doesn't have all the information we have, so sometimes it's better to just ask them what they think. When letting other people review your content, ask them to let you know:

- What do you remember the most from this page?
- How did this text make you feel?
- Do you have any questions about what you've just read?
- What parts do you feel need more clarification?
- What parts feel too long or repetitive?

You don't need to take every single critique to heart because we all have opinions, but if a particular issue was mentioned repeatedly, you should probably look into it.

Finally, there is also the design piece. Website design has two components: user experience and aesthetics. They're distinct, but intertwined—better aesthetics leads to a better user experience, and vice versa.

**User experience** (UX) is concerned with making the website easy to use. Placement of elements on the webpage and their emphasis can lead to a drastically different experience from the user's view. For example, a search bar right in the top middle of the screen (as seen on Google and PowerThesaurus) makes the search function unmistakable. Placing the search bar in the top right corner of the page makes it less likely to be noticed. Even choosing to have a search bar or not is a UX decision. Since we can't emphasize every single thing and make it visible at all times, we need to make some difficult choices:

- Which goal is most important for the user?
- Which goal is most important for my business?
- How can we meet both of these goals?

Your goal as a business owner is to sell more of your services. The goal of your client is to learn what they need to do to get the results they want. Their goal may not be to buy from you—it's to make the best decision for *them*. Help them make a good decision by providing them with what they need, without putting hurdles in their path (like pop-ups, ads, and other nuisances).

A common UX flaw I see on small business websites is that it's not obvious which page elements are interactive (clickable), and which are not. In web design, we use color, shape and text decoration to differentiate links from regular text. Keep your text links in articles underlined, and never underline text that's not a link (use bold and italic for emphasis instead). Choose a contrasting color for links, and only use this color for links and buttons—don't use the same color for headings. If you're creating banners for your services, also offer a text-based link to the same page, because internet users have developed banner blindness* and may miss the link entirely. If you're using color to differentiate actionable items from the regular text, color blind people may not be able to tell them apart. Use tools like Toptal Color Blind Filter or a browser add-on to see an approximation of what your website looks like to people with partial or total color blindness.

Auto-play music and videos are problematic on many levels. They interrupt users and waste their mobile data. Let the user decide when and how they want to consume your media. **User experience affects the brand perception just like aesthetics does.** If a person has had an unpleasant experience with your site, they won't come back. With so much competition at their fingertips, why should they give you another chance?

A great example of how user experience sends a message to your visitors about what your brand is like is a so called 'exit intent popup', which has been popular in 2016–2017. (I hope that if you're reading this book a couple of years into the future, the trend has crashed and burned.) Exit intent popup appears on websites when you move your mouse toward your browser tabs in an attempt to close the tab. The pop-up asks one last time if you'd like to sign up to their newsletter. I've heard prominent marketers claim that *"if*

---

* *"Banner Blindness: Ad-Like Elements Divert Attention"* by Kara Pernice, Nielsen Norman Group (March 9, 2018)

*they're going to lose the visitor anyway, it doesn't hurt to be pushier."* Here's what the usability experts at Nielsen Norman Group have to say about this:

> *"Every website has a personality. The visual design, the interaction design, the copy, and tone of voice all contribute to how your users perceive your site and your brand. Needy patterns like the please-don't-go popover and the get-back-to-me tab chip away at the presentation of a professional, confident website. They also damage users' perceptions of credibility.*
>
> *As a thought experiment, ask your brand manager whether "we're desperate for attention" is one of the company's stated brand values. If not, why signal such desperation to customers?"* *

Every action you're taking to get your prospects' attention tells a story about your brand. Do you want to come across as a pushy, desperate brand? Or would you rather be perceived as a relaxed and confident brand? Marketing folks are most concerned with metrics: they do split-testing† and compare which page has performed better—but we don't know for sure *why* a certain method performed better. It could be because it's a better solution for the user, or because the user didn't see any other alternative but to complete a sign up form in order to continue. We need to be careful not to rely on certain tools just because a famous marketer claims that it works.

We've talked about the **aesthetics** in the seventh chapter in detail, so I'm only going to point out a few things that are specific to websites. People view websites on a variety of screen sizes, so choosing a font size that's easy to read on most of them is key. Since people typically have shorter attention spans while reading web content than they do with books, it's important to make your text 'scannable':

- Break it apart into shorter paragraphs.
- Use subheadings to divide content & attract attention to key points.

---

* *"Needy Design Patterns: Please-Don't-Go Popups & Get-Back-to-Me Tabs"* by Kate Meyer and Kim Flaherty, Nielsen Norman Group (May 15, 2016).
† Split testing is a method of serving different web page variants to different visitors and measuring which one has resulted in more sales, registrations, newsletter signups, etc.

- Use lists (like this!)
- Add descriptive photos and illustrations to keep interest.
- Highlight most important information with bold text.
- Add generous margins around paragraphs and headings.

Large photographs, especially those including people, attract attention and increase trust. A few years ago, my client Kristijan Ljutić ordered professional photographs of his team at his civil engineering consulting company 4D-monitoring. As a result, they got tremendous engagement on social media after we've published the new website design and started using the new photos. (Now they share impromptu field photos of their team on social media regularly.)

Illustration is being used more and more on corporate and startup websites, and it's been used on creative small business websites since the early days of internet. The style of illustration can be whimsical and fun, like the website of the designer Robby Leonardi, or elegant and sophisticated like the ones used by the jewelry designer Angela Georgiu. Even peppering a couple of custom icons here and there can make a difference.

Statistics on mobile web users report significant growth over the past years, and in March 2018 this number has grown to more than 51% of mobile users globally.* **Responsive websites**, which adapt the design based on the device screen size, have become the norm. This ensures a better experience with your website on mobile phones. If you're hiring a designer or a developer, request a responsive website. If you're looking for a ready-made theme, watch for the 'responsive' feature and test it on your phone before you buy it.

When you publish content on your website, you'll probably want to share it on social media to get it in front of more people. Add **featured images** to your pages or blog posts that will appear alongside the post title when shared. If you don't specify a featured social media image, Facebook will pick up the first image on the page. (Other social networks may or may not do the same.) Create a template for your featured image that you can reuse

---

\*   *"Desktop vs Mobile vs Tablet Market Share Worldwide – March 2018"*, StatCounter Global Stats (April 2018)

to save time and create cohesion among your website graphics.

If your blog posts contain original photos and art, you'll probably want to protect them with some sort of **watermark**. This way, if someone shares your images on their blog or social media without linking to the source, at least your credit will be there. You can use your logo, signature, full name, or website URL as a watermark.

We've covered all the website aspects in broad strokes, and I hope this will help you get started. If you'd like to dive in more into the user experience and website design, here are some resources that go into more depth:

- *Don't Make Me Think* by Steve Krug
- Smashing Magazine
- Skillshare
- Khan Academy
- Codecademy

Websites require regular upkeep. Even if you make the very best website you can when you first launch it, after months of people using it, you'll notice that some things could be improved. In some cases the improvements are as simple as changing the text, but other changes may require fiddling with code and redesigning entire sections. If your business has grown significantly and you're looking to update your brand perception, this is a good opportunity for a full website **redesign**. If you're considering a website redesign, there are several methods you can use to take stock of what your current website is doing well, and what could be improved:

- Imagine yourself as your ideal client who wants to learn about your services, and navigate the website like you're seeing it for the first time. Write down any questions or frustrating experiences you might notice.
- Ask a friend or a relative who has never been on your website before to try to complete a goal (like, send a message through your inquiry form). Record or write down their comments.
- Install a tool like Hotjar to see how people are using your website.

- Offer a random person on the street (who matches your target demographic) a gift card in return for using your website with a phone and providing their comments.

- If you're using Google Analytics or another advanced website statistics software, examine which pages get the most traffic, which have the highest and lowest bounce rate, and note your conversion rates (so you can compare how these are affected after redesign).

If you want to make an exclusive website for a select audience, be aware who you're leaving out and why. The boundaries around your business should be based on your core values, worldview, style of expression, and the services you offer. Try not to exclude people with disabilities or marginalized minorities from benefiting from your work, and keep them in mind as you're considering the design and the content of your website.

## SOCIAL MEDIA

Social media is an excellent channel for timely updates and work in progress, and its less formal nature allows you to share your work in a more intimate way. There's no one right method—it depends on your boundaries and your comfort level.

First, decide which of your social media channels will be public and related to your business, and which you'll only use privately.

**The best social media channels for your business are those most suited for the type of content you enjoy creating, and where your ideal clients also spend their time.** If your ideal audience isn't there, then no matter how often you post on a certain social media channel, it will be a waste of time. We've discussed this in chapter six in more detail, and it's useful to check the notes you've made in your workbook to get ideas where your ideal clients hang out, and show up at those places.

Some business owners share their hobbies and vacation photos on social media. Some talk about social justice and environmental issues, and this creates another point of connection with their right people. If you're the type of 'open book' business owner who wants people to get to know the person behind the business, do it. Don't let anyone else tell you you're *"doing it wrong"* or are *"alienating your audience"* if your audience gives you positive feedback.

Another choice is whether to handle your social media channels by yourself, or hire an assistant to do it instead. If you're a solo business owner, or your online presence is personality based (like a writer or an artist), I suggest managing your own social media interactions to maintain your personal connections. If you need help, absolutely get help—but don't detach yourself from your channels completely. Running popular social media channels is hard work, but if Neil Gaiman, Stephen King, and Amanda Palmer can do it, so can you. People follow them specifically because they're willing to engage with their audience and be authentic.

If you run a business with several employees, the one who is most qualified can run your social media channels (likely a marketing or a sales person). You could also hire a social media manager, depending on the workload. It's important to vet this person carefully, because what they publish will form the audience's opinion of your business. Even if you're too busy to check on social media, make it a habit to examine what happens on your channels on a weekly basis to ensure it's aligned with your brand.

If I had one rule to follow on social media, it would be this: **never mock or mistreat your clients and followers.** If you act like a jerk, people will (rightly) think you're a jerk. Treat people as you wish to be treated: if you decide to put up boundaries regarding certain behavior on your social media channels (which is fine), then adhere to these boundaries yourself. If you don't tolerate insults, don't insult people. It sounds like I shouldn't even be writing this because it's 'common sense', but everyday experience teaches me it's anything but common. Even high profile entrepreneurs and celebrities struggle with this apparently simple concept. **Always remember there are other people watching your interactions.**

You're allowed to block anyone at any time for any reason, and there's no need to justify yourself—protect your sanity. Some people have a thing for getting into arguments online, like J.K. Rowling who is famous for her sassy responses to political opponents. Since she's famous and very outspoken about her personal values, she attracts more haters than the average small business, and this is how she chooses to deal with them. She's witty and funny, and can turn these things in her favor with grace—something *very* few people can do well. Her snarky retorts often end up in the newspaper, so it gets her free publicity. However, I'm sure not even she has a perfect track record. If you're called to adopt such an approach because your comedian personality can handle it, great—but be aware that it can backfire.

Now that we've gotten the basics of social media etiquette out of the way, what can you use social media for? The short answer is: whatever you can think of. Creative ideas are welcome, because it's a dynamic and saturated environment that keeps evolving. Here's a list of ideas to start with:

- Announcements of new services, special offers, events, etc.
- Features of new projects or case studies.
- Sharing your articles, videos, interviews, etc.
- Behind the scenes photos of your team at work.
- Photos of your work in progress.
- Snippets from your articles or books formatted as quote graphics.
- Short, condensed text posts (can be used as 'beta tests' for longer articles).
- Illustrated diagrams or infographics.
- Short video updates about timely topics.
- Live video question and answer sessions.
- Live video streams from industry events.
- Interviews with your clients and people you admire.
- Client success stories (written or video).
- Polls about future services, content, products, etc.
- Questions for your audience.

Many business owners also re-share other people's memes, quote graphics, illustrations, and other visual content, probably because they don't have enough content of their own to fill their posting schedule. I'm not a fan of this approach because it can dilute your brand. If you want to use other people's quotes, create your own graphic templates. (Always credit the original sources—if the quote author is alive, tag them in your post.)

Try to avoid posting graphics that don't align with your brand. There are of course exceptions to this: if you're speaking at an event, or are interviewed on a podcast or a magazine, the publisher will provide their own graphics that match *their* brand. This can actually help you boost your profile, especially if it's a well-known event or publication. It pays off to break the consistency if it's to demonstrate that other organizations or publications endorse your work.

While many people believe you should be available on social media every single day, I don't share that opinion. I find it overwhelming and distracting when I'm trying to focus on large creative projects of my own. Computer science professor Cal Newport argues that social media is not essential for 'knowledge workers', and that in many cases social media can prevent our best work from happening: they're *"massively addictive and therefore capable of severely damaging your attempts to schedule and succeed with any act of concentration."*[*]

It's possible to have a successful service based business without a social media presence. I know many service businesses who have never had a Facebook profile, or never tweeted, and they're doing just fine. It's better to do fewer things well, than try to do many things at once and fail at it.

## NEWSLETTERS

Newsletters are regular email updates that people voluntarily receive from organizations or individuals. (Adding people to your list without asking them is considered unethical, and in many countries illegal.)

A collection of your email contacts is not the basis for your newsletter. **You need to get confirmation from every single person that they want to be on your newsletter list**, and keep written records of how and when your subscribers have joined in order to comply with the international spam and privacy laws like GDPR and CAN-SPAM Act. Modern newsletter applications keep record of all the subscriptions and unsubscribes, so if you use a system

---

\* From "Deep Work" by Cal Newport, copyright © 2016. Reprinted by permission of Grand Central Publishing., an imprint of Hachette Book Group, Inc.

like MailChimp, InfusionSoft, ConvertKit, etc. you're safe as long as you don't add people into it manually.

Newsletters are typically associated with sales. You sign up to be notified of seasonal discounts, or to find out when your favorite art teacher will be giving a workshop in your area. Being notified of sales and events can be enough of a value in itself, but they're also a great channel for building **lasting relationships** with your audience by providing even more value though free content. Many marketers advise sending a weekly newsletter to stay top of mind. Some business owners find that too overwhelming, and choose a monthly schedule, or even quarterly.

Since newsletters are delivered directly to one's email inbox, I see them as a more intimate way of communication than websites or social media. **Newsletters are exclusive**—they're not freely available to the public, but only to those who share their contact details with you. This gives you an opportunity to provide an even better experience for them, and treat them like a special club of insiders. Even if your newsletter only repurposes the information you've published on your blog, include a personal introduction, and an outro at the end that makes it read like a personal email message.

You can send them content that you don't publish anywhere else to create even more exclusivity. **You can be more transparent and vulnerable in your newsletter than on social media or your blog.** This is one of the most powerful tools for building a Human Centered Brand—one that connects you to your right people more directly and authentically. Approach writing your newsletters as you would writing a letter to a dear friend. If you want to keep a bit of professional distance, write as you would to a business partner you've been working with for years.

On the aesthetic side of things, there are two camps in regards to newsletter formatting:

1. Newsletters should resemble regular emails as much as possible.
2. Newsletters should be visually attractive.

The creator of ConvertKit Nathan Barry argues that the simplest newsletter designs are superior to graphic-heavy designs:

*"So when you send an email, what part of the communication delivers the most value? That's right, the content. So we should be stripping away everything else that isn't necessary in order to focus on the content. Multi-column layouts, background images, logos, and all the other nonsense that typically fills marketing emails doesn't deliver value to the recipient. Instead it is all about you, the sender. Flip that around and start delivering value."* [*]

I'm not convinced that we must all drop all the graphics completely. I always place a small logo at the top of my client's newsletters. As Nathan states, this focuses on the benefit the company is getting from the reader (brand awareness). But if you go all the way to provide valuable content, it's fine, as long as it doesn't negatively affect usability and user experience. Seeing that logo at the top may help people remember who is writing to them in the first place.

The signature area of a newsletter may be larger than that of a regular email. You may include social media links, a call to action to your services, or even your own photo and a short biography for people who are new or haven't read your emails in a while. The signature area also *must* include your contact details and the *"Unsubscribe"* link so that people can stop receiving your emails whenever they choose.

To figure out what to include in your newsletter and how to format it, observe what your favorite bloggers and business owners do. What do you like in their newsletters? What seems excessive or not very user friendly? Are they doing anything that's uncommon, but totally works for their brand? What would something like that look like for *your* brand?

Newsletters can be easily changed from issue to issue, so you can experiment until you land on a format that works best for your business. From that point forward, as usual, keep it consistent.

## VIDEO MARKETING

Video enables you to be present with your online audience through voice, appearance, movement, and body language. Using video marketing, you can

---

[*]  *"Why beautiful email templates hurt your business"*, Nathan Barry (May 6th, 2013)

speak to millions of people, while recording your talks or performances in your own home, office, or studio.

People shy away from video marketing out of fear of looking ridiculous, not liking their own appearance or voice, or the tech overwhelm. I can empathize with all of these reasons, and I feel self-conscious every time I post a video as well. Like anything else, it gets easier with practice. You can do it using minimal equipment, like a smartphone with HD video recording capabilities or a webcam. If you don't have access to professional lighting yet, you can film during daylight, sitting opposite of a window. Sound quality is fairly important, so an external microphone should be your first investment.

The easiest and most common type of videos is **'talking head'**. They show your head or bust as you're talking about a topic related to your expertise. (My tips for client video meetings apply here as well.) The limitations of video cameras and microphones typically require you to sit close to the camera, but if you have access to professional filming and sound equipment, you can also create talk-show like videos where you're sitting or standing with your entire body in view.

**Interviews** feature two or more speakers which are recorded in the same room, or while in an online video call (using Skype, Zoom, or Hangouts). Business owners typically interview experts who can speak on the topics that their audience is interested in, or people their audience can relate to (like clients, students, or peers).

**Demos** show you as you perform your processes—usually with live commentary, added-on commentary, or subtitles. This is a great option for hands-on skills including technical, creative, and bodywork techniques. Since the focus is on the work performed, the camera will be zoomed in on your hands, instead of your face so it's good to create a talking head introduction to connect with the viewers.

**Screencasts** enable your audience to view your screen as you're performing a task. This can be used for demos and tutorials, as well as software reviews, website or social media critiques, etc. Popular screen sharing software includes Camtasia, Snagit, and Open Broadcast Software.

**Explainer videos** are illustrated videos used to break down complex topics in an entertaining way. This option is great for creatives who are able to design their own graphics and learn how to animate them. Those who can't create their own video graphics can purchase this service from many companies that offer it nowadays.

Videos can be pre-recorded or live. In case of **live videos**, viewers can ask you questions or share their comments in the chat box, or you can even bring them on to join you via video if you're using software like Zoom. Live videos are more forgiving because the interactive element keeps people engaged even if your delivery isn't perfect.

With pre-recorded videos, you need to work harder to keep the audience interested. Make a script or an outline before filming to avoid filler words and going off on a tangent.

Once you've recorded your video, you'll need to edit before uploading it to the web. Editing can involve basic tasks like cutting and stitching video sections, speeding up the video (useful for demos that last too long), changing the lighting and color, adding static images, adding background music, making transitions between sections, etc. Popular video editing software includes Adobe Premiere, Final Cut Pro, Apple iMovie, OpenShot, and Blender.

Videos created for your business should have a short branded intro and outro—the shorter the better, preferably no longer than 5 seconds. The intro typically consists of your company logo, video title, and intro music. The outro contains all the credits for people and resources that helped with your video, and your own website link. Elaborate intros can contain video snippets or photos with text and graphics whooshing by. Examples of intros like that can be seen on newer videos by money mindset coach Denise Duffield Thomas and negotiation specialist Devon Smiley.

Any music you use should either be purchased, or offered by their creators through a Creative Commons license to avoid any issues with video hosting services. Websites that catalogue music available for free use include Free Music Archive, ccMixter, Incompetech, and Purple Planet. Affordable music can be purchased on some of the aforementioned websites, as well as AudioJungle.

The final part is distributing your videos. You have the option to host them on your own website, or on paid remote servers like Wistia, VideoPress, or Vimeo Business. You can also upload them to free services like YouTube and Vimeo, and directly on your social media channels.

**The main brand signifier in videos is your own personality and appearance.** Get calm and relaxed so that your real self can come out. Take time to prepare for filming to get yourself into the right mood. Marketing consultant for creative businesses April Bowles Olin recommends to *"be yourself after two cups of coffee."* This means: be slightly more expressive on video than you are in person, because video tones everything down. Your clothing can also affect how people perceive you and your brand, and I'll get into more details on that in chapter ten.

Check the section on presentations for more information on how to create more engaging and attractive designs if you plan to use them in your videos. Ensure that the style of graphics and animations you use are consistent throughout the entire video, and as well as your other videos.

Create consistent video thumbnails using your brand colors and typography, so that they all look nice when viewed on your channel or blog archive. (For an example of this, check out the thumbnails of the Summer Hen YouTube channel, which Naomi Dunford has created in Canva.)

While videos take more time, energy, and technical skills than other types of content, they offer an intimate connection with your viewers, and help them imagine what talking to you one on one would be like.

## PODCASTS

Podcasts are self-produced independent radio shows, either in an interview format, or featuring the host alone. You can publish them on your own website, on another podcast network, or on services such as iTunes, Mixcloud, Soundcloud, or Stitcher. Podcasts are usually published on a regular (weekly) schedule resembling a real radio show, although some podcasts have seasons and breaks between them.

The essence of the podcast is the sound of your voice. Being more expressive and making dramatic pauses will help keep your listeners tuned in. Some podcasts utilize sound effects, like the *Tea & Jeopardy* podcast hosted by the sci-fi writer Emma Newman, which is a blend between a regular interview show and radio drama. Emma's audience are sci-fi geeks who welcome a bit of role-play, so this format is very well received.

Like videos, podcasts also typically have a short intro and outro featuring music. Your intro will be heard both by new listeners and regular listeners, so keep it short. This is your opportunity to make your brand voice work hard for you: spend a bit of time to come up with an intro that evokes the feelings you want your listeners to experience with your podcast.

Your podcast also requires a few visual elements. One is the podcast **cover art**, which remains the same for all your podcast episodes. Adding cover art to your audio files may be a bit more involved depending on the software and distribution channels you're using.* The second visual element are your blog and social media **sharing graphics**. Your sharing graphic (or featured image) should contain the podcast episode title, and the name of your guest (if you have one). Interview podcasts often use the guest's photo in their featured image.

If you want to learn more about podcasting and what you'll need to start your own, The Podcaster's Studio and NPR Training are great free resources.

## INTERVIEWS & GUEST ARTICLES

Being interviewed or having your content featured in other people's publications is a great way to expand your audience. Of course, not just any publication will do: select those whose audience profile is closely aligned with your ideal client profile. When featured on other platforms, you don't have as much control over how the content you provide is presented, and the design of your content will be determined by the publisher's visual brand identity. Let's explore what you *can* do within these limitations.

The most important element is your short **biography.** I know, everyone hates writing their own biography, but it's essential if you're going to do any public speaking or writing. Take this as an opportunity to implement what you've learned in the previous chapters. Here's a structure you can start with and build on:

1. Open your biography with your name, occupation, and your unique value proposition.

---

* A good tutorial I've found on this topic is *"How to add or change your podcast cover art"* by Daniel J. Lewis.

2. Share who you work with (your ideal client) and what you help them achieve.

3. Offer *just enough* credentials and facts to prove your expertise.

4. Mention your most successful projects, clients, awards, publications, etc.

5. Close with a call to action (if appropriate).

Refine and reword the biography so that it reflects your brand voice qualities, and presents you in the role that you want to be seen in.

Your biography will change over time as you get more successful. Someone who is new to their industry may emphasize university education as their largest credential. Book authors will mention the names of the books they've written (and note their bestseller status), while consultants who work with well-known brands will name-drop their clients. As you add more achievements to your biography, you can drop the less impressive ones to keep is concise.

If you're allowed to make a **call to action**, use it to promote a no-brainer offer like a free gift, a free discovery session, or an affordable evergreen offer. If you're doing the interview specifically to talk about a current offer, then promote that. The call to action can be a part of your biography, or within the content itself. Guest posts typically don't allow any links or calls to action within the content, but interviews might.

The third and final piece is your **profile photo**. Use the same profile photo you're using on your website and all your social media channels, so that people can easily recognize you. Send your most current photograph in a fairly large size for the web (around 1000 pixels on each side), or the largest size you have available if the interview is published in print. Gather your best **visuals** of your services or products and send them along with your other information, since the media loves visual content.

If you're planning on doing many interviews, package your biography, high-resolution profile photo, and any additional image resources into a **media kit** (press kit). Upload it all to a cloud hosting service or your own website. That way, you can simply point reporters to the link where they can download everything they need.

In order to get on other people's platforms when no one is sending you invitations, you'll need to send them a **pitch**. Some websites have steps you can follow to ensure your pitch goes through, while others just provide general contact information. Your pitch can be a simple email where you describe how you can contribute to their publication with relevant content, or if you feel confident, you can send them a finished content sample.

In addition to the more informal email pitch, there's also a formal type of story pitch called the press release, more common in traditional media like the newspapers, radio and TV. (More on that in the following section.) As your business and brand grows in fame, the media will start reaching out to you for an interview, so you won't need to pitch anymore.

## Public Relations

Public relations (PR) is communicating with journalists and submitting stories to them. They get something interesting to write about, while your business or a project gets a free mention in front of their audience.

Media mentions help you establish credibility—if someone thought you or your business were interesting enough to talk about, this holds a lot more weight than when you toot your own horn through your marketing. Being featured in well-known publications looks impressive in your biography and on your website. Different media you can get featured in includes:

- Newspapers
- Magazines
- Radio
- TV
- Web portals
- Blogs
- Podcasts
- Video shows

The best way to get featured is to do something of special interest, like organizing an event, performing in a local show, exhibiting your work, running open days, starting a charity campaign, publishing a book, etc. The media won't report on 'business as usual'—there has to be an element of newsworthiness to your story.

If you want to increase brand awareness in your local community, pitch stories to your local media outlets. If you want to get featured internationally, look up publications whose values align with your own, and whose audience is likely to be comprised of your ideal clients. You can also create an account on the website Help A Reporter Out (HARO) and start replying to journalists and bloggers who request quotes from experts to feature in their articles.

In order to get the attention of the reporters and TV or radio show hosts, you need to send a **press release**\* to their email address. In addition to the press release text, provide the media with a small selection of high-resolution photos and graphics they can use. Make sure all the photos are credited to the original photographer, as newspapers and magazines have strict crediting guidelines.

After sending a press release, get ready to receive phone calls from journalists who want to interview you for their show. Radio and TV stations prefer to host people, instead of just reading a press release to their audience. These calls will come at all hours of the day. Some live shows may require you to get up early, or stay up late. As impractical as this disruption to your life may be, a successful media campaign can make a tremendous impact on your business.

## Live Events

Conferences and fairs that your ideal clients visit are an excellent way to make new connections. Speaking is a great strategy for consultants to raise interest in your work, and you can reach many people at once. For business owners selling hands-on services or custom commissioned art (like massage therapists or book illustrators), fairs are a way to get lots of foot traffic to your booth. In addition to participating in events that others have organized, you can also organize events of your own, like workshops, classes, retreats, etc.

Industry events offer an opportunity to meet the people you admire and want to collaborate with. What happens on stage matters, but off-stage conversations may be even more important. No one is too big or too important to

---

\*   *"Press Release Format, Instructions & Easy To Use Template"* by Jeremy Marsan, FitSmallBusiness (January 3, 2018).

*"Writing and Formatting Tips for News Releases"*, PR Newswire.

talk to. Most people are very gracious and will gladly answer your questions if you show genuine interest.

**Don't pitch your services to people you've just met.** If your short introduction highlights your unique value proposition in a compelling way, people will start asking you questions about your work. If the other person expresses interest, exchange business cards and invite them to connect with you so you could talk again and see if there's a fit.

Even more important than talking about your own services is to find out as much as you can about the other person's problems and needs. That way, you'll know whether you're the right person to help them, or if you can recommend someone else. Even if someone is not your ideal client, be helpful. Besides it being a nice thing to do, they may actually know someone who is your ideal client and recommend you to them.

In this section I'll mention brand identity and client experience elements that are unique to events, but your event presence can also benefit from printed advertising materials like brochures, flyers, and business cards.

## PRESENTATIONS

Presentations are an essential component of conference talks, workshops, classes, and webinars. The most important part of an effective presentation is the **topic**. We've talked about the topic you most want to be known for in the fifth chapter, and this is one of the ways you get known for it—talk about it *everywhere*. The best topics offer takeaways that the audience can apply, or provokes them to think about something they haven't given enough importance to.

The second component is the **organization**. The same topic can be presented in various ways: as a linear story, as a list of steps, focus on one tiny segment of a topic, etc. Break things down for the audience that may not be familiar with your topic, and let each point logically follow the previous ones. A mistake I make all the time is cramming too much content into my talks and workshops. Time your presentations while you rehearse, and cut out everything that isn't necessary.

The third component is your **delivery**. To get better at public speaking, rehearse your talk at home for a couple of days before the event, and speak at as many events as you can, as often as you can. The calmer and more confident you get before a presentation, the more authentic you'll seem, and the better your impact on the audience. There's no shortcut, but the good news is it does get easier over time.

The fourth component are effective **visuals**. Presentation slides are a valuable teaching aid, but they also give you the opportunity to subtly promote your brand. It's quite easy to stand out from the typical conference presentations by applying slightly higher design standards than most business owners have. The purpose of a presentation slide deck is to reiterate the points you're making verbally, or to provide visuals that enhance the understanding of the topic. Here are my tips on designing better presentations:

**Use the same fonts and colors as you do in the rest of your materials.** Don't use any pre-made presentation templates which clash with your other visuals. Use the simplest template you can find, and build your own from that.

**One idea or sentence per slide.** You don't need a dozen bullet points that repeat what you're saying. Often these bullet points are too small to read from the back seats anyway, and it keeps people busy with a task that they shouldn't be doing anyway.

**Make the text larger.** No, larger than that. Nope, larger still. The text should be easy to read from the last row. Test this by standing back from your computer, and see how far you can go until the text becomes difficult to read.

**Show visuals that aid in the understanding**: graphs, charts, illustrations, photos, screenshots, or video.

**Use a background other than white.** Pure white backgrounds look aggressive in darkened rooms, and can cause eye strain. You can use white text on a dark background, or dark text on a light gray background instead.

**Header or footer, but not both.** Some company presentations go overboard with a logo in the header, and full company name and contact information in the footer of every slide, which takes up a lot of screen real estate. Put your logo, website link, or email either in the header *or* the footer of the slide template.

**If you're not projecting from your own laptop, use the PDF format.** If you move your PowerPoint or Keynote presentation to a different computer, your text formatting may change. This can throw an otherwise great presentation completely out of whack. PDF is the safest format because it retains font formatting no matter where you view it. (Unfortunately, some advanced features such as speaker notes and next slide preview will be lost.)

The presentation slide deck is not used just for the duration of your talk: it's a resource you share with your audience to take home. You can also reuse the visuals from your presentation in your blog posts, white papers, and videos.

## BOOTHS

Business owners who frequently exhibit their offers at fairs have the challenging task of setting up a booth that attracts visitors and gives a great first impression. It requires investing in displays, or building your own. You'll need a nice tablecloth to cover up the often banged up tables that the fairs provide. It's possible that the first fair you attend will only cover your expenses for setting up the booth (not to mention the booth rent), but once you've paid off that initial investment, you'll get to keep more of your profits.

Booth design sets the atmosphere for your goods and services. Think of it as a portable office, studio, or salon: what can you bring on the road to recreate the atmosphere with only the few items you can carry? Obviously you can't control the entire fair space and the show is going to be noisy, but your own booth can become an oasis for your ideal clients to take a break and enjoy.

Your booth setup can make your creations look appealing, or unappealing—and I've seen plenty of both. A nice tablecloth in your brand color and a few of your key pieces propped up on an easel can make all the difference.

My friend and former client Barbara Kosmač who creates enchanting handmade jewelry at Alcyone Crystals did something exquisite for her booth at one of the events: she brought a fallen branch she found in the woods, covered it with pieces of moss, and placed some of her jewelry and wood elf figurines on it. This made perfect sense for her brand: her work is inspired by nature, made of natural materials, and her products are often photographed on a natural backdrop.

What do you do if you're selling services? I've seen booths with the person sitting next to an empty table with a piece of paper, and I never bothered to even stop and look closely at what they sell. If people can't read what you offer from a few meters distance, your sign is not working. Ideally, your sign should be completely vertical, either stuck to a wall behind you, or on a rollup banner standing next to your table (more on that later). The next best thing is a sign propped against an easel—slightly leaning back, but still easy to read from a distance.

If you have any promotional items like brochures, flyers, and business cards, or free goodies like bookmarks and stickers, fan out a small number of each around your table.

If you're selling sessions right on the spot, it's even more important to make your booth look like a space where this transformative work can happen. Aromatherapy lamps or incense sticks can help create a relaxing atmosphere. You can decorate your booth with beautiful artwork or inspiring cards. If the venue allows it, you could even make tea for your clients using a small electric kettle. My friend and client Jasna Legović of Claire Fortune used to have a Tarot reading booth at local events that featured ornamented tablecloths, candles, incense sticks, the crystal ball, china figurines, and of course—her gorgeous Tarot cards. At a few events she even had a tent which gave her clients more privacy, and made the experience more intimate.

Think of your booth as a portable office or salon, and approach to it as you would to decorating your own brick and mortar place.

## ROLLUP BANNERS

Rollup banners are large, tall posters printed on a thick plastic canvas sheet with a metal support that enables them to stand upright. You can see them at fairs, conferences, and other events, typically covered with sponsor logos.

As large as they are, the only usable space of a rollup banner is the top third. If they're placed at the ground level, the bottom two thirds will be obstructed by booth tables and people walking by.

If your audience if familiar with your brand and expects you to visit the event, a rollup banner helps them spot your booth from a distance. For those who don't know about your business yet, seeing your logo from far away won't mean much, but it will be in their face as they walk by your booth, and may intrigue them to check out your offers and talk to you. The most important information to feature at the top of a rollup banner is the logo or business name, tagline, and website address.

A rollup banner can turn your modest booth into a professional-looking trading space, so it may be worth investing in it.

## FREE GIFTS

Also called goodies or *swag*, free branded gifts are given out to event visitors. They can be packaged in the official event swag bag (an honor reserved for event sponsors), or given to people who stop by your booth. They also make great holiday gifts for your employees, clients, and business partners.

**The main aim of free goodies is to show generosity to your prospective clients and stay in their memory.** A secondary aim may be for these gifts to be seen by others if the person wears them in public. If the gift recipient has a large audience, them appearing with your swag on a stage or on video can give you a significant boost in brand awareness. (Which is why brands send so many freebies to 'influencers'.)

If you're organizing an event of your own like a workshop or a retreat, giving your attendees something physical to keep after the event increases the perceived value of the event. If you give items that they can share with their family members, this also helps create more goodwill with people that they care about the most and whose opinion matters to them.

While most branded goods are offered for free by companies for promotional purposes, in certain industries they are goods that are sold. Musicians sell T-shirts and prints with their album art, and people gladly pay for them to support their music. Indie cultural festivals without the budget to give away goodies to everyone may upsell these as souvenirs.

Since freebies are so ubiquitous, it's hard to do it right. We already have too much *stuff* in our homes, and if something isn't either exceptionally useful or exceptionally beautiful, it will probably end up on the landfill. If you care about the environment at all, this is something to keep in mind as you brainstorm for what kind of gift to create.

The **usefulness** criteria is subjective because it depends on your target audience—people will consider different things useful. Examine the lifestyle of your ideal clients, and see what small and cheap things might come in handy as they're going about their day. For example, I get free key chains all the time, and they're useless to me because I only need one in my life. But when I got a keychain that was also a bottle opener, I immediately put it on my keys and threw the old one into the trash. On the other hand, I always pick up bookmarks from booths and bookstores because I can never have too many of those.

The **beauty** of a product is the measure of how attractive it is to your audience. A question to ask yourself to evaluate your gift is: *"Would a person pay for a product like this?"* If it's a plain white T-shirt with a huge company logo on it, the answer is probably not. If it's a colored shirt with a subtle mark or an illustration, and they're the kind of people who wear those colors and style, they probably buy shirts like that often. Popular gift items include:

| | | |
|---|---|---|
| • T-shirts | • Badges | • Postcards |
| • Hoodies | • Lapel pins | • Bookmarks |
| • Umbrellas | • Stickers | • Water bottles |
| • Mugs | • Bags | • Blankets |
| • USB drives | • Notebooks | • Socks |
| • Pens | • Writing pads | |

As people receive more and more of these gifts, it's difficult to stand out. Investing thought and effort into a good design can make a difference between a throwaway item and a cherished part of someone's daily ritual.

My client Iva Silla, storyteller and tour guide at Secret Zagreb, gave badges featuring the illustrations I've created for her as gifts to the participants of her gamified quests. Here the memory of a great experience is paired with a keepsake.

Being primarily a visual creator, I use postcards in lieu of business cards, and hand them to almost everyone I talk to at events. The front of the postcard features on of my artworks or a hand-lettered inspirational message, and the back has writing space, my logo, and contact information. I also send custom hand-written greeting cards to my clients and business partners every holiday season.

Jennifer Lee, whom I've already mentioned a couple of times in this book, created a mug that features an illustrated chart with 'left-brained' abilities on one side, and 'right-brained' abilities on the other side of the mug. It's a great example of a gift that reminds people of the essence of your message.

In addition to these common gift items, explore options that have a symbolic association with your brand. Connie Solera, artist and art teacher at the Dirty Footprints Studio, gives branded aprons to the artists who take part in her retreats. This apron then becomes an integral part of their creative practice, and the act of putting it on and taking it off are the rituals that mark the beginning and the end of every painting session.

What could you give your prospects or clients that will become an essential part of their daily rituals, especially as it relates to the work you do? A personal trainer may give away custom wristbands. An editor may give bookmarks with common grammar do's and don'ts on the back. A therapist may print a small set of cards with easy self-soothing techniques. Many artists nowadays create free coloring pages. A successful client gift is useful, appealing, rare, and reminds people of how you can help them.

## Advertising

Advertising consists of a wide range of printed, audio, and video media designed to attract the attention of your audience, and provide more information for those who might be interested in your services. Compared to content which may mention your business is a subtle way, advertising is explicit in describing services, products, and the benefits of working with you.

Good ads are helpful, relevant, and user-friendly. You may be super annoyed at ads that have nothing to do with your needs and cover up the content that you want to read, but you will gladly pick up a travel agency brochure about trips to Paris, or click on a Facebook ad offering discounted flights to Paris if you've decided to visit Paris this year.

- **Helpful** means that the advertisement provides a next step toward the solution of the prospect's problem.

- **Relevant** means that the prospect is actively looking for a solution to this problem right now.
- **User-friendly** means that it won't impede the prospects ability to easily ignore the advertising if it doesn't interest them.

The main aims of any advertising is to attract the attention of your ideal clients and create interest, so they decide to visit your website or contact you immediately.

The most important thing to get right is to **feature the advertisement in places where your ideal clients are likely to spend their time.** You don't have to pay for large billboards downtown if the venues where your ideal clients hang out have spaces where you can advertise for free. Places like libraries, waiting rooms, yoga studios, and universities sometimes have a designated spaces for flyers or posters. Some companies stuff flyers in people's mailboxes, which can be annoying and actually create a *negative* impression of your brand. If an apartment building has a shelf for flyers, use that instead. Respect *"No advertisements"* labels on mailboxes.

Advertising methods range from cheap to expensive, and your choice will largely depend on your budget. Different forms of advertising you can explore are:

- Brochures
- Magazine & newspaper ads
- Posters
- Flyers
- Banner ads
- Social media ads
- Radio advertisements
- TV advertisements
- Sponsored content

Some forms of advertising are small or only seen from a distance, so you can't put too much information on them. Cut down the text to make it *as short as possible*, but at the same time try to keep your brand voice in it. (And while you're at it, balance on your head while stirring polenta with your feet.) Copywriting for advertising is hard, so you might want to get a professional to help you. Share your brand style guide with them so they know who you're targeting, and what you want your ads to sound like.

If you have lots of room on a brochure or a flyer, include more information about your services, a map to your office, and even feature client testimonials. Provide your website link in every ad you run, so that people can find more information. Photography, illustration, video, and animation can capture your audience's interest if the visuals resonate with your ideal clients. Movement attracts attention more than static imagery, and people tend to memorize animated ads better.*

Piquing curiosity is a start, but if your clients actually *desire* what you offer, you're more likely to make a sale. If the prospect is interested in your offer, they're wondering *"What do I do next?"* Tell them what the next step is with a clear **call to action**. You don't have to be pushy or hyper—speak with your natural brand voice, but don't beat around the bush.

Most of the time your advertisements are going to appear next to other ads or content. Context can greatly affect how your ad is perceived.† If you can make your ad look different from all the other ads, or make it seem related to the content, there's more chance it won't be ignored completely.

Online advertisements have the added bonus of leading people directly to your website. Once you've attracted the prospect on your **landing page**,‡ you have an opportunity to give them even more useful information and explain your unique value proposition in more detail.

With traditional advertising, you and your creative team will decide what to feature in the ad, but when it comes to sponsored content, you'll need to work with the editor of the piece. Share your media kit with them and explain what you want to achieve with your piece. Make the content valuable to the reader, even if they don't end up buying anything from you. Some media companies don't allow businesses to write sponsored content for them, but will propose ways they can write content that fits with their

---

\*   *"Assessing the Effects of Animation in Online Banner Advertising"* by Chan Yun Yoo, Kihan Kim and Patricia A. Stout, Journal of Interactive Advertising (Volume 4, 2004 - Issue 2, Pages 49-60)

†   *"Context is King: A Million Examples of Creative Ad Campaigns Getting it Right"* by Daniel Marks, Moz (June 21, 2016).

‡   A specific page on your website that you direct people to from advertising campaigns.

publication. This gives you less control, but rest assured that the content authors are keeping the best interest of their audience in mind, which is a good thing.

## Physical Space

Professionals that are location based or that travel to their client's home or office to perform their services have plenty of additional opportunities to improve their client experience and make it a memorable and pleasing one. Here are just a few of the ways you could upgrade the presentation of your office, studio, or vehicle.

### OFFICE SIGNAGE

If your business has a brick and mortar presence, make it super easy for people to find you. Even with the help of GPS maps, we can still get lost among the numerous offices or stores in a single building. Another benefit of having clear and visible branding elements on your physical space is **attracting foot traffic**. Some businesses discourage walk-ins, but if you'd like more people to know that your business exists, use the space you're already paying for to double as advertising space. Some countries require businesses to have a **sign** featuring specific information affixed next to the building entrance, regardless of whether your office is open to clients or not. The size of your signage will be dictated by your budget, and by how much foot traffic your place attracts. Dry cleaners, car mechanics, cosmetic salons, and other highly frequented shops typically use larger, backlit signs above the doors. Businesses that work on appointment only may use smaller, subtle signs.

### INTERIOR DESIGN

Use your brand mood as inspiration for the colors and textures of your office. Even affordable furniture comes in a wide range of colors and materials, so finding something that matches your brand shouldn't be too hard. Inexpensive decorative items like pillows, curtains, and vases can quickly turn an otherwise bland space into a charming oasis.

White walls and empty shop windows can appear sterile and off-putting.

Large glass surfaces may even pose a safety hazard, because people tend to walk straight into them. Wall and glass **decals** can make your space feel more inviting and cozy, reduce the chances of people hurting themselves, and let you advertise through your street-facing windows.

If you're on a tight budget, print shops offer ready-made motifs. You can also order prints of your own logo, patterns, icons, or illustrations, or hire a mural painter. If you're filming videos in your office, decorating the wall which may be seen behind you offers a great way to feature your visual brand identity on all your videos.

**Wall art** such as paintings, photography, and posters can liven up the space and affect people's mood. If you happen to have a creative hobby, you can use your own art to decorate your walls. This way your clients can get to know a different side of you, and it will also make the space more pleasant for you to spend time in. For those who aren't artistically inclined, there are different options to look into:

- Commissioning custom pieces from artists.
- Purchasing prints or originals from artists and photographers you like.
- Ordering printed infographics or inspirational posters.
- Collecting posters you like and framing them.
- Renting art from local artists.

**The most important criteria to base your art selection on is what emotions it evokes in your clients.** Tattoo parlors may go for edgy art with bold motifs. A doctor or a psychologist might prefer calming motifs, such as landscapes, baby animals, underwater scenes, etc. Architects and engineers may opt for modern cityscapes or techy-looking abstract art. Massage and bodywork studios can feature expressive art inspired by the human body.

Consider the state of mind your clients are in when they walk into your office. What kind of art, colors, furniture, decor, and music would encourage them to enter into a state of mind that helps them get more benefits out of working with you? You may want people to be calmer, more excited, more focused, or in some other state. Observe the type of office decor that makes *you* feel this way, and provide it for your clients. If you're having trouble with this or just don't have the time, an interior designer can recommend the furniture, decor, wall paint, wallpapers, and art that matches your desired studio 'vibe' and is within your budget.

### VEHICLE GRAPHICS

Cars, vans and trucks are an excellent method of getting your brand seen by many people in your local area every single day. For a single investment it takes to design and get your car decals printed, you get long lasting free advertising. You can place smaller decals on the flat surfaces, or get the entire vehicle wrapped in plastic. You can place decals on your personal car too, in which case you'll probably want a more subtle look.

What information you include on the vehicles depends on how much space you have available. You can include the logo, tagline, website, and phone number. What you want to achieve with this is for people to immediately realize *"This is relevant for me"* or *"This is irrelevant."*

Croatian company Ases Usluge does urgent interventions of the plumbing variety. Their trucks and vans are emblazoned with illustrated characters and the tagline *"Your shit, our bread!"* That tagline attracts the attention of every passerby, and was featured in Croatian media.* It takes guts to own a brand like that, and these people have plenty of it.

## Uniforms

Some companies require their client facing staff to wear uniforms, which helps the customers easily identify them, and gives off a more professional company appearance. This is common in the hospitality, health, construction, and repair industries. These uniforms may have logos printed or embroidered on them.

Easy-going places like cafés, pubs, hostels, and ranches may provide branded T-shirts and aprons for their staff, with few rules for the bottoms.

---

\*     *"Njihov je posao većini nezamisliv: 'Kad stignemo, ljudi u nas gledaju k'o u Boga'"* by Matina Tenžera, Dnevnik.hr (April 14, 2017).

Fancier places like restaurants, gelaterias, hotels, and bed & breakfast places may provide branded button down shirts, pants, and skirts and have strict requirements on appropriate shoes.

People who get their hands dirty wear coveralls, which come in a variety of colors. Health and wellness professionals often wear lab coats that protect their clothes from coming into contact with bodily fluids, hairs, and chemicals. They're usually white, but you can also get them in other, friendlier colors. Quality is important, because flimsy clothing items have to be replaced more often, while quality clothing keeps its shape and color even when washed often.

## Packaging

You may offer a mix of services and products in your business, or do custom commissions, which counts as a service despite the result being a physical item. Beautiful packaging can enhance the customer's experience of the product, and restate its value. The more expensive and premium the product, the more important the packaging.

**Boxes** are unavoidable if you're selling goods that may get damaged in transport, or if you're selling luxury items—nobody wants to receive a $300 custom gemstone necklace in a bubble-wrapped envelope. For jewelry and accessories, packaging isn't just about the first impression, but for safe-keeping of the item when it's not in use. Depending on your budget, your options are (from most to least expensive):

- Custom boxes.
- Printing on ready-made boxes.
- Printing labels on ready-made boxes.

You can also customize regular envelopes and shipping boxes with branded labels. Seeing your logo on the box while feeling the excitement of the item arriving at the door can create stronger positive emotional associations with your brand.

**Gift bags** can be used for smaller or cheaper items that don't require a box, or they can be used to carry boxed items. They come in a variety of shapes, sizes and materials—choose the kind of bag that best fits your core values, brand qualities, and product. Depending on your budget, you can print your logo on two largest sides of the bag, or a pattern across the entire bag.

**Tags** are attached to items such as clothing, accessories, and jewelry and can be made out of cardboard or plastic. They typically contain the logo, product price, size, materials, and country of origin (check your local laws for mandatory information). They may also contain other messaging, for example that the product was created using recycled materials, that it's made using sustainable methods of production, or that the business gives a portion of the proceeds to a charity.

**Wrapping paper** can serve two functions: to wrap the box (like most gift shops will do when you request this service), or to wrap the item prior to placing in a box (think of shoes or wallets). They provide an extra step in the 'unboxing' ritual. There are also online printing services that can print your logo on fabric **ribbons** or washi tape. If this isn't something you want to invest in at the moment, carefully selected wrapping paper and ribbons that are available at your local store can do the trick without breaking the bank.

**Keep in mind that the recipient of the product may not be the person who bought it.** If it was given as a gift, the new owner may have never heard of your business, and your packaging is their first introduction to your brand. If you don't have contact information on your tags or boxes, include a business card in the package.

If you want to see some beautiful packaging examples, the Friday Likes category on the Brand New blog is my favorite place to get a regular shot of eye candy.

There are many more ways to enhance your client experience that I haven't mentioned, but this is more than enough to start with. If you cover those that apply to your business, you'll have done way more than most small businesses owners do in their entire careers. Just take it easy, and remember that every completed step is worthy of celebration.

In the next chapter, we'll take a birds-eye view on how your brand strategy affects wider areas such as your business offers, company culture, hiring practices, social impact, and even your fashion style.

*chapter X*

# Beyond Branding

We're coming close to the end of the book, and by now you've learned what the elements of a Human Centered Brand are, you've gone through the exercises to discover your own, and explored many different ways you can weave your brand through your client experience. We're almost done, but before you go I'd like to talk about the more expansive impact of your brand.

A brand includes all the factors that can affect people's image of your business. While most of this is focused on positioning, target audience, and stylistic choices, there are elements that are too wide to be covered by a brand strategy. In this chapter, I'll offer thoughts on these adjacent, but still very relevant parts of your business that can work with or against your carefully crafted brand. We'll examine the importance and the effects of:

- Choosing a business model that suits your personality.
- Pricing that meets your needs & reflects the value of your services.
- Social impact of your business and marketing practices.
- Creating a healthy company culture.
- Expressing your personality through fashion.

You may be wondering, *"What do these topics have to do with my brand?"* and the answer to that is: **everything has to do with your brand**. There isn't a publicly visible portion of your life or business that does not affect your brand. People form opinions and develop impressions based on what they see and hear you share, and what other people say about you. Anything that comes out of your office can work in your favor or to your detriment, which is why we need to address the potential opportunities and pitfalls.

## Business Models & Offers

When we launch a new business without any prior experience in this particular niche, we're making a lot of assumptions. We assume:

- Who our most likely buyers are.
- What our buyers need and value the most.
- How much they're willing to pay.
- What kind of experience they expect us to deliver.

It doesn't matter how well you've done your research, once you start working with your ideal clients, everything can get turned on its head. You may start with one unique value proposition, only to learn you've been sitting on a far better one without even realizing. You may get sudden clarity when you receive a client testimonial that describes the essence of your work better than you could. Flexibility is a trait that every business owner needs, because things rarely go according to plan.

The rule of Human Centered Branding is that **if you change one level of the pyramid, you need to reexamine all the levels above it**. If your unique value proposition changes, you need to evaluate your brand voice (or at least the topic and role portion), your ideal client, and your visual brand identity. Perhaps they'll withstand this shift, or maybe they'll need to shift as well to keep up in step. Your core values are least likely to change, but what may change is your self-awareness. Maybe later you'll discover a core value you didn't know you had, and this will cause a ripple effect through your entire brand.

### BEWARE THE SHINY OBJECTS

I'm assuming that you're a smart, talented person with a lot of experience and skills under your belt. You could potentially be doing a lot of different things in addition to what you're already doing. Maybe your friends, colleagues, clients, or fans are asking you to expand into other services or products that you haven't considered. They may make it sound like it's a great idea and that people would shower you with money if only you did that, but it may not in fact be the best course of action for you.

Other people don't know your values, your vision, and your passions as well as you do—not even those closest to you. What may seem like you're leaving money on the table to them, may actually be the best possible business decision for you. We have a limited amount of time and energy, and we can't be all things to all people. It's your decision who you want to be, and what service you're willing to offer to the world. No one should make that choice for you.

Take for example productized services. A few years ago, productized consulting and recurring revenue were all the rage. Freelancers were coming up with easy to understand offers with clear deliverables and short timeframes, and the option to engage them on a monthly basis. Many swear that it has transformed their business. *"The real money is in continuous support"* they say, and I believe them. Yet, the very idea of working on the same project for a prolonged period of time makes me cringe. My core values and my personality lean towards independence and flexibility, and I couldn't stand doing support work or incremental improvements. My brand of creativity is envisioning new ideas and launching new projects. I'm great at making drastic makeovers, and I'm very bad at maintenance. What my brand proposes to my clients is *"I can do things for you that you can't even imagine. I will surprise you in the best possible way."* Productizing and incremental improvement would suck the soul out of my offers. It would downplay my defining value, and it would force me to keep a more rigid schedule. This business model may work perfectly for some business owners, but it doesn't work for everyone.

Some people jive better with separate projects and repeated launching, while others prefer keeping a steady commitment and having their schedule cut out for them a year in advance. This isn't a question of which one is 'better', it's about which one is sustainable for you. Be careful when anyone tries to sell you their business model as a revolutionary *"must try now or you'll miss out on big bucks."* It's okay to test some ideas, but if adapting your business to a new business model would make it look more like your competitors', and less like your own, that's a dangerous gamble.

Your best offers are those that give the highest value to your clients, while simplifying your life. Too many different offers can be overwhelming for you, *and* for your audience. One-off offers that don't fit within your larger client journey may confuse people.

**If you want to get repeat business without having to resort to recurring maintenance, craft a journey.** Imagine your ideal client at the point where they're most ready to work with you and buy your service for the first time. Then think about this client once they've gone through your service—how else might you support them? What can you do that takes them deeper into their own transformation? What new visions will they be open to once they've felt the initial results of working with you? Note that this expanded vision is often not available to people who haven't worked with you yet, so you shouldn't lead with it, unless you you're in the company of people who you know are ready.

The next question is what do your *almost* ideal clients need in order to turn into ideal clients? Is there a way you can provide support to them to get them to a state where they're ready to work with you? If the answer is no, that's okay. Not everyone needs to have a group coaching program, a self-paced course, or a book. But if you choose to do this, it's important to position this offer as a step in your journey, not something that competes with your more valuable and higher priced services.

Heart of Business offers training and coaching, and their client journey is laid out in a model titled The Four Stages of Business Development. Their group training *Foundations 1: Clients and Money* focuses on businesses in the earliest stage, so they can generate cash flow as quickly as possible. The next group training course *Foundations 2: Expand Your Reach* is focused on marketing fundamentals and creating website content, and is suitable for 'stage 2' businesses that are already making money, but need to reach a wider audience. Their next step for businesses in the third and fourth stages is individual coaching.

MNIB Consulting has developed a different model to categorize businesses into four stages, and they only help businesses in the third ($15.000–$30.000 per month in revenue) and fourth stage (more than $30.000 per month in revenue). They know what they're best at and what they most enjoy doing, and stick to that. This makes their marketing simpler and more targeted.

When observing what other people do in their business to get inspiration and ideas, keep in mind that you don't have all the information, and this business model may or may not be working well for them. Businesses can look very successful on the outside, when in fact they may be struggling. You won't know the truth until they admit to it publicly, and turn it into a rags to riches story.

## Pricing Your Work

Talking about money tends to bring out our deepest insecurities to the surface. Before we move on, I want to stress that you deserve to be paid well for the value you provide. The system we live in doesn't value all services fairly. It's *absurd* that most artists can barely make a living, only to have their work sold for millions once they're dead. Instead of ranting about how capitalism has failed humanity, let's talk about what you can do on an individual level.

Many service businesses set low prices to match that of their competitors, and then try to cut costs and make their business more efficient, so they can work with more clients in the same amount of time. That is certainly one way of making your business more profitable, but not the one I've chosen for myself, and certainly not the one I recommend.

Instead, you can charge in the highest bracket that a business of your size can get away with, and then improve your service to make it worth that much to your clients. Sean Low, the business consultant and founder of The Business of Being Creative explains his take on pricing categories:

*"When you price above or below a category, you are not in that category. Period. Why? Clients cannot understand the relative value you offer. (...) Own who you are today. That means know your category and strive to be the highest priced business in that category. (...) Of course, to raise your price you will have to define the extra value you are offering to justify the increase."* \*

---

\*  *"Be The Most In Your Category"* by Sean Low, The Business of Being Creative (February 14, 2017).

Price speaks volumes about your brand, and forms clients' expectations about the quality they're getting. It can help you position your offers as more valuable and capable of delivering better results, or it can drive the expectations down and push your clients into the comparison shopping pit. The price should never be the primary choice why people choose you—instead, what you want people to say about your services is *"They were among the most expensive providers, but they're worth every cent."*

You owe it to your own well-being to charge prices that make your business sustainable. Most small businesses can't afford to be cheap, because they don't have the necessary volume of sales to make it profitable. People who charge less than they need to make are driving their business into the ground. I've experienced that, so I know how bad it is to feel like you're working all the time, and only just covering your expenses—no buffer, no savings, no investments, no travel.

As you're forming the prices that take care of your needs, you might lose a certain demographic that won't be able to afford working with you anymore. You can either embrace that (like MNIB Consulting did), or you can create 'pay what you can' offers or scholarships for those who would otherwise be a great fit, but can't afford it (like the Heart of Business). These offers still shouldn't cost you so much to jeopardize the sustainability of your business, so don't jump straight into it without crunching numbers and deciding where the extra money to make up for this loss is going to come from.

No matter how low or how high you charge, some will think it's too expensive, and some will think it's too cheap. Too low a price may cause people to not take you seriously. If your offers have a tremendous value and you're able to explain it well through your copywriting but the price seems "too good to be true", this may result in fewer sales because people don't believe it's that good. Scientists did several studies on the placebo effects of pricing, and they consistently show that for the majority of participants, the same product (like wine) with a higher price tag *tastes better.** It's not just

---

\*   *"Do More Expensive Wines Taste Better? Evidence from a Large Sample of Blind Tastings"* by Robin Goldstein, Johan Almenberg, Anna Dreber, John W. Emerson, Alexis Herschkowitsch, and Jacob Katz, Journal of Wine Economics (Volume 3, Number 1, Spring 2008, Pages 1–9).

that they say it tastes better, brain MRI scans show that their reward brain centers respond more strongly to more expensive products.* The wisdom we can glean from this is that we shouldn't undercut ourselves by lowering our prices below those of our peers, because this causes clients to believe our services are of lower quality, and it turns into a self-fulfilling prophecy. Businesses with a strong unique value proposition that form a deep connection with their audience can charge prices that are higher than their competitors'. If someone wants to compare your price to someone else's you can legitimately state: *"Our work is different, and the value we provide is higher, which is why we charge more."*

People who want to work with you above anyone else won't be deterred by the price. If someone states the price as their main reason why they went with someone else, they're not your ideal client, because your ideal client recognizes that there is no one else who can serve them better than you can. An ideal client who can't afford your services will keep an eye on you, and save up money until they can.

Your website copy needs to reflect the needs of your ideal client at the moment when they're ready and able to work with you, and this will inevitably discourage those who have different needs from applying. Quoting the price range or a minimum level of investment on your website helps your clients make an informed decision before they contact you. By the time they start talking to you about their project, they're already sold. You don't have to justify or defend your prices, or give in to requests for discounts.

If you aren't publicly displaying your prices or expected ranges, it wastes everyone's time and puts people into an awkward position. I've been on both ends of that conversation when it's clear that the service provider and the prospective client had vastly different budget projections. What often happens is that the prospective client starts avoiding you because they're embarrassed to even have been in that position. Save your client's face and be upfront about what working with you costs.

---

\*   *"Individual Differences in Marketing Placebo Effects: Evidence from Brain Imaging and Behavioral Experiments"* by Hilke Plassmann and Bernd Weber, Journal of Marketing Research (January 2015).

### PRICING & BRANDING MISMATCH

After forming a price that reflects the value of your work and meets your financial needs, ask yourself: **can your brand handle this price point?**

If your brand looks distinctly budget, but your offers and prices are premium, it can feel like a bait and switch. Similarly, a brand that looks too luxurious but charges low fees can create confusion and put people off. If your brand is broadcasting one thing, and your prices are stating another, your clients can sense a discord which may stop them from buying.

As consumers, we demand certain quality standards for certain price points. We not only expect the contents to be good, but we also expect the production quality to be at the same level. That's the effect that being immersed in marketing since birth has had on us: **we came to expect that the packaging reflects the quality of the contents inside.**

I experience this discord as a customer regularly. One example that I still remember very well happened some years ago. I was in a free strategy call with a coach that was a very gracious, kind and generous person. Everything about their brand—website design, headshots, documents—was crafted with great care, but the materials were clearly not designed professionally, and didn't tell a coherent brand story. Colors, typography, and graphics were all over the place and had a budget vibe. When they presented their offers and stated the prices, I was taken aback because their brand didn't prepare me for those prices. Had I known before, I wouldn't have even applied for the strategy call.

Granted, I'm way more sensitive to design than the average person, but that was precisely why I'm able to make this observation. The average person may not realize *why* something feels strange. Fortunately, in the previous chapters I've laid out all the ways you can use design to your advantage and create the appropriate expectation of the value your clients get.

Another thing to be careful with is so called **charm prices** that end with the digits 9 or 97. The purpose of these prices is to make a product or a service seem cheaper than it is: $39 looks cheaper than $40, because buyers are focused on the left-most digit and the number of digits when making a judgment. Even though the former is only 1 dollar cheaper than the latter, the psychological effect of charm prices is significant.* The problem with these types of prices is two-fold:

1. They're manipulative.
2. They attempt to position your offer as a bargain.

Bargains may be fine if you're selling a cheap product, but if you're selling a $5.000 retreat, setting the price to $4.997 may actually work against you, since it changes how the price is perceived. Round numbers say *"Our prices are high, and we believe they're worth it."* Charm prices say *"We want you to think this is cheaper than it is."*

Set the prices that send the message *you* want to send. Just because all the marketing blogs quote the science on charm prices and use it as proof that you should do it to, doesn't mean you have to. It's your business.

## Social Impact

Your business doesn't live in a vacuum. Everything you do ripples out to a wider community. You help your clients, they help their clients and invest in their community, and their families and friends benefit secondhand from your work. However, in this day and age trickle-down empowerment is not enough.

Considering the impact your business has on the world is worthy in its own right, but it also affects the perception of your brand. People are getting tired of being used and manipulated by corporations, and many of them are actively looking for other options. In the coming years, small business owners' awareness of social issues will not only be welcome, in many communities it will be a requirement.

Marginalized people and their allies are paying attention to what businesses are doing, and calling out unethical behavior. I've witnessed backlash against many high profile entrepreneurs because of a reckless comment, hosting an expert panel that wasn't inclusive enough, or using imagery

---

* *"Effects of $9 Price Endings on Retail Sales: Evidence from Field Experiments"* by Eric T. Anderson and Duncan I. Simester, Quantitative Marketing and Economics (2003, 1: 93).

that's alienating people of color or indigenous people. We have all these 'new' words to learn (which aren't really new, but are only now reaching the mainstream), like cultural appropriation, micro-aggressions, internalized oppression, toxic masculinity, toxic whiteness, rape culture, etc.

People who resist this effort to create a world that's more inclusive towards traditionally marginalized communities are lamenting about 'PC culture',* and how one can't even make a joke these days without being called out. Political correctness is simply caring for the impact our words have on other people. It means doing the right thing instead of the easy thing.

How everyone chooses to address social impact in their own business is their choice, but every choice we make has an effect. Be prepared that people might call you out on your behavior, and it's their right to do so. No matter what you do, you're going to lose some clients, and gain others. **The important question is: which clients would you rather lose, and which ones would you rather keep?**

In February 2018 after Parkland (Florida) shooting, people of the United States with high school students at the forefront have started vocally protesting against the National Rifle Association (NRA), which lobbies for rights to own firearms. Someone realized that the NRA members are getting benefits from many US corporations like airlines, banks, car rental companies, software companies, etc. and urged social media users to pressure them into cutting ties with the NRA. In response, many of those companies have succumbed and decided that they would rather lose business from NRA members than those who oppose the NRA. Some chose the opposite. Before this protest, these businesses thought they could take money from both groups. In 2018 they've realized they had to choose.

Our own choices may not be in the public eye, but this doesn't make them any less important. Being a Human Centered Brand is a double-edged sword: while it gives us an opportunity to authentically connect with our audience, we also have a greater responsibility to hold ourselves to better standards than the big corporations hold themselves to. **If we fail our audience, it feels like a betrayal because our connection to them is more personal.**

---

* Political correctness

If you're just getting started with your business, forming your ethical principles might take a while. Sometimes you might end up doing projects that you only realize in retrospect were not a good fit. Making mistakes is good, as long as we own them and learn from them.

Artists, designers, writers, musicians, inventors, engineers, developers, teachers, consultants, and other creative and service based entrepreneurs can choose not to be complicit in things that we ethically oppose. You're allowed to uphold your values in your personal and your business life. You're allowed to say no to any project you don't feel comfortable working on, or to any people you don't feel comfortable working with.

The first and most immediate step you can take is to choose your clients carefully, so you don't inadvertently support doing harm to people and the environment. Instead, you can work with clients who are committed to doing good in the world. You can also support non-profit organizations and marginalized people by offering your services pro bono (if that's something you can afford to do).

The second step is choosing how to show up in the marketplace. Your marketing practices may either be ethical and inspiring, or they may be manipulative, divisive, and bringing more suffering to the world. We can't just copy what 'influencers' are doing, because many of those influencers are using practices they've learned from old school marketers that cause harm. These people were not the least bit concerned with how their actions affect their buyers.

Mark Silver wrote a great free guide *Don't Buy Now*\* which spotlights some of the manipulative and harmful marketing and sales methods. Writer Kelly Diels examines how certain practices that are taken for granted perpetuate kyriarchy,† especially in the female entrepreneurship space. Before

---

\*　Available for download at *heartofbusiness.com/pdf/dontbuynow.pdf*
†　Kyriarchy is a social system or set of connecting social systems built around domination, oppression, and submission. It encompasses sexism, racism, speciesism, homophobia, classism, economic injustice, colonialism, militarism, ethnocentrism, anthropocentrism, and other forms of dominating hierarchies in which the subordination of one person or group to another is internalized and institutionalized. (Source: *Wikipedia*)

reading about this topic from these and other writers, I knew there was something off, but I wasn't able to form a coherent explanation why it bothered me. Thankfully, today many people are speaking out eloquently about alternative ways of marketing and sales that aren't based on exploitation, in a way that is accessible even to those of us who didn't graduate from social studies.

It's no longer enough to make our work accessible only to white, able-bodied, cisgender, well-off men and women. It's no longer enough to center people who look just like us in our marketing materials. It's no longer acceptable to build prosperity on the backs of marginalized groups and child labor. Each person living in the industrialized society is syphoning more resources than we're giving back. Our entire life's legacy won't come close to repay for the burden we've caused—burden on other people, and on nature. It's more important than ever to examine where we're putting too much of a burden, and where we're not pulling our own weight.

If you feel there's something in the world that needs to be addressed, examine the possibilities of using your business as an engine for this change. You may not have the bandwidth or the energy right now to make a big campaign, but you can at least join a community where you'll be exposed to different people, their challenges, and needs. This will open your eyes to how different other people's experience of the world is to yours, and how your own privilege has protected you.

Even if you don't have the solution for the big world problems yet, and the depressing news makes you feel like there's no point in even trying, we need to remain open and strong. Keeping a portion of our attention on those big problems may spark some inspiration down the line on how you can use your own creativity, skills, and passions to bring your core values into the world with an even greater impact than you thought was possible. I can't tell you how to do this, because I'm only just learning how to do it myself. But what I do know is that connecting with people who are as motivated to bring the positive change into the world as you are is a crucial step.

We don't only connect with our clients through our core values—we also connect to our colleagues and fellow change makers. Find a community that appreciates your core values, and shares your vision of a better future.

Support others who are taking a stand and making a difference. Amplify voices that have an important message to share, but aren't getting enough attention from the mainstream media. Positive action is contagious, and it will rub off on you. When you're ready to go out and change the world, you'll know there are people who have your back.

## Company Culture

If you're hiring employees or plan on doing so in the future, choosing the right people is crucial to your business' success. I've never employed people in my own business, but I've managed a non-profit organization, so I know a bit about successful teamwork.

Companies used to search for employees that can tick certain skills checkboxes, but now many of them realize that's not enough: they also need employees who fit their company culture. The book *Organizational Behavior* shares the following definition of culture:

*"Organizational culture is the set of assumptions, beliefs, values, and norms that are shared by an organization's members. This culture may have been consciously created by its key members, or it may have simply evolved across time. (...) This idea of organizational culture is somewhat intangible, for we cannot see it or touch it, but it is present and pervasive."* *

Your business has a culture even if you're the only person working in it: it's your clients that define your culture. We've talked a great deal about clients already, and here I'd like to emphasize that another way poor-fit clients harm your business is that they derail and dilute your company culture. Your ideal clients are all a part of the same culture, no matter how different their businesses are. Be explicit about what kind of culture you want to develop, and what boundaries you're putting in place to protect it.

The sooner you define your culture, the easier it will be to find a great

---

\*  *"Organizational Behavior: Human Behavior at Work"* by John W. Newstrom and Keith Davis, McGraw-Hill (1997).

fit for your first employee. Luckily, by doing the core values exercises you've already defined the key piece. The second big piece of the culture is your brand voice, or how your business communicates with its clients and the role your business plays in their life. Other elements of organizational culture is how employees talk to each other, what type of actions are acceptable or unacceptable, dress code, etc.

Changing a culture retroactively is more difficult than setting it up in the first place. Instead of waiting for problems to appear, think of potential issues that might come up as soon as you start thinking about bringing in your first hire, and how you plan to address them. Set clear boundaries about what kind of language is permitted, what actions are unacceptable and grounds for termination, and what objects or living things may and may not be brought into the workplace.

We've already established that a good working relationship with clients and contractors requires a good **personality fit**. Employees are no differ-ent—especially if people are sitting in the same office and collaborating daily. I don't mean that your employees need love all the same stuff and talk in exactly the same way as you. Each of us brings our unique perspective into our businesses, and if you're hiring someone, it should be specifically *because* of the new perspective they're adding, not just to repeat the same things you've done on your own. A personality fit means that:

- You can be honest and transparent with each other.
- You can communicate clearly without misunderstandings.
- You're able to find common ground without too much friction and drama.
- You share some of your top core values.
- They get along with your clients, and sincerely want to help them.

**Your brand is represented by the people your clients are in touch with**: the account manager, the receptionist, the mechanic... They'll either disappoint or delight your clients, and your reputation depends on them.

Your team members need to feel like the work they do is meaningful. People who work in a job in which they don't find **meaning** often become detached, and even depressed.* People who find meaning in their work are motivated to keep their work to a high standard. They're willing to learn more about the field and see their future in it.

Employees who don't find meaning in their job will jump at an opportunity to work elsewhere for higher pay. Those who feel their jobs are meaningful and are surrounded by a great team of people they get along with, value these benefits over financial ones. While yes, more money is a great incentive, it's not the most important one. Entrepreneurs endure all sorts of adversities in the name of meaning. Employees are more risk-averse, but have many of the same human needs that we have. Knowing this can help you define job roles that your employees will enjoy, not simply endure.

## Fashion Style

Choosing a clothing style is a personal decision, but it influences how people perceive us, so it's worth mentioning in the context of Human Centered Branding. It also affects how we feel about ourselves—feeling 'overdressed' or 'underdressed' compared to people around us can mess with our self-confidence.

People adjust their clothing style to the occasion: we wear comfy clothes and footwear at home and during exercise, fancy and less comfortable outfits for special celebrations or a night out, and practical, weather resistant, and durable clothes for nature trips. People's definition of 'comfy', 'practical', and 'fancy' varies greatly. I know university professors who wear sneakers and jeans, those who wear high heels and a ton of makeup, and anything in between. In some industries such as law, sartorial rules are more rigid: everyone wears classic two piece suits, ties, button down shirts, and leather shoes. Wearing inappropriate clothing in court is frowned upon.

For those who choose their own clothing, there are virtually limitless options, so much so that choosing an outfit for a professional photo shoot or a speaking engagement can get overwhelming. Some people hire stylists to help them choose a professional wardrobe—in that case, your stylist needs

---

\*    *"The impact of work environment on mood disorders and suicide: Evidence and implications"* by Jong-Min Woo and Teodor T Postolache, The International Journal on Disability and Human Development (2008; 7(2): 185–200).

to be familiar with your values and your brand voice qualities, so that your clothing selection reflects them. Your brand mood board can also inform your choices of colors, forms, and fabrics.

If you already know what you like, the only thing to be wary of is whether your clothes is appropriate for the occasion and your ideal clients. Whether a certain style will be tolerated also depends on the local culture. For example, Western European countries tolerate body modification and unusual hairstyles much better than Eastern European countries.

Some professions are allowed greater freedoms than others. Creative professionals are half-expected to do crazy things with their hair, get tattooed, or dress in an unusual way. Lawyers and doctors aren't that lucky, and any person that goes against the established expectations in their industry will be equally admired and criticized for it.

A professional that specializes in serving a certain demographic or subculture (like youth, artists, hip-hop musicians) will be accepted by them more readily if they dress in a way that's consistent with this subculture. A psychotherapist that works with teens may appear more approachable if they wear pop culture related T-shirts. This can help their young clients to see them as someone who understands them, as opposed to yet another authority figure that's here to tell them how to behave.

A unique fashion sense can help people tell you apart from your peers. It can be your brand amplifier. When your work is high quality, your fashion style should not deter people from hiring you, but if it does—I'd say that's a good sign. By pushing the boundaries of what is expected from your profession you're creating another filter for your clients, but it can also make people perceive you more positively:

*"A series of studies published in an article in June 2014 in the Journal of Consumer Research explored observers' reactions to people who broke established norms only slightly. In one scenario, a man at a black-tie affair was viewed as having higher status and competence when wearing a red bow tie. The researchers also found that valuing uniqueness increased audience members' ratings of the status and competence of a professor who wore red*

*Converse sneakers while giving a lecture."* *

While I believe most people could use a little more creativity in their wardrobe, it's better to stick with what you can comfortably pull off. If someone who has only worn jeans all their life puts on a cocktail dress, they're going to feel uncomfortable for a bit since it's a whole different bodily sensation—the body is legitimately confused about how to move in that thing. Test your wardrobe before you wear it to a conference to make sure it doesn't scratch or feel too tight anywhere. I'm all for taking fashion risks, since this is an area of life where few things can go wrong. As long as your private parts are fully covered, you'll be fine.

If upgrading your wardrobe to become more 'on brand' feels like a project you can't commit to right now, even purchasing a few statement pieces you can wear on special occasions helps. This can include eyeglasses, jewelry, ties, belts, handbags, hair accessories, shoes, scarves, etc. No matter your gender or your religious restrictions, there is *something* you can find that makes your outfits more interesting. What's great about accessories is that you can wear them all the time—unlike clothes which we do need to wash and rotate between uses, your accessory can be a permanent part of your outfit, and people will start to associate it with you (like Seth Godin's yellow glasses). If you can find this piece in your brand color, that's even better.

On my best days, my own fashion style is elegant with Victorian and pin-up influences—meaning, most of my wardrobe is black, seasoned with lots of frills and lace. (People ask me *"Who died?"* quite often.) I usually balance one unusual clothing article with items that can pass as completely normal. Practicality and comfort has become increasingly important as I got older. I also use statement jewelry pieces, as well as socks and tights with interesting design to spice up an otherwise boring outfit. My speaking gig outfits usually include a red item, to echo my main brand color. When it comes to client meetings, I'm more flexible with color choices, and dress down a bit compared to public appearances.

---

\*    *"Dress for Success: How Clothes Influence Our Performance"* by Matthew Hutson and Tori Rodriguez, Scientific American (January 1, 2016).

Our outfits are our way of expressing our personality, but they also serve as an armor. Unfortunately, our current culture often makes up excuses for harassment and abuse, especially towards women, based on what the victim was wearing. When we get catcalled on the street, it's "our fault" because we were showing too much skin. People in high stakes situations, like negotiations or a court hearing, dress to protect themselves from being underestimated and judged. Being a young-looking woman that often negotiates with much older male clients, I find myself dressing more on the conservative side in some client meetings to reiterate that I'm not just some artsy girl, but a mature business owner.

Depending on your line of work, you can 'dress up' or 'dress down' to challenge assumptions. If your work puts you in a position of authority, which is the case with medical and mental health professionals, perhaps a more casual style would help your clients be more at ease.

What's most important about your clothes is that you feel good while you wear it. Even if no one sees you, your appearance may influence how you feel about yourself, and how productive you are. As we grow older, certain styles we liked in the past may no longer reflect who we are, and this clothes may start feeling like a drag—donate it to someone who will find new joy in it. Free your wardrobe from clutter, and only buy clothes you absolutely love. Take it from someone who has nine 'little black dresses' in their closet: having more isn't better if you barely ever get to wear it.

## Reviewing Your Brand

After completing The Human Centered Brand Workbook, your next step is to examine all the most important pieces of communication and steps in your client process, and check if anything about them needs to change in order to better align with your brand. (Chapter nine provides many suggestions and ideas.)

Which pieces count as 'important'? Good question. If you've been in business for a long time, you probably have hundreds of website pages and a myriad of documents—going through every single one of them sounds like a chore. Here are some examples of things that make the biggest impact:

Big thanks to my amazing beta readers: Mihaela Marija Perković, Cherry Jeffs, Beth Barany, Deborah Claire Procter, Devon Smiley, Igor Rendić, Mihovil Mikulec, Marie Mikkonen, and Višnja Željeznjak for offering their valuable perspectives and resources for the book.

A lot of thanks to my teachers and mentors Jennifer Lee, Naomi Dunford, Tara Gentile, Goran Čandrlić, Mislav Marohnić, Marko Dugonjić, Boris Golob, Sean McCabe, Havi Brooks, Mark Silver, Andrea Schroeder, Chris Oatley, Franjo Škrabec, and everyone else I might have forgotten to mention, who helped me develop the necessary skills I needed to grow as a designer, business woman, artist, and human.

Many thanks to Paul Zelizer, the Awarepreneurs community, Heart of Business community, plus all of my friends and colleagues, for celebrating with me as I shared my journey, supporting me through my challenges, and helping this book make a splash.

And finally, thanks to my loyal readers, some of whom have been following my work for over a decade, for your wonderful letters and comments of encouragement over the years. This book was written with you in mind.

I'm incredibly grateful for having all of you in my life.

- Your website home page.
- About Us page.
- Services pages.
- Landing pages.
- Contact page.
- Thank you pages.
- High-traffic blog articles and pages.
- Newsletter subscription boxes.
- Free resources.
- Documents that you send to all your clients (proposals, contracts).
- Email communication that goes out to everyone (email signature, newsletter templates).
- Pre-written email replies you use regularly.
- Your short biography.
- Social media profile images and cover graphics.
- Applications you use to collaborate with clients.

As you're going through the list above, write down all the content that comes to mind that you need to check and possibly change. These are the things I'd suggest addressing immediately.

Other things may be changed as you need them. You may leave old blog articles and graphics alone, but if you're linking to old content in your new articles or wish to promote it on social media, you can edit the content and redesign the graphics so that they match your new brand, because this may be the first piece of content your new visitors see.

Now that you've made a list, it's time to address each item on it one by one—I have yet another resource to help you with that.

## THE BRAND ALIGNMENT CHECKLIST

Use this checklist to review your existing pieces of content, as well as any new piece you create starting from today: blog posts, newsletters, videos, social media graphics, documents, advertising materials, etc. Keep your workbook and your brand style guide handy so you can refer to them. Focus on **one** piece of content, communication, or client touch point you want to examine, and answer the following questions:

1. **Does this piece reflect my core values?**
   If not, how can I change it so that it does?

2. **Does it help bring more of my core values into the world?**
   If not, how can I change it so that it does?

3. **Does it cover the topic I want to be known for?**
   If not, how can I change it so that it does?

4. **Does it prominently feature my unique value proposition?**
   If not, how can I change it so that it does?

5. **Does it highlight my unique perspective?**
   If not, how can I change it so that it does?

6. **Does it reflect my brand voice qualities?**
   If not, how can I change it so that it does?

7. **Does it speak to the needs of my ideal clients?**
   If not, how can I change it so that it does?

8. **Is it relatable to my ideal clients?**
   If not, how can I change it so that it is?

9. **Does it help solve my ideal clients' problems?**
   If not, how can I change it so that it does?

10. **Am I using the fonts and colors defined in my visual brand identity?**
    If not, which ones do I need to use?

11. **Am I using photos and illustrations that are harmonious with my brand?**
    If not, which ones would fit my brand better?

12. **Am I using the correct logo version, and is it clearly visible and easy to read?**
    If not, replace with the correct version and change its size if needed.

(The Brand Alignment Checklist is also included as a printable PDF with your book bonuses.)

After you've determined what you need to change about a particular piece of content, make the change immediately, before moving on to the next piece. This way, you'll see the effects of your effort sooner, and this will motivate you to keep going.

As you gain more experience with creating content that's completely aligned with your brand, you won't need to use this checklist as often anymore, but it's still smart to run through it for your most important new creations.

# Closing words

The Human Centered Brand is an approach to business that allows you to stay rooted in your essence, despite the onslaught of information that fills your inbox and news feed every day. It enables you to stop the rat race of always trying to come on top of the latest trends, and instead make choices that align with your unique gifts.

**Human Centered Branding allows you to connect with yourself, so that you can more fully connect with your clients.** The work you've done, and that you'll continue doing along this journey, will help you lead a more fulfilling, meaningful, and joyful career. I can't guarantee you that you'll make a lot of money this way, but at least you'll feel really good working for it.

Before jumping onto the next big bubble, reflect back to the notes you've written about your brand while reading this book, and ask yourself *"Is this really what my business needs right now?"* Just because someone says you need to do something, it doesn't mean it's true. (Even if it's me saying it.) There are a million ways to grow a business, and you don't need all of them—just a few reliable techniques that work for you. Feel free to experiment with new things when you have the time, but don't do it because you feel pressured.

The realization that you're not required to be everything and do everything gives you tremendous freedom of choice. You can relax, knowing that **you're enough just as you are.**

If you feel like you need someone's permission to start using more friendly and conversational language, to offer a service no one has ever heard of before, to raise your prices, or to ditch clients who always haggle and call you at odd hours—I offer it to you. **You're allowed to make your business whatever you want it to be.** Your clients, colleagues, parents, mentors, friends, spouse, children, and random online people may have *opinions* about your choices, but their opinions don't outweigh your own experience. People like to judge others for doing things they dare not to do. Don't take all the things you hear to heart.

Creative, innovative businesses can't just repeat what others are doing—we need to move further. The world is counting on us to come up with new things and break new ground. You have something unique to offer. Don't let other people's fears stop you from sharing it with us.

Your own Human Centered Brand is your compass when you feel lost and confused. All you need to do is to read over your notes and compare if a certain action is aligned with them or not.  If you've read this book from start to finish and used all the free resources that accompany it, you've now got a pretty solid brand strategy in place.

- You know who you are, as a person and as a business owner.
- You know what you and your business stand for.
- You know what you want to offer to your clients.
- You know who your ideal clients are.
- You know how to express yourself, both in person and online.

Staying true to your Human Centered Brand is an exercise in **self-trust**. When you know that there's no one single right choice for everyone, but only choices that are more or less aligned with your essence, you can release the pressure to perform according to someone else's standards. You're free to act from your values, and drop the fear of missing out.

## What's Next?

The information in this book is helpful in its own right, but its true power is revealed only through implementation and personal experience. Many of the things I've written about are common sense, and not especially new or revolutionary. You may have said to yourself *"I knew that!"* as you were reading some of the information. But does is count as knowledge if you haven't implemented it and tested it? I read lots of smart ideas and tips every single day, but only a fraction of them sticks with me. If I don't make a *commitment* to try it, I'll forget about it within days. I don't want this to happen to you, which is why I've created the workbook which guides you through the exercises so you can immediately start creating your own brand.

If you still haven't downloaded The Human Centered Brand Workbook and other bonuses, you can do so at: **humancenteredbrand.com/bonus** After you're done with the workbook, you'll have three choices on how to continue:

1.  Do nothing and go back to 'business as usual'.
2.  Implement your new brand, by yourself or with your team.
3.  Find trusted professionals to help you envision and execute your new brand.

Whichever direction your take, your Human Centered Brand Workbook will provide an immensely valuable source of insights and guidelines, whether you're typing an introduction email, presenting a talk, or designing your social media images.

The **Book & Brand Style Guide Bundle**\* also includes templates and instructional videos, so that you can create a professional brand style guide to share with your team, contractors, partners, and the media to ensure everyone you work with represents your brand in the best possible way.

If any of your branding questions have remained unanswered after reading this book, feel free to write to me at **hi@neladunato.com**—I'll be answering reader questions on my blog, and will also take them into account for potential new editions of this book.

### AS TO WHAT'S NEXT FOR ME...

It's been about 18 months since I've first created an outline for this book using post-its in my tiny studio office. When I envisioned this book, I wanted it to be the most comprehensive guide on branding for small business owners—a resource that readers will enthusiastically recommend to their friends, colleagues, and clients. But even more importantly, I wanted to encourage people to embrace their authentic self-expression, and trust their own guidance

---

\* *gum.co/hcbbundle/bookdeal*

when it comes to making important business decisions. I sense there's a lot more for me to learn in this arena, and I look forward to discovering new layers and sharing them with you on my blog, and who knows—perhaps another book.

## SPREAD THE WORD

If you've enjoyed this book and want to share it with others who may need it, I'd love it if you told people about it on social media, or your local business meet-up. The best place to send people to is **humancenteredbrand.com** where they can get the free sample and all the bonuses. (There are also some graphics and text snippets you can use.)

If you have a friend who literally can't afford to buy this book but really needs it, I encourage you to lend it to them—my books are DRM-free. I only ask that you don't make it publicly accessible.

If you run an organization, school, or a book club and want your members or students to read this book, **contact me** and I'll be happy to provide a bulk discount.

## STAY IN TOUCH

The best way to receive more tips and resources on Human Centered Branding is to stay signed up for email updates. If you haven't confirmed to receive my newsletter while downloading your free bonuses, you can do so now at: **humancenteredbrand.com/letters**

## ONWARD AND UPWARD!

Thank you for reading this book and giving The Human Centered Brand framework a try. I sincerely hope that you've enjoyed this journey and have found this information helpful and applicable in your own business. I wish you lots of success and good fortune in your future creative adventures.

May you always walk the world in your full brilliance and power, and may your path guide you towards kindred souls who cherish you.

# Acknowledgements

While I take great pride in doing as much as I can by myself, I couldn't have possibly created this book without the help of many kind people who have contributed to it, supported its launch, or cheered me on as I was deep in the trenches.

First of all, I want to thank my partner David, and my friends Jasna, Maja, Domenika, and Korana who are always there for me when I need to vent, talk me off my ledge when life becomes too much, and support me in my crazy creative dreams. I've often neglected you because of my work, but you still haven't kicked me out of your life and that means a lot to me.

My gratitude and love goes to my family: mom, dad, my little brother, and my late grandma. We've had our issues and we may not always agree, but I know I can always count on your help.

Special thanks to Irmin and Gunter for encouraging and fueling my creativity—especially for giving me my first computer, which made all of this possible for me. I'll never be able to repay you for your kindness.

Massive thanks to my brilliant editor Siobhan Colgan for helping me make this book more integrated, cohesive, and refined, while championing my vision. Letting your writing be seen by someone else for the first time is vulnerable and tender, and your encouragement in that moment meant so much, and helped me stay motivated to keep writing.

Huge thanks to my wonderful clients—this book wouldn't have happened without you. Working with you has transformed how I think about business relationships. Seeing how pleasant and easygoing it could be made me eager to 'crack the code' of how to intentionally develop such business friendships and share this knowledge with other people. You are my inspiration, and I'm looking forward to seeing your business grow.

# References

ANDERSON, Eric T.; Simester, Duncan I. (2003) Effects of $9 Price Endings on Retail Sales: Evidence from Field Experiments, Quantitative Marketing and Economics, 1:93.

BARRY, Nathan (2013) Why beautiful email templates hurt your business.

CUDDY, Amy (2012) Your body language may shape who you are, TED.

DANISH National Agency for Enterprise and Housing (2003) The Economic Effects of Design.

DION, Karen; Berscheid, Ellen; Walster, Elaine (1972) What Is Beautiful Is Good, Journal of Personality and Social Psychology, Vol 24, No. 3, 285-290.

GENTILE, Tara (2015) It's Not You: 3 Things to Consider in the Face of Failure.

GOLDSTEIN, Robin; Almenberg, Johan; Dreber, Anna; Emerson, John W.; Herschkowitsch, Alexis; Katz, Jacob (2008) Do More Expensive Wines Taste Better? Evidence from a Large Sample of Blind Tastings, Journal of Wine Economics, Volume 3, Number 1, Pages 1–9.

HARGRAVE, Tad (2012) No One Cares About Your Project.

HAWKINS, Christopher (2017) Make Freelancing Serve Your Own Dreams with Paul Jarvis, 100k Freelancing.

HOLLIS, Nigel (2011) Starbucks' New Logo: A Risky Move, Harvard Business Review.

HORN, Robert E. (2001) Visual Language and Converging Technologies in the Next 10–15 Years (and Beyond).

HOY, Amy (2014) How Your "Fuck This!" Moment Changes Everything.

HUTSON, Matthew; Rodriguez, Tori (2016) Dress for Success: How Clothes Influence Our Performance, Scientific American.

JALIL, Nurlelawati Ab.; Yunus, Rodzyah Mohd; Said, Normahdiah S. (2012) Environmental Colour Impact upon Human Behaviour: A Review, Procedia – Social and Behavioral Sciences, Issue 35, 54 – 62.

JUST, Marcel; Ludtke, Melissa (2010) Watching the Human Brain Process Information, Nieman Reports.

KAHANE, Josiah (2015) How Your Brain Understands Visual Language, Fast Company.

LANGLOIS, Judith H. (2000) Maxims or Myths of Beauty? A Meta-analytic and Theoretical Review, Psychological Bulletin, Vol 126 No. 3, 390-423.

LITTLE, Anthony C.; Jones, Benedict C.; DeBruine, Lisa M. (2011) Facial attractiveness: evolutionary based research, Philosophical Transactions of the Royal Society B: Biological Sciences, 366(1571): 1638–1659.

LOW, Sean (2017) Be The Most In Your Category, The Business of Being Creative.

MA, Xiao; Yue, Zi-Qi; Gong, Zhu-Qing; Zhang, Hong; Duan, Nai-Yue; Shi, Yu-Tong; Wei, Gao-Xia, You-Fa (2017) The Effect of Diaphragmatic Breathing on Attention, Negative Affect and Stress in Healthy Adults, Frontiers in Psychology.

MARKS, Daniel (2016) Context is King: A Million Examples of Creative Ad Campaigns Getting it Right, Moz.

MARONEY, Terry A. (2016) Emotion in the Behavior and Decision Making of Jurors and Judges, Emotion Researcher.

MAYER, Richard E. (2001) Multimedia Learning.

MCCABE, Sean; Toalson, Ben (2016) The One Rule You Must Remember to Get High-Value Clients Who Pay You More to Work Less, Seanwes.

MEYER, Kate; Flaherty, Kim (2016) Needy Design Patterns: Please-Don't-Go Popups & Get-Back-to-Me Tabs, Nielsen Norman Group.

MIHAJLOVIĆ, Živorad Slavinski (1995) Kreaton.

NEWSTROM, John W.; Davis, Keith (1997) Organizational Behavior: Human Behavior at Work, McGraw-Hill.

NEUMEIER, Marty (2016) Branding By Business Type.

NEUMEIER, Marty (2016) The Onlyness Test.

NEWPORT, Cal (2016) Deep Work: Rules for Focused Success in a Distracted World, Grand Central Publishing.

NORMAN, Donald (2002) Emotion & design: attractive things work better.

PAVLINA, Steve (2004) Living Your Values, Part 1.

PERNICE, Kara (2018) Banner Blindness: Ad-Like Elements Divert Attention, Nielsen Norman Group.

PLASSMANN, Hilke; Weber, Bernd (2015) Individual Differences in Marketing Placebo Effects: Evidence from Brain Imaging and Behavioral Experiments, Journal of Marketing Research.

RUSSELL-KRAFT, Stephanie (2018) Shearman & Sterling Spent Three Years Rebranding Itself, Bloomberg Law.

SCHELSKE, Marc Alan (2015) Are Your Core Values Real or Aspirational?

SHADEL, Matt (2014) A Brief History of Branding, Convoy.

SILLENCE, Elizabeth; Fishwick, Pam Lesley; Harris, Peter (2004) Trust and mistrust of online health sites, Conference on Human Factors in Computing Systems.

SILVER, Mark (2005) Why Marketing Often Feels Sleazy (and How to Avoid It).

SPERA, Stefanie P.; Buhrfeind, Eric D.;Pennebaker, James W. (1994) Expressive Writing and Coping with Job Loss, Academy of Management Journal, Vol. 37, No. 3.

STATCOUNTER Global Stats (2018) Desktop vs Mobile vs Tablet Market Share Worldwide – March 2018.

VAN EDWARDS, Vanessa (2014) Body Language for Trainers and Teachers, MNIB Consulting.

VOGEL, Douglas R.; Dickson, W L; Lehman, John A. (2005). Persuasion and the Role of Visual Presentation Support: The UM/3M Study

VUKUŠIĆ, Nenad (2017) Kako smisliti superslogan za firmu ili obrt.

WALSH, Amy (2017) On getting comfortable with pictures of ourselves: we contain multitudes!

WARD, Michelle (2011) Your Win Book: What It Is, Why It Rocks, and How to Make Your Own.

WEINSCHENK, Susan (2012) 100 Things Every Presenter Needs to Know About People, New Riders.

WHEELER, Alina (2013) Designing Brand Identity, Wiley.

WOLPERT, Stuart (2013) How the brain creates the 'buzz' that helps ideas spread, Science Daily.

WOO, Jong-Min; Postolache, Teodor T. (2008) The impact of work environment on mood disorders and suicide: Evidence and implications, The International Journal on Disability and Human Development.

YOO, Chan Yun; Kim, Kihan; Stout, Patricia A. (2004) Assessing the Effects of Animation in Online Banner Advertising, Journal of Interactive Advertising, Volume 4, Issue 2, Pages 49-60.

YOUYOU, Wu; Stillwell, David; Schwartz, H. Andrew; Kosinski, Michal (2017) Birds of a Feather Do Flock Together: Behavior-Based Personality-Assessment Method Reveals Personality Similarity Among Couples and Friends, Psychological Science, Vol 28, Issue 3, pp. 276 - 284.

ZMUDA, Natalie (2010) Filling in the Gap of a Rebranding Disaster, AdAge.

# About
# Nela Dunato

Nela Dunato is a multi-passionate artist, brand designer, teacher, and writer based in Rijeka, Croatia. She's been working as a graphic designer since 2005, both as a freelancer and as an in-house agency employee. In 2013 she started her own design consultancy, with the focus of helping small businesses craft expressive brand identities and exceptional client experiences.

She teaches graphic design as a course instructor, leads in-person workshops, and speaks at conferences. Although this is her first published book, she's been writing about design, branding, marketing, business, and creativity for over a decade on her multiple blogs.

Her artwork and illustrations have been published, exhibited, and awarded internationally, though nowadays she prefers painting and drawing for her own pleasure. She is a huge sci-fi and fantasy nerd, lover of Victorian and Art Nouveau aesthetics, cat person, and a dedicated shadow worker.

Learn more about Nela and her work at: **neladunato.com**
Write to Nela at: **hi@neladunato.com**

# Index

CPSIA information can be obtained
at www.ICGtesting.com
Printed in the USA
LVHW080357300120
644905LV00007BA/46